THE POET SPEAKS

The Poet
SPEAKS

Interviews with contemporary poets
conducted by
Hilary Morrish, Peter Orr, John Press
and
Ian Scott-Kilvert

General Editor
PETER ORR

Preface by
FRANK KERMODE

NEW YORK
BARNES & NOBLE, INC.

First published
in the United States of America
1966

by Barnes & Noble, Inc.
New York, N.Y.

© *The British Council 1966*

Printed in Great Britain

Contents

CONTENTS

Editor's Foreword

THE INTERVIEWS which appear in this volume are substantially, although not word for word, the same as the recordings from which they have been transcribed. These recorded conversations were originally designed to accompany tape recordings of contemporary poets reading their own works, a series produced by the British Council in collaboration with the Poetry Room in the Lamont Library of Harvard University. The interviews are, of course, unscripted and unrehearsed, and what emerges is not anything in the nature of a prepared statement, but rather the poet's immediate response to a series of fairly simple, and sometimes apparently naïve, questions about his craft. When I first put the idea of these interviews to Jack Sweeney, of Harvard, the aim was to present the poet as something other than a disembodied voice reading his own poems; in fact, to put it simply, as a person talking about his own work. We have tried to produce, as far as possible, the flavour of a conversation which might crop up between friends who share a common interest—in this case, poetry. We have, I sincerely hope, avoided any suggestion of the inquisitorial technique which seems to have become fashionable of late in interviews on radio and television.

As a general rule, these interviews were recorded without any real preparation or conscious connivance between the poet and interviewer, although it has often happened that a preliminary conversation over the lunch table has provided a starting point for discussion. In editing the transcriptions for this volume, I have excised the repetitions inevitable in such proceedings, removed obvious irrelevances, made such alterations in syntax as seemed necessary to assist the reader and allowed the poet licence to clarify any points which seemed obscure in their initial expression, but basically the substance and shape of each interview as it appears here in print is faithful to the original.

I have resisted attempts by some poets to alter drastically the sense and form of what they said at the original encounter; other poets have understandably exercised their right not to have their utterances reproduced in print. I have much sympathy with one young poet, a good friend, who writes that if he is to leave a testament, then the poetry is it.

Readers of this volume will be able to judge for themselves the value of whatever testimony reposes in these pages. For myself, I believe that these interviews have a quality of immediacy which cannot easily be captured otherwise: the gems are rare, but they are, I think, occasionally to be glimpsed in the pages of dialogue which follow. Tentative a great deal of it may be—though as E. M. Forster once remarked to me during a similar exercise, everything one says is tentative—but here and there gleams a poet's instinctive and real response to the world around him and the art by which he is possessed. It was for these reasons that I had the temerity to think that these conversations might bear reproduction in print, and I was encouraged in this thought by a number of the contributors who now appear in this volume.

It is to the poets who have so cheerfully submitted themselves to this ordeal that I owe my first debt of gratitude. Without their willing co-operation, such a volume as this would never have seen the light of day. Then my thanks are due to Jack Sweeney, who has, over the four years of work represented here, kept up a constant stream of encouragement and help which has made the task in itself worthwhile. I am glad to acknowledge the assistance and advice of my colleagues at the British Council, Ian Scott-Kilvert, Hilary Morrish and John Press, who have undertaken many of these interviews, Philip Henderson and Jo Caesar, who have relieved me of much of the arduous routine of checking and editing the transcripts of the recordings, and finally my thanks go to the several secretaries who have painstakingly transcribed the original recordings into the form in which they now appear.

Many of the poets whose interviews appear in this book can be heard reading their own poems in a recorded anthology on six long-playing records (RG 451–6) which I have edited for Argo. Full details of this anthology, also entitled 'The Poet Speaks', may be had from the Argo Record Company Ltd., 113 Fulham Road, London S.W.3.

PETER ORR

The British Council, London
December 1964

Preface

by

FRANK KERMODE

It is now almost commonplace to lament that ours is an age in which the medium is more important than the message it bears—the pseudo-events of television, the half-lies of advertising, have reduced our interest in actuality and truth. So it might seem sadly appropriate that we take more interest in poets than in their poetry. Most people, cross-examined, would agree with Peter Porter that 'the sort of chap' a poet is outside his work is a matter of trivial interest; they might even hold that his opinions, in so far as they are independent of his essential function, have no more claim on our regard than anybody else's. Yet biography and literary criticism sell better than verses. And then there is a newer *genre*, favoured by the B.B.C. and now in this book; a hostile commentator might call it the pseudo-conversation, arguing that no one enters into such a discussion unprepared, unmasked, and that the tape will necessarily be indeterminably less than the whole truth, since the poet will protect himself according to his ability. Indeed, it might seem reasonable enough for a man to decline an invitation to such an encounter on the ground that those elements of his life which have objective interest are somewhere in his poems. There is a danger that the poet might be too self-conscious, perhaps working up some *ad hoc* ideology he would prefer to be without. I know a distinguished novelist who has abjured these interviews because he thinks they were affecting his work.

Still, most poets enjoy this degree of attention; one of them opened an interview here printed with a spirited protest, but later the lady clearly consented, and seems to have enjoyed the experience as much as the others. One need not exaggerate the novelty of poets interested in being sought after, or of a public seeking information about them. The birthplace of Homer was a subject of vigorous dispute; Dante began his big poem with a brief biographical statement; Spenser put himself in as Colin Clout, and his girl as a supernumerary Grace; and Milton put himself in as Milton, 'long choosing and beginning late'. We boast

ix

sophisticated notions about the poetic *persona*, and about the 'impersonality' of poetry; but it would be inhuman to abstain from human interest in the Pope of the satires, the Pound of the *Pisan Cantos*, or, indeed, the Eliot of the *Quartets*. We must be cautious, remember the difficulties and avoid naïve expressionism; but we may also remember what Wallace Stevens said was incessantly forgotten, the importance in a body of work of 'the presiding personality'. Of course the chat of poets is incidental to the true epiphany of the *œuvre*; but this means only that we should read the poems as well as listen to the talk.

The talk is largely about poems; whether or no we find it good in itself we may be sure that historians will use it when they are trying to characterize the poetry of the 1960s. Not all the poets are here, but the important 'movements' (except perhaps the survivors of the Movement itself) are represented. There are old and young, well-known and unknown poets. Mr. Orr's may not be a random sample—I don't know how far he has let his own preferences affect the selection; and certainly the reader will be able to think of ten more or less regrettable omissions. But this loss is, I think, made up for by the presence of the young, obscure and no less dedicated practitioners. The historian will no doubt agree.

It is not easy to guess what he will make of it. He may comment on the high level of technical competence, as Roy Fuller does. He may note that except for Sylvia Plath, who was an American anyway, there is little apparent interest in the contemporary American 'confessional' poetry, or in the 'projective' or typewriting style that has grown out of Charles Olson's manifesto. He may endorse Stephen Spender's view of English poetry as the work of amateurs, especially by comparison with the professionalism of the Americans. We have little self-evidently *avant-garde* poetry, and many of the poets here seem to share the relief of Julian Ennis that 'we have at last moved out of the "modern" experiments'. Those experiments belonged to an era in which it was understood that order had to be demolished before it was made new, to the *anni mirabiles* in which the modern act of 'decreation' —to use a word of Simone Weil's—preceded the establishment of modern imaginative order. Its monuments are *Ulysses*, *The Waste Land*, the early *Cantos*. . . . We are Alexandrian in the sense that we prefer the smaller forms and use them with critical accuracy; we turn our backs on Eliot as he tried to do on Milton; he is our Chinese Wall, 'a very damaging influence', says Michael Baldwin. As for Yeats, he 'imprisoned a generation of Irish poets', says James Liddy.

Not the least interesting experience in reading these conversations is the wide, apparently random variety of writers named, in the space that would formerly have been reserved for Eliot, Yeats and Pound, as 'influences'. John Wain's far-out writer in *Hurry On Down* answered the question pat: 'Dante, Spinoza, Rimbaud, Grieg'. There are combinations almost as odd as this, the reader will see. Poets choose their own masters; more or less unconsciously they conform with certain inherited assumptions—for example, that good poems are likely to be short poems—but they also assume, and in fact possess, considerable liberty of action, and this affects their theoretical pronouncements on poetry. Let us see if any kind of consensus can be got from what they say.

Poetry, it would seem, is no longer 'the scholar's art'. These men may be learned, but their learning is not essential to their poetry, and they have no common tradition of scholarship. Most of them dislike critics as much as Robert Conquest and Norman Nicholson say they do, and they distrust the universities: Ronald Bottrall argues that teaching uses 'very much the same energy that you use in writing poetry', and Christopher Middleton thinks it's all right only if you don't touch the literature of your own language. Reading these conversations one cannot avoid being impressed by the manner in which all avoid speaking by the book; ancient, belaboured topics are treated as if the speaker had worked them up from scratch, as if there were no libraries left. This is not necessarily bad; and it does help the appearances of untrammelled activity, as well as emphasizing the variety of opinions.

No one, for instance, discusses the issue of communication in terms of what has been said before, though it is difficult to be original about it. Taner Baybars needs an overhearing audience, not wishing to go on 'echoing in his own valley'; Thomas Blackburn calls poetry 'a solitary art'. This is a confessional view, but held at a level less dangerous and exciting than that frequented by the American poets, Lowell, Sexton, Plath, who write professional confessions. The English poet cares less about his audience, perhaps, being amateur; and he may be more inclined to treat his craft as a lofty game, played mainly for his own satisfaction. Hilary Corke's interesting observations on rhyme—which he thinks of not merely as a useful resistance, but as 'a fruitful source of ideas'—stresses, I think, this private, unrhetorical approach. What one gets out of poetry, perhaps, is the satisfaction of giving apprehensible form to transactions that disturbingly take place below the level of one's consciousness—a notion touched on by John Arden, and having D. W. Harding as its best theoretical exponent—and this is the primary purpose of writing. Many would agree to this; but there is, as you would expect, variety even in areas where general agreements hold.

The poets react on the whole favourably to the revived fashion of speaking verse aloud. But even here there is dissent. James Reeves, the older man, does not think speaking aloud important except in children's verse; Alexander Baird, the younger, goes to the extreme of saying that poetry on the page is less rewarding than a musical score. Poetry never made itself thoroughly typographical; the restoration of the oral isn't very surprising in the age of the tape-recorder and the record-player. And it implies a listening audience, which poets on the whole really do like, if only as an extra benefit. (It is remarkable how many of them have a slightly terrified longing for the poetic drama.) Some show a decent concern for the comfort of their auditors; they expect them to work, of course, but for reward. Fruitless obscurity, one of the less desirable consequences of the *anni mirabiles*—for the epigoni did not always understand what the great ones were being obscure *for*—is not condoned. A modest tone is nowadays preferred. Miss Pitter—and if I were allowed to step off the platform for a moment I should call her my own favourite contributor—puts the point admirably when she says, 'take your meaning as far as you can take it, and then if you are forced into obscurity your obscurity will be valid; there will be some sort of blessing on it. . . . But you must take your meaning as far as you can.' I suppose most contributors to this book would agree about this, even though their agreements have the air of being merely fortuitous collisions within a given field of force.

It seems to me that the interviewers and the editor have brought out the agreements and differences very judiciously. Their work may give some readers cause for regret; nobody here seems girded for the Herculean task of re-imagining order, of making it new. Only the senior contributor, Sir Herbert Read, uses the serious language of the great years, and thinks of the arts as working incalculably beyond themselves; as the spirit of human civilization, the leaven in the lump. The mood is modest. Nevertheless, it will give pleasure now and, later, instruction to the historian as he sets about interpreting our times. If he notes the poets' modesty he should observe their variety; and like any other historian he will benefit from reflecting on Stevie Smith's shrewd blow at Hegel: Mr. Orr asks her whether she thinks of herself as 'a 1961 contemporary poet', and she replies, unanswerably, 'The times will just have to enlarge themselves, won't they, to make room for me, and for everybody else.' By and large, I think this book encourages us to say that poetry in the 1960s, though not as far out as we might like, is waving, not drowning.

John Arden

JOHN ARDEN was born in 1930 in Barnsley, Yorkshire, and studied architecture at King's College, Cambridge, and the College of Art, Edinburgh. He worked for two years as an architectural assistant, but has been writing full-time since 1958, largely for the stage. He is married and has four children.

His published plays include *Serjeant Musgrave's Dance* (1960), *Live Like Pigs* (1961), *The Happy Haven* (1962, in collaboration with Margaretta D'Arcy), *The Business of Good Government* (1963), *The Workhouse Donkey* (1964), *The Waters of Babylon* (1964), *Armstrong's Last Goodnight* (1965).

ORR: John, you are best known, of course, for your work as a playwright, but you also write quite a number of poems. Where does this poetic activity fit into your scheme of things?

ARDEN: Well, I think it's very much a subsidiary activity. I sometimes write an occasional poem when I haven't got a play on hand. Usually I find most of my more satisfactory poems are integrated into the plays in some way, in the form of songs or speeches which can, in some cases, be detached.

ORR: Play writing is your *job*; is writing poetry something you do for your own pleasure?

ARDEN: No, I don't draw the distinction, in fact. I earn money from writing plays, but not from writing poems. But I do them both for pleasure. It's a question of the appropriateness of ideas. The idea behind a poem of ten lines is of a different nature from the idea behind a two-and-a-half-hour play, and I find that my own invention tends to run towards full-length plays rather than short poems.

ORR: Do you find that the discipline of a short, concentrated work like a poem of a dozen lines or so is valuable to you, though?

ARDEN: Yes, I do. It helps to clarify one's mind for the writing of a

I

poem which is, as you suggest, a useful discipline when you are writing a play.

ORR: And do you pay much attention to the formal conventions of poetry: rhyme schemes, regular metrical structure?

ARDEN: I have a prejudice in favour of poems that scan and rhyme. It's only a prejudice, I don't think there's any sort of ideology behind it. This is more applicable to the verse passages in my plays. I think that there is a necessary artistic distinction to be drawn between stage dialogue in verse and stage dialogue in prose, and that when I write verse in a play, I prefer it to be clearly verse with obvious rhythm, and possibly rhymes, to distinguish it from the dialogue in prose.

ORR: And you also strive for clarity and intelligibility in your poems?

ARDEN: Well, I do now. I was, some years ago, under the influence of Dylan Thomas, as I think a lot of young writers were at that time, and I tended to write poems of a sort of murky and obscure content. But I now find that I prefer, on the whole, the most simple forms of verse: the ballad stanza or the decasyllabic couplet.

ORR: This is interesting, because I think there is, in much of your work, a strong interest in mediaeval times, mediaeval crafts and literature, isn't there?

ARDEN: There is, yes. I have a great interest, actually, in mediaeval plays, most of which are not interesting to be performed today, although some are. But they do normally have dialogue in verse written in tight stanzas, which seems to me a form that can be adapted to the modern theatre.

ORR: What about your environment and your upbringing? How important a part does this play in the sort of writer you've become?

ARDEN: Oh, I think that's impossible to say. My upbringing was very conventional: a middle-class family in Yorkshire, public school, university. I don't think that it is necessarily reflected in my work to any great extent.

ORR: You don't think, if you had been brought up, let us say, in St. John's Wood or Kensington, you would have been a very different sort of writer?

ARDEN: I have no idea. It's possible, of course. But I think that I am perhaps more interested in a sort of historical or legendary approach to my work which one could equally well have found anywhere else, perhaps. On the other hand, the Yorkshire countryside and also the Irish countryside, where I sometimes live, is conducive to this type of imagination.

ORR: But I think it's true to say that you are not, even today, what could be called a metropolitan writer, are you? You don't mix, as people do here, with other metropolitan writers?

ARDEN: I don't know whether this is a matter of choice or accident, in a way. It's partly economic, that it is more expensive to live in London with a family than it is in the country. I like to come to London and meet other people. Ideally, I think, I would like a house in the country and somewhere in London where one could come for a few months each year.

ORR: Do you find it helpful, and even necessary, to meet other writers, musicians and artists and actors and so on?

ARDEN: I find it enjoyable: I don't know how necessary it is. When I am writing I like to be well away.

ORR: You do believe in writing in absolute isolation, then?

ARDEN: Well, I can write in crowded circumstances, but I feel happier if I am away in a country cottage, or somewhere.

ORR: What I mean here is, that the idea, which has sprung up in London, of this sort of group poetry doesn't appeal to you, does it?

ARDEN: Not really, because I don't think poetry is a group activity. I know a number of writers, and I meet them when I am in London, and we talk about our work. In general, I don't think any of these writers take any notice of what any of the others say. In fact, this is purely a social meeting of colleagues rather than any sort of collective experience from which art can grow.

ORR: Can you describe how a poem takes shape in your mind: the processes that go on before it is finally committed to paper in a final form?

ARDEN: To begin with a general idea, a very vague idea: I want to write a poem about a soldier going off to the wars, or whatever it might be. I sit around and brood until a first line comes into my head; decide on a form for the poem, based on the first idea, the image, and then slog away at it and perhaps change the whole idea halfway through. I do believe, to a large extent, in the old idea of inspiration: that the traditional image of the poet being inspired by his muse, as envisaged as a sort of angelic lady whispering in his ear, does have a certain psychological truth; that the things that will make a poem a poem, rather than just a prosaic statement in metrical form, derive from the subconscious and one has to clear one's mind and let them swim up, as it were.

ORR: But does this mean that you can't sit down one morning and say:

3

'I am going to write a poem', in the same way as a cabinet maker, let's say, goes into his workshop and says: 'I am going to make a cabinet'?

ARDEN: Well, I do do that, not always with successful results. It happens in two ways. Sometimes I do that, not because, in the way of a cabinet maker, one has to do so much work a day or else you lose money, but more for the fact that my mind has been itching for several days in an uncomfortable fashion, and that one knows from experience that this means you want to write a poem (there isn't necessarily a subject in your mind); and under such circumstances I sit down and try and make my mind as blank as possible for a long time in the hope that something will emerge. This, I think, has been the traditional practice of poets. I think it was Shelley (I may be wrong about that, but one of the nineteenth-century poets) who used to attain this sort of trance-like state by having decomposing apples on shelves in his study and the smell put him into a mood. I find that I can obtain something rather similar by putting a record by Handel or Bach or Vivaldi on the record-player and becoming involved in a kind of hypnotic state from the rhythms of that music, to which I am very susceptible. The other thing is, that sometimes an idea for a poem will just suddenly arise when I am doing something quite different, like shovelling the coal in the coal-house, or digging the garden.

ORR: Your poems read extremely well: what I mean is, they read *aloud* extremely well, they have strong rhythmic impulse and an immediate impact. Is this something which you consciously strive for, and is it something which perhaps comes out of the fact that you are a playwright as well?

ARDEN: I think it comes out of the fact that I am a playwright, because when I am writing for the theatre I always say everything aloud as I write it, because otherwise I find that you write lines that actors find difficulty in speaking. And this is, in fact, the distinction between writing for the theatre and writing for the printed page, in a novel or whatever, that theatrical dialogue is no good at all unless it's practicable for an actor's voice. And I suppose this happens, too, with occasional poems that I write.

ORR: Do you have an audience, or a particular sort of person in mind to whom you wish to communicate when you write your poems?

ARDEN: Well, my wife: that's about as far as it goes. But I think a poem can be written for somebody one knows well like that, or possibly for a circle of a few acquaintances. Again, one has to know them

4

fairly intimately and their reactions to your ideas and thoughts. The business of writing poems for a large unknown, unseen audience I do not find possible. I don't even find it possible when writing plays, where it is unfortunately necessary.

ORR: Does what you read have a great influence on what you write, or are the two activities completely separate?

ARDEN: Well, if you mean am I influenced by any specific authors, yes and no. I am very rarely influenced by contemporary authors. I feel that my own contemporaries and myself are, as it were, like ships passing in the night: they go their way, I go mine. I read their books and enjoy them, or do not enjoy them. But I do read them purely as an ordinary reader; they don't have any great bearing on what I am writing, or very rarely do they. But if I am influenced, it is mostly by older writers: classical writers of any sort, the Greeks or the mediaeval writers, or the Elizabethans. But I think that these people are sufficiently far distant in time, so that I can take ideas from them and influences without being in danger of imitating the detail of their content or their style.

ORR: Are you a keen judge of your own output? Can you stand back from it at all and assess it?

ARDEN: Well, I try to: I find it very difficult. I much prefer to have somebody else to do it for me. I always submit my scripts first of all to my wife, who is slightly less biased in their favour than I am, and then after that I am never happy unless the plays are put on by a director in whom I have confidence and who can act as a critic as well as a producer.

ORR: But your poems, as distinct from your plays, are they perhaps rather more of a personal utterance?

ARDEN: Well, I am not very interested in publication of my poems. I have had a few printed in magazines and things. But, by and large, they are things that I write to satisfy a sort of personal need at the time and I don't care if people don't read them.

ORR: Do you ever feel drawn to writing anything else: novels for example, or critical work?

ARDEN: Well, not really critical work. I occasionally write articles about the technique of the theatre and things like that. I prefer to write them about the technique rather than about the meaning of my plays, or anything of that sort. As for writing novels, I don't know. I have toyed with the idea now and then, but I don't really think that prose narrative is quite my form.

ORR: John, you were at one time an architect—in fact, I think you are still an architect. Is writing all-excluding? Is this something that you had to do in preference to everything else?

ARDEN: Yes, I am not actually an architect any longer. I used to think I was until last year I found myself converting a cottage to live in and realized with horror that I had forgotten everything that I had learnt through lack of practice. I still take an interest in it, and read the architectural journals and so forth. But I did, after working two years in an architectural firm, decide that I was really more suited to be a writer, and I think that that is what I am.

24th January, 1964.

Alexander Baird

ALEXANDER BAIRD was born in 1925 in Liverpool and educated at Emmanuel College, Cambridge. He served in the Royal Air Force 1943–47. He specializes in the pronunciation of English and has taught in England, Japan and India. He is a lecturer at the University of London Institute of Education. He is married and has two daughters.

His publications include two novels, *The Micky-Hunters* (1957) and *The Unique Sensation* (1959), and a volume of verse, *Poems* (1963).

ORR: Mr. Baird, do you remember when you began writing poetry?

BAIRD: I don't remember exactly, but I'm sure that it was at a pretty early age.

ORR: What sort of poetry was it?

BAIRD: Well, at that stage, of course, it was very conventional poetry with lots of rhyme and lots of metre, and I suppose as the years went by I began to relax a little more and pay a little less attention to form and get a little more interested in saying something.

ORR: *Why* do you write poetry? Is it some inner compulsion, or is there a sense of duty to write poetry?

BAIRD: I don't know about a sense of duty; I've never suffered from that, but I'm pretty sure it's a compulsion, the very same kind of compulsion which makes people do far worse things than writing poetry.

ORR: Do you write for an audience?

BAIRD: Very definitely. I don't write for myself and I scarcely believe people who say they write for themselves. The audience is very much in mind all the time, although it's a rather nebulous and obviously a many-headed audience.

ORR: Do you think of the sound of your poems when you're writing them?

7

BAIRD: Very much so. For me, the dynamic features of poetry are intonation and juncture and I suppose these things go to make up what we generally call rhythm. This seems to me to be the most important side. The words themselves, which have got rather more attention than they've deserved over recent years, are, in fact, to me less important than what we might call the supra-segmental elements of the poem as a whole. So really, the poem as it's written down in the book is even less adequate a form than, say, the score of a symphony. People can read the score of a symphony quite happily and get some pleasure out of it without listening to the music, but I think to sit and read a book of poems is a very inadequate way of appreciating the poetry.

ORR: Do you intend, then, for your poems to make an immediate impact on a listener?

BAIRD: Yes, I think one does think along those lines inevitably. I wouldn't really call one's tactics 'shock tactics', but one does always have the desire to draw attention to some point and one always likes to feel that the new reader is there, bringing something new to the poet, in just the same way that you are bringing something new to him.

ORR: You were talking about form a few minutes ago. Do I take it, then, that form is a very important part of poetic composition to you?

BAIRD: Obviously it is a part of poetic composition, because I can't believe that you can divorce poetry from form.

ORR: Does this mean that you place particular value on some of the stricter forms, the sonnet form, or a regular metrical system in your poems?

BAIRD: Yes, I think certainly. These are very simplified aspects of form, but form itself can express itself in many different ways. I think if you examine even the most apparently loose form of *vers libre* you will find that it has a very strong form running through it all the way and, in fact, looked at linguistically and phonetically, you'll find that form, that pattern, is very strongly marked.

ORR: You say linguistically and phonetically: this is another part of yourself, too, isn't it, in that this is your profession?

BAIRD: Yes, that's true, and naturally I'm interested in linguistics and phonetics from the point of view of a poet, and I suppose that's the way I came to these subjects, really.

ORR: Do they have much to do, one with the other, your profession and your occupation as a poet?

BAIRD: They seem in my mind to be very closely linked, and the mere act of writing poetry means that I am preoccupied with problems of expression and those problems of expression are also very closely concerned with problems of sound, and so, quite inevitably, I find myself thinking in linguistic terms.

ORR: Let's turn a little now from the mechanics of poetic composition to the content of some of your poems. Is there a particular theme, or a set of themes which attracts you strongly, which you feel impelled to write about?

BAIRD: There are times when I find myself in situations in which I write a lot of poems: situations which may last a matter of months or weeks or even a matter of years. Then there are other situations in which I hardly write at all. And so, quite inevitably, blocks of poetry tend to be concerned with certain themes. The curious thing for myself is, I find that these themes are mainly concerned with place.

ORR: With places you have actually visited?

BAIRD: Very definitely. All my poems arise out of personal experience.

ORR: You don't draw any of your inspiration from books, then, do you? Not only literature, but history, philosophy, religion?

BAIRD: Only in so far as those books are part of me and I have digested them in the past, but I don't like to think there is any literary origin in any poem that I write; though the word 'inspiration' rather suggests that one has read something very fine by somebody else and feels compelled to write something oneself, and I have never really had that kind of feeling. But I have had the feeling of being in a certain situation which I must express in poetry.

ORR: Do your poems occupy a long time in composition?

BAIRD: They vary quite incredibly. Some poems may be finished in a couple of days and there is really nothing more one can do with them, and at least one poem in my recent book took, I think, fifteen years to write, on and off, and it meant that I was looking at this poem at intervals of one or two years and thinking: 'Surely there is something more I can do with this', and yet I couldn't think what that thing was. And then, as my life went on, I added to this poem. That poem isn't at all an exception. There are others which have taken quite a long time to come to fruition.

ORR: How do you decide, when what you have in your mind starts to come out, whether it is a short story, or a novel, or a play? How does it drop into this little bottle, which we can call a poem?

BAIRD: Well, the odd thing for me is that poetry is the primary form

9

and, although I have written novels, there are passages in those novels which started out by being written as poems. And, as I began to write them, I saw that I was dealing with something which was not perfectly crystallized as a poem seems to be—the thing was jelling in another way and I suddenly realized that I had stopped thinking of it as a poem and I had started thinking of it as prose. There is no clear demarcation line for me. Obviously, when you look at a page you can usually tell whether it is a page of poetry or a page of prose; but in real life, in actuality, they are both very much concerned with form and problems of juncture and intonation and, although these things aren't clearly put down on the page, nevertheless prose and poetry form for me a continuum.

ORR: Have you ever felt drawn to express yourself in verse drama?

BAIRD: Yes. At one time, at a very early age, I was attracted by verse drama, but the problems which this involved were so terrifying that I very soon gave it up because, I suppose, my own life hasn't been dramatic enough, and for me poetry is very closely concerned with personal experience.

ORR: Does what interest you may have in the other arts affect your work as a poet? Your interest perhaps in music or in the visual arts?

BAIRD: My interest in the visual arts certainly seems to preoccupy me and to creep into my poetry. As for music, for me much of poetry takes the place of music and I must admit that I am not an enthusiastic musician.

ORR: Do you believe there is any correlation between these two arts: that parts of one belong to parts of the other?

BAIRD: I do, and I feel that there is a kind of satisfaction which the human mind requires and this satisfaction can be gained either from poetry or from music.

ORR: Are there any writers, poets or prose writers, who have had a particular influence on you at any stage?

BAIRD: Well, oddly enough, those that have influenced me most are those I was forced to read at school and, as I had a classical education, it meant that the poems I read most closely in English were those I was required to translate into Latin or Greek verse, which means that sometimes they were not very good poems and they were not very good poets. But I don't think this matters. I think that it is important to make a student or a schoolboy pay close attention to some kind of poem. It doesn't matter very much if it is only a second-rate poem, but he must pay close attention to it if he is to understand what poetry is at all.

ORR: How do you find that these writers influence you, though? Stylistically, in the way you *think*, or in matters of craftsmanship?

BAIRD: Stylistically, certainly, they influence me and to some extent that is linked up with matters of craftsmanship. I like to think that I think in my way and not in anybody else's way.

ORR: Do you find yourself much in the company of other poets?

BAIRD: Well, no. I have no close friends who are poets, though I have some acquaintances who write poetry.

ORR: Do you read much contemporary poetry?

BAIRD: I read quite a lot of modern poetry, and I can't always say that I read it with pleasure, because I feel that I am in the game too and in some ways, I suppose, reading modern poetry for me is sizing up the opposition. But still, one learns and one sees how other people are working and what they are working towards and this is interesting, because I think, on the whole, I am working towards the same goals as many people who are writing today. And, frankly, I should welcome the opportunity to meet one or two people whose work I admire.

ORR: You say you are *in the game*. Does this mean you feel you are part of a movement which may in a hundred years' time be labelled 'Mid-Twentieth Century Poetry'?

BAIRD: I am afraid that is inevitable, really. Either one is part of mid-twentieth century poetry or one isn't anywhere at all. And so, of course, I am forced to say that I like to think I am in that main stream. And, quite inevitably, that mass, that block of mid-twentieth century poetry will have something in common. Whoever writes it, there will be a common theme to that block, merely because the people who write poetry are usually aware of the world in which they live.

ORR: Do you find that the young poet today is labouring under a tremendous disadvantage in that the whole weight of the tradition of English literature is pressing on him in a way that the American poets, for example, with very little tradition of their own, do not have to labour under?

BAIRD: I think that's certainly true. I admire the dynamism of American poetry and, in fact, when I spoke of the poets whom I would like to meet, I was thinking in one or two cases of American poets, because their work seems to me to be rather more alive than some of the work which is being written over here, and much more closely related to personal experience. And this seems to me to be a very important element.

ORR: Is the writing of poetry something which brings you a deep and lasting satisfaction?

BAIRD: No; if you mean by that when I have written a poem, does it give me satisfaction, no! Frankly, the act of writing it was satisfying. The finished product gives me very little pleasure at all, and of course inevitably I am concerned with the next one. But this is not a continuous experience, as I said before, it comes in patches and I suppose I could conceive of a time when I might go for a year or so and never write a poem. That would seem quite natural. It would depend on the situation I was in at that time. I suppose you might say that that could only happen when I was completely contented, and God forbid that we should ever be completely contented!

11th July, 1963.

Michael Baldwin

MICHAEL BALDWIN was born in 1930 in Gravesend, and educated at the local grammar school and at St. Edmund Hall, Oxford. He has written books, articles and broadcast scripts on educational subjects, and has worked for television and the cinema. He wrote a verse play, *The All American Bust*, a satire based on Chaucer's *Knightes Tale*, for the 1963 Poetry Festival at the Royal Court.

He has published several novels and collections of poetry, including *Grandad with Snails* (1960), a poetic account of childhood, and the double volume *Death on a Live Wire* and *On Stepping From a Sixth Storey Window* (1962).

ORR: Michael, do you enjoy writing poetry or is it a kind of labour of love that you feel you have to undertake?

BALDWIN: I think both, because different poems write themselves in different ways. Some poems have been an awful sweat to write. Others have written themselves pretty easily and I have had an idea which has excited me and it has worked itself out in a way which has seemed to me exciting. Other poems I have really had to go at for a long time.

ORR: Have you ever tried to analyse why you write poetry?

BALDWIN: This is perhaps a risky thing to say, but a long time ago I did so mistakenly with the Miltonic idea that fame was a spur and it was only when I got older and disillusioned that I realized that there was no fame to be had from writing poetry and I should have thought of something else.

ORR: But when you were a young man, you had great romantic visions of being a wonderful poet, did you, and achieving great fame and applause for this?

BALDWIN: When I was a boy, I had wonderful visions of this and by the time I was a young man it was a habit and I found I'd got used to trying to crystallize my problems in this form.

ORR: Do you remember when you wrote your first poem?

BALDWIN: Yes, it was when I was twelve years old. It was an invasion scare and the idea was that church bells would ring if parachutists were dropped anywhere in the South of England. It was a very frosty night and I heard what was, in fact, just church clocks striking from miles around, and I thought these were church bells ringing and I wrote this very wet sort of prayer in verse, and that was my first poem, quite certainly. I did not write another one until about a year later, when I was involved rather intimately in a local thunderstorm and actually saw the lightning hitting the ground very close to me, and I wrote a very derivative poem in form, but a true poem in so far as it arrived from that experience.

ORR: It strikes me, and I would like you to tell me if there is a general truth in this, that a large number of your poems arise out of specific incidents, which either have happened to you or which you witnessed. Is this true?

BALDWIN: I think so, because my conception of the role, as it were, of the poem today is that it should be an entirely personal vehicle and not an impersonal one and I think this means that I am a romantic in my attitude to the poem and to the poet.

ORR: Are you greatly disturbed (and I am speaking here of you as a poet, not as a man in the street), are you greatly disturbed as a poet by world problems—by, let's say, the fear of the hydrogen bomb, the tragedies and the difficulties of present-day life?

BALDWIN: I think, yes, more as a poet, because poetry represents one's deeper honesty. I think it is in my poetry that the sort of wider honesties tend to break through and I have written poems which are frankly 'agin the Bomb'. Again, it was by writing a poem about Caryl Chessman that I became convinced that I was against capital punishment, whereas my conscious convictions until then had been in favour of capital punishment. So I tend to find that I reach a greater honesty in my poetry and a greater involvement (which often converts me) than I find in my ordinary living.

ORR: Do you find yourself, then, adopting a definite moral standpoint in your poems which, perhaps, you don't adopt in your normal day-to-day life?

BALDWIN: I don't find myself 'adopting', I find it being taken up for me. It is there waiting for me in the ordering of the poem which, I suppose, is just an example of one's primitive imaginative forces winning over one's intellect, and I think it is a good thing that they should do so.

ORR: Let's come back now to something that you said earlier. You said of your early poems that some were very derivative. Do you find that you are, or tend to be, influenced by other writers in your work?

BALDWIN: I think I would be very foolish if I said that there weren't influences. One of the dangerous things is that one can recognize that certain writers could have influenced one for bad. I tend to know now, almost for the first time, what is good and personal in my writing and I feel that I am less and less going to be influenced by other people. I sometimes even see that it is in me to influence other people and that at last I am getting my own back on literature.

ORR: Are there any particular writers that have had a tremendous influence on you?

BALDWIN: Yes, at varying times in my life, generally before the age of twenty (and I am sure they are very important years), quite diverse personalities: George Barker, Pablo Neruda, for example, were poets who influenced me very, very deeply.

ORR: What about some of the earlier writers? I mean it is almost a cliché now to say that one is influenced by Yeats or by T. S. Eliot.

BALDWIN: I would hope not to be influenced by T. S. Eliot, because I deeply dislike his poetry, but I think it would be impossible, probably, for anyone writing today not to be influenced by him to a small extent, even by virtue of trying to avoid him. But I think he has been a very damaging influence on poetry, quite as damaging as Milton (or as he claims Milton has been) with, of course, a lot less excuse in his case.

ORR: Do you feel that it's essential, or even a good thing, for the poet today, or at any time, if you like, to be something of a scholar, something of a literary critic as well as a writer himself?

BALDWIN: My own view about writing (and I write other sorts of things than poetry; in particular, I am interested in novels) my view about writing is that the less of a formal education you have had, provided that you have had a full education in the senses and particularly in the relationship between the senses and the imagination and words, then the less of a formal education you have had the better. Certainly my time at Oxford did me nothing but harm as a writer and resulted in a very bad volume of poetry.

ORR: What else do you do in your life apart from writing poetry?

BALDWIN: I teach at a Teacher Training College for women at present.

I'm a pretty committed educator. I do write books and broadcast and give lectures on some of the theory of education. I write novels which have been published, or which are going to be published, but my over-riding ambition is to write plays. I do write plays, but these have been far less successful: they got people interested, but they don't get themselves towards production, or they have not done so far.

ORR: Are these plays in verse?

BALDWIN: I have written some plays in verse. Curiously, they have been more successful, they have been successful with amateur groups, but I do not write verse plays now and I think that a verse play really is an anachronism. I see no point in writing a verse play in 1963.

ORR: Why?

BALDWIN: Because I think there's more to drama and to poetry than the formal shape of verse. I think a poetic apprehension, as related to the stage, does concern itself with other things, such as the essential poetry in a scene, the essential poetry in character, the deeper symbolisms and layers that you can get in a piece of dramatic writing: something quite apart from the shape that you give it, often the distracting shape today, by putting it in verse.

ORR: All these various activities of yours, as an educator, as a writer of novels, as a playwright, do all these belong to separate compartments or do they all belong one to the other and somehow add to your stature, to your depth and experience as a poet?

BALDWIN: I certainly think that a poet today has got to apply himself to more media than just writing, shall we say, lyric poems. The novelists whom I most admire are people like Faulkner, for example. I believe Faulkner has, in his youth, published poetry, but he writes *as a poet* in the deepest sense. So I am sure these things do spread one into the other. There is no doubt about the fact that my work as an educator has influenced my poetry, in all sorts of ways. It does, probably, give me that slightly didactic streak and that is a pity; but it has also taught me a great amount about imaginative processes by looking at the way they happen to other people, particularly to children. I think there is a very fertile area for a poet to be exploring.

ORR: Do you find yourself thrown into the company of other poets and other writers?

BALDWIN: In general, I don't like writers at all. They are often curiously incomplete individuals, and I suppose that is one of the reasons that they write, that they are trying to complete themselves in words. I prefer not to meet writers, quite certainly, unless they are interesting to meet as people and I generally don't find that.

ORR: Do you write your poems with the idea in your mind while you are writing them of having them read aloud?

BALDWIN: I think I am always aware of the aural qualities in a poem. It isn't true of all my poems, but I do try and hear, at least with the inner ear, every word, every line that I write.

ORR: Are you a stern critic of your own writing?

BALDWIN: I am pretty stern, once time has passed. Just occasionally I know that I have done something good and that conviction does not change. I produce a great amount of work, which really only can appear in what I think is its true light to me after a number of years have passed. I don't like much of my own poetry, but it does take me a considerable time before a poem which I wrote in rather a hurry shows itself in its true value, and I often tend to include in a collection of poems work that I have written eight or ten years before, for the reason that it suddenly seems to belong and it suddenly seems right.

ORR: When you look back on your early poems, do you look back on them with a sense of satisfaction and with a sense of the same enjoyment that you had in creating them at the time, or do they seem to belong to some almost different person?

BALDWIN: A lot of my early poetry is, I think, quite deeply neurotic. It excites me because it is colourful, but I find it hard to think that it is written by the same person, not because I am necessarily an unneurotic person now, but because the neurosis seems to have changed. I don't read it with a great deal of enjoyment, no, though with certain gleams of recognition of something. I don't think I would include much of my early poetry in any collected volume, if I ever get that far.

ORR: How much should, or do, the poems of a particular writer introduce you to the man himself? In other words, do you think someone reading your volumes of poetry would then expect to meet the sort of person that you are?

BALDWIN: I would hope that a volume of poems would show you the real man, the man stripped of his social layers and so on. There is no doubt, though, that my own poetry on occasions strikes attitudes, rather grotesque attitudes and postures, which I think are over-extreme. It would be true, though, to say that some of this attitudinizing is true of my own nature. I think, probably, my current poetry does at least make an image of what I am like as a person. So I would be unhappy if I felt that a person's poetry did not make an image, a pretty recognizable image of what he or she was like as a person. But then, of course, it has got to be an image of something which is pretty much inside. I think you have got to make an allowance for the social layer before you can talk about this.

ORR: Do you think then, perhaps, that there's a temptation for, let us say, a timid or inarticulate person in company to go away and write the most bold and outspoken verse?

BALDWIN: Yes, I think this is true. A lot of poets in the past have been extremely inarticulate verbally, haven't they? I believe Swinburne was, for example. I am sure one does go away, if one has a pimply chest, and beats it in one's verse to some extent.

ORR: Michael, is the writing of poetry simply a task which you feel you have to go on doing and that there's no point at which you can look back on it with a sense of fulfilment?

BALDWIN: It never brings me any real sense of fulfilment or satisfaction. It is just something which I honestly feel I cannot escape doing. It's a compulsion: I mean to that extent it is a personal indiscipline rather than a personal discipline. I could not stop doing it. Although when I am doing it, it can be painful to me, I would never want not to do it. But it does not bring much satisfaction with it, no.

ORR: Does it matter very much to you whether people read your poems and, if they do, what they think of them?

BALDWIN: Yes, it used not to, but more and more it does. I feel about all my writing that I want it to be read by as many people as possible and one sets oneself target figures. I have always wanted to write a novel which I can lean back and say has been read by, what shall we say, a hundred thousand people, which is a very big figure indeed in contemporary novel terms. I still want to write a book of poems which I can say has been read by, shall we say, ten thousand people, which again would be an absolutely astronomical figure in contemporary terms.

ORR: Do you think at all of your poems being read in, let us say, two hundred years? And if you do, does this interest you, appeal to you?

BALDWIN: It is very hard not to be terrifyingly egotistical about this. In fact, yes, I would like to think that. I am not yet sure that I have written poems that deserve that to happen, but I think all the time one is trying to write something which will seem to say something for all time. It is a fact, of course, that a year or two after you have written it, you know that it cannot possibly say it for your own time or even for you, and it is this that drives you on to trying to write again.

21st March, 1963.

Taner Baybars

TANER BAYBARS was born in 1936, and was educated privately and at the Turkish Lycée in Nicosia. He came to London to study law but never did.

His first collection of poems *To Catch a Falling Man* appeared in 1963, his novel *A Trap for the Burglar* in 1965.

ORR: Taner, where were you born?

BAYBARS: Nicosia, Cyprus.

ORR: And when did you start writing poetry?

BAYBARS: At the age of eight, which was also my first publication date, and after that I just kept on writing.

ORR: Your first poems, then, were written in Turkish?

BAYBARS: They were, yes.

ORR: And did you obtain the same mastery of English quickly, as you had of Turkish?

BAYBARS: Well, I don't know how it came about, but I just started writing in English and the poems I sent out were rejected continuously and, all of a sudden, I started having them published.

ORR: Let me ask you, are you well read in English literature? In other words, have you explored the great tradition of English literature thoroughly and minutely?

BAYBARS: Not thoroughly and minutely, but as far as I could.

ORR: Do you feel this is part of the poet's stock-in-trade, to have an extensive knowledge of English literature and of literary techniques?

BAYBARS: I, personally, wouldn't have thought so, no. I think he is writing what he feels in the first instance and not what he has learned from books. He doesn't elaborate on the knowledge he has acquired from the tradition of the the best literature. From this point of view I think it's a good thing to be rather ignorant in writing poetry.

ORR: You don't feel, then, that it's absolutely necessary to have a bird's-eye-view of modern European literature?

BAYBARS: I think a bird's-eye-view is very useful, but to go into it as a scholar might and afterwards to try to imitate it as a poet would, under the circumstances, is a wrong thing.

ORR: How is it useful to you, though, if you're not going to imitate it?

BAYBARS: Well, imitation comes in two forms. Imitation of technique and imitation of the spirit. If you are imitating a technique, then perhaps it's a good thing, because, after all, you learn a great deal from other people's techniques. But to start imitating their spiritual entities would be a very harmful thing indeed.

ORR: Do you find it helpful, or even vital, to your writing to live in what, for want of a better phrase, I might call a cultural environment, such as a big metropolitan city like London?

BAYBARS: It might sound paradoxical, but I do, yes. I couldn't live, for instance, in a village either in England or elsewhere—Spain or Turkey—isolated from all literary activities. I want to be in the hub of things. And I want to feel the liberty of either going into that activity or remaining outside it. But to be away and not being able to do either would depress me a lot.

ORR: But you do find, in the midst of all this, you have to find a spot of isolation for yourself?

BAYBARS: I do, yes, and I think the best isolation I have found is achieved in a crowded city like London and not in a quiet village up on the mountains.

ORR: Let's turn now and look a little more closely at the actual process of composition. How do your poems occur to you and how do they take shape? Is there a sort of process that you can identify? You can say, 'Ah yes, I feel a poem coming on', as some of us say, 'I feel I've got flu this morning.' And then how do you get rid of it?

BAYBARS: Well, I like that medical analogy, but I couldn't altogether agree with it. I don't feel that a poem is coming on because I've got the symptoms of a poem. But a poem might strike me just suddenly as an image, and I would capture the image as I would capture, probably, a butterfly. This perhaps is a wrong analogy as well; but, nevertheless, it is an immediate capturing and after that you build your poem around it. I don't agree altogether with revisions, because revisions inevitably destroy a great deal of the first capturing moment. I belong to the school, the old school perhaps, who take poetry as a first, instantaneous, spontaneous commitment to the paper.

ORR: But, then, do you undertake a refinement of language? Are you very meticulous about the use of language and finding exactly the right, precise word?

BAYBARS: I think every poet should. Without that I don't think anyone could write poems at all, because if you used ordinary language without rhythm—I don't mean rhyme at all, because rhyme is not important, as far as I am concerned—without rhythm or without vision then, of course, it would be a great flop. And I should say that composing a poem requires this spontaneity, not only in images and ideas but also in language. And so, to me it's a kind of synchronization of the three aspects all at once: language, image and thought.

ORR: What sort of things inspire you to the creation of a poem? Are there larger themes which are constantly in the back of your mind or are there just sudden little chance events, or sights, or apprehensions, that set a poem in motion?

BAYBARS: What I have been trying to explore in my poems are the fundamental fears of human beings. These might be written in the form of, say, walking in a tunnel, or falling, or not being able to go to bed with one's wife because one has a fear. I mean, different forms of fear I have been trying to explore. But I don't think that to write a sequence or, rather, a kind of heroic poem in the line of de Vigny or Hugo would help me. Well, at least, not in the present age. So, it's best to see the different aspects of these fears and write about them in different circumstances and present them in different situations.

ORR: So, in fact, a collected volume like this of yours entitled, from one of the poems, *To Catch a Falling Man*, could perhaps present a mosaic which in itself creates a pattern of its own? Would you agree?

BAYBARS: I would agree with that.

ORR: Taner, this is a very difficult question, but have you ever paused to consider why you write poetry?

BAYBARS: No, I haven't. I am very thankful for that, and I don't want to start thinking why.

ORR: But this is something you would do in preference to anything else, is it?

BAYBARS: I think it is an urge. It's an unavoidable thing and you can't help being a poet if you are a poet.

ORR: Do you write for yourself or do you write for an audience, an imagined audience or a real audience?

BAYBARS: Ah, well, there are dangers nowadays that certain groups and audiences force themselves on the poets and, therefore, before they write anything on paper, first of all they picture an audience and without using their own critical faculties they start thinking, 'What is he or she going to think when I have written this line?' I try to avoid that. It is terribly difficult, but I do try to avoid that and I feel that most of my successful poems are those written for my own self.

ORR: Do you pay great attention to the sound which your poems make? In other words, do you think of your poems as things being read aloud, being voiced, rather than just merely scanned on the printed page?

BAYBARS: I do, a great deal, yes. I think sound is very important, very important indeed. I would in this instance suggest what Pound said in *The ABC of Reading*, that poetry is language charged with dynamism and also that if poetry gets away from rhythm it atrophies.

ORR: Do you strive all the time to avoid obscurity in your poems? Do you try to make them as clear as they possibly can be?

BAYBARS: I suppose that I do try up to a point to present an obscure problem that I am experiencing as clearly as possible, so that I can communicate to other people, otherwise I would be just echoing in my own valley.

ORR: The principle of communication, then, is one that is important to you?

BAYBARS: Of course, terribly important.

ORR: What I mean is that you're not behind the shelter of your pen and your paper, putting on a great big frightening disguise to try and appear as something other than what you really are?

BAYBARS: No, that mustn't be done. It is dishonesty in poetry. Everything must come from the heart.

ORR: And do you think there is a purpose in this? Do you ever think what the end of this is to be?

BAYBARS: I don't really want to go into psychoanalysis, but I mean it is quite obvious that a poet is somebody who is trying to share his pleasures, sufferings and thoughts with other people; or the primordial idea of a poet is this. And I should have thought, in the Jungian terminology, that this would be as obvious as a man just going out and weeping in the middle of the street. There is no end to his weeping probably, but all the same, he is communicating something to the passers-by.

ORR: And do you want to communicate to as many people as possible?

BAYBARS: That again brings up the question of an audience. A poet must write primarily as a free person without thinking of an audience,

24

but also bearing in mind that he is trying to communicate something to other people. It is a kind of transmission. If you haven't got the right receiver, you don't get that station, you see. Whether you are a workman or you're a gentleman, it doesn't matter. The transmitter is there all right, so it all depends on your receiver.

ORR: Is the writing of poetry something which brings you cumulative satisfaction as each poem goes down on to paper, or is it something rather in the nature of a continuing frustration between poems?

BAYBARS: There is a little of both, I should say. It's a great satisfaction, of course, to see that you have done something and to see it on paper. Also there is a great satisfaction that you are thinking of a new thing and you are anticipating its coming: a kind of pregnancy. And after that, perhaps, you're not pleased with what you've done. To me, frustration starts then, not between the two poems, but after the failure. As soon as you conceive another idea which pleases you, then you feel greatly satisfied again and you just forget about the miscarriage.

12th September, 1963.

Thomas Blackburn

THOMAS BLACKBURN was born in 1916 and educated at Bromsgrove School and Durham University. After twelve years as a school teacher he was Gregory Fellow of Poetry at the University of Leeds for two years. He is now Head of the English Department at the College of S. Mark and S. John in Chelsea. He has recently completed a study of Browning's poetry.

He has published six books of verse, of which the most recent is *A Breathing Space* (1964), and one book of criticism, *The Price of an Eye* (1961).

PRESS: Your first collection appeared in 1951. Had you been writing for many years before?

BLACKBURN: I had been writing, but without any thought of publication at all. Partly because the war took one's time up. So it was a fairly late start as far as publication is concerned.

PRESS: But not actual writing?

BLACKBURN: No, no, I had been at it since I was very young indeed. I used to write sermons instead of doing prep at school; due to the fact that my father was a parson perhaps. They were very bad, and I tore them all up.

PRESS: In these early poems and indeed in many of your later poems Yeats seems to be a very powerful presence. Is this deliberately sought or did he, as it were, possess you?

BLACKBURN: I got steeped in the poetry of Yeats as a young man, I knew a great deal of his work by heart and it was only when there were certain things that I wanted to say that Yeats hadn't said that I began to seriously want to write. And it has given me tremendous trouble to get his rhythms and accents and so on out of my work. I do feel he is the great figure towering over our age and it is terribly difficult to avoid his influence.

PRESS: In your earlier work you rely on myth to a far greater extent

27

than in the verse of your two most recent volumes. Is this a gradual change or did you decide to make a break?

BLACKBURN: I think it represents a closing-in on experience. First of all I wanted to talk about my own problems through myths, Oedipus, for example, and Pasiphaë; I only got excited by those great themes because they touched off something in myself. They were a kind of bridge between myself and the audience. But later I wanted to write very much more directly about what went on in my own life. But I suppose that one's life is a kind of myth, that one is lived by things, written by things, almost beyond one's control. I wanted in my last two books to make poetry about everyday experiences and show how they touch off into all sorts of mysterious areas and significances. Quite little things, like a quarrel or watching birds from a stone by the sea, can arouse innumerable echoes.

PRESS: Are you a follower, a disciple, of Jung?

BLACKBURN: Again, like Yeats, I feel he has permeated my thought; that there has been through Jung, I suppose through Freud too, a revolution in what we feel about ourselves: the mind of man has expanded into all sorts of mysterious continents which were unknown before. One is not only trying to assimilate one's own personal problems but to assimilate this new conception of the human being. It isn't so much that I am a follower of Jung, but the sort of experience I have had leads me to read him, and his work substantiates what I have felt about life.

PRESS: Your father was an Anglican clergyman. You frequently use Christian images and themes. Do you regard yourself as an orthodox Christian or do you think of yourself as being, so to speak, a Christian heretic rather like a third or fourth century heretic?

BLACKBURN: I am trying to remember what you said in your book *Rule and Energy* about that. You had a few words about it, didn't you, which I rather agreed with?

PRESS: I suggested, I think, that you might be a gnostic.

BLACKBURN: Yes, and I might have been burnt in a more civilized century.

PRESS: In a more *faithful* century.

BLACKBURN: Faithful century, yes. I feel that Christianity was there, is still here, but now it is bursting through the seams of churches and orthodoxy and that we have somehow to take the characters of its divine drama, Judas, Christ, etc., and bring them back inside ourselves, into the Armageddon of the human being himself.

PRESS: Many of your poems seem to be an exorcism of your own private devils. What about the social function of poetry?

BLACKBURN: I wonder, you know, about that. If you could get your own private devils exorcized I feel that you would be doing something for society, because if you manage to come clean of these various things then the way you react to society would be quite different, wouldn't it? I find no difference between the clarification, elucidation and understanding of one's own personal problems and those of society. After all, one is busy with society and the reaction one has depends on how much one has understood of oneself.

PRESS: Your poems very often have extremely strong, forceful, clearly marked rhythms. Are they designed to be read aloud?

BLACKBURN: I certainly compose aloud, sort of boo and bah it over to myself and make the words come off the tongue. I feel that is an essential part of composition. On the other hand, I have tried to break up the rhythms. I felt that in my earlier books I had too marked a rhythm and have tried in my new collection to bring the rhythms and the rhymes to the heel of more colloquial speech by breaking them up and by half rhymes, assonance and so on.

PRESS: Do you write swiftly?

BLACKBURN: In the end I do; I get an idea, a sort of germ comes, and if that comes I know the poem will be finished. But it may take me weeks and weeks of brooding and thinking about this exciting idea, and then suddenly the poem will arrive; but it takes a long period of gestation; then once that birthpoint has been reached the thing is written quickly; but then comes the working over and that's a long process.

PRESS: You say a germ. By that do you mean an idea, a visual image, a cadence, a form of words?

BLACKBURN: I find it's difficult to separate the idea from the cadence and the visual image. It is usually an idea married to an image and a cadence.

PRESS: Are you angered, amused, depressed, by severe and adverse criticism?

BLACKBURN: I had a lot of bad ones this time certainly, but on the other hand my previous book had good criticism. If you take the good seriously then you've got to take the bad, so I suppose one ought to detach oneself from both good and bad. But obviously, being human, one is annoyed and may teeter a bit in one's confidence because poetry is such a difficult thing to know about. You cannot tell till you've been dead for about fifty years or have lived so long that you are as good as posthumous, whether you've written poetry or just a snappy ersatz modern number with nylon voice-box and plastic back. But still something insists that one does the work.

PRESS: Do you think that the practice of group poetry, to use a convenient shorthand phrase, has anything to commend it?

BLACKBURN: Not to me! I have been to one or two groups and found them intensely depressing. Poetry is a solitary art. I do like meeting the occasional poet or two, you know, but the idea of going along and having a kind of seminar of practitioners to me would be anathema. I'd hate it.

PRESS: What about for young poets? Would you approve of their being trained technically, as musicians are, to write in certain metres, certain poetic forms; really severe technical academic training?

BLACKBURN: The one time that really did happen in England was with the translation of Latin and Greek verse, wasn't it? What the value of that was I don't quite know. I would have thought that most young poets seeped themselves in the writing of earlier poets and that that does something to them, but I can't myself see that any technical academic training would help. It would only impose some sort of strait-jacket and it would stop the particular individual brooding and gestation that is an essential for poetry. The writing of poetry by children is very puzzling. If one really wanted to make a child a poet, presumably one would dig a fairly deep hole and drop them in head first and cover it with tar and a bit of glass and leave them there for about six months and then by the end of that they would either be dead or they would be a poet perhaps. It seems to come from something other than the school, often from rather difficult early experiences in the home, although, mind you, I suppose that means nothing in itself; there's got to be this mysterious thing technique, though where that comes from, I don't know.

PRESS: The technique, as you call it, you feel is not really akin to the technique of the other arts?

BLACKBURN: I don't think it can be acquired from external influence and schools in the same way as it can in the other arts.

PRESS: Are you much influenced by the other arts?

BLACKBURN: I was very influenced, both through his personality and his work, by Francis Bacon. He would take quite ordinary themes, like a businessman laughing, and show this action dropping off into great dark areas of significance; that I found tremendously stimulating.

PRESS: He is the only painter who has had this effect on you?

BLACKBURN: The only modern painter. I mean, I was influenced by other artists but I would find it very difficult, except in the case of Francis Bacon, to show how definite it was.

PRESS: You are a very keen mountaineer. This obviously is both a skilful and a dangerous sport. Do you link this with your writing of poetry in any way?

BLACKBURN: I think I do. I think when you write a poem you must feel the absolute value of the writing, you brush away all other considerations but the poem. This is supremely important and the whole of your energy must be, as it were, offered like a kind of sacrifice to the poem. And in the same way, mountaineering is the only sport where you offer the whole of yourself; when you are making a difficult move on a rockface, you know very well that if your muscles are not co-ordinated rightly and if you don't take a great deal of care and judgement, then you will fall down and break your neck. And I love that, the sense of one's whole life being pushed up and caught by one small physical movement. This intensity of the moment.

PRESS: And the writing of poetry is a spiritual parallel?

BLACKBURN: I hadn't thought about it before, but I think there is this sense of the whole of one's being offered to the activity and summed up by it, so it matters supremely .

PRESS: It is often said that, for Victorian agnostics, walking on the mountains was a substitute for worshipping God. Is there any element in your mountaineering of this particular reaction?

BLACKBURN: I would not like to make it specific. I know that being in these places has this effect. I have to live in town because of my job, but in the mountains you do feel exposed to a solitude which can be tremendously fructifying, a silence which speaks. I think in my poem on Wordsworth there is this sense of something coming through silence, of listening to silence, but I would not like to say specifically this was a religious experience.

PRESS: Do you feel the need to make any striking technical innovations in the art of verse?

BLACKBURN: The real revolutions in the art of verse have been very small modifications of technique. Those are the ones that matter. Usually when you have had absolutely outrageous and strange changes, poems in the form of mice and one word on one line and everything broken up, these have been, as it were, sports, things which were ephemeral and were soon lost. The important major changes seem to me changes in moving towards a more colloquial diction or away from the rhythms of everyday speech.

PRESS: I can see this applies to Yeats, but surely not to Eliot?

BLACKBURN: No, when I said that I was thinking of Yeats, as regards modern poets. Eliot seems to be a person who did make almost a radical break, but I wonder how much he really has changed the techniques of verse.

PRESS: You yourself have not been deeply moved by Eliot or deeply influenced?

BLACKBURN: Not influenced: deeply moved. 'The Waste Land' is a great and revolutionary poem but in a lot of his other ones Eliot keeps fairly close to traditional forms. One tends to generalize too much from 'The Waste Land' which, I believe, was cut about a lot anyway by Pound.

PRESS: Do you feel the need to write a long dramatic poem, a play, a libretto?

BLACKBURN: Well, yes, more and more. I have just finished a libretto for a friend of mine, a composer. We have done a couple of short oratorios already—and this piece is to be on Judas Iscariot. I found the work very satisfying.

12th November, 1964.

Edmund Blunden

EDMUND BLUNDEN was born in 1896 in London and educated at Christ's
Hospital and Queen's College, Oxford. He served in the Royal Sussex
Regiment 1915–19 and was awarded the Military Cross. Professor of
English Literature at Tokyo University 1924–27, Fellow of Merton College,
Oxford, 1931–43. U.K. Liaison Mission, Tokyo, 1947–50. Professor at
Hong Kong University 1953–64. D.Litt. Leeds University, D.Litt. Leicester
University. Companion of Literature, Benson Medallist and Fellow of the
Royal Society of Literature. C.B.E. 1951. He was awarded the Hawthornden
Prize in 1922, and the Queen's Gold Medal for Poetry 1956. He is married
and has five daughters.

His published works include *Undertones of War* (1928), *Nature in English
Literature* (1929), *English Villages* (1941), *Shelley, a Life Story* (1943), *Shells
by a Stream* (1944), *After the Bombing* (1948), *Poems of Many Years* (1957),
A Hong Kong House (1962), *Lee Lan Flies the Dragon Kite* (1962).

PRESS: Your first book of poems, I think, came out in 1914 when you
were still at school. Was this the result of a sudden outburst of writing
or had you been writing verse since your early teens?

BLUNDEN: The first book was called *Poems 1913 and 1914*, and I think
I had done something before, which naturally I didn't want to print.
I'd got to the superior age of seventeen or eighteen when I printed
this book, so I threw away what had been written earlier. Apart from
reasons of sentiment, the reason I began to write probably was
imitation.

PRESS: When you say imitation, do you mean imitation of English
poets?

BLUNDEN: And French poets, because we began to cope with them at
my big school—and the earlier one. And by imitation, I mean not
exactly literal imitation, but rather the attempt to find in the world

33

the sort of things they had already found. Even old-fashioned writers seemed to me suddenly to be wonderfully good. I particularly enjoyed (it seems strange now) Thomson's *Seasons*, and one day in the grammar school picked up a little anthology. We had plenty of poetry at home, but it just happened one afternoon in the grammar school I picked up a schoolbook and there was a great quotation from 'Paradise Lost', the one you know so well: 'Him the Almighty Power/Hurl'd headlong flaming from th'ethereal sky', and that suddenly struck me again as beyond the confines of prose.

PRESS: You were one of the earliest people, I think, to admire John Clare?

BLUNDEN: Yes. When did I begin? I think about 1913 or 1914, and a little dedication to him shows it about that time. He had been very beautifully selected by Arthur Symons, so there was no difficulty in getting him then. Lately it's been made out that he was discovered by myself, with a dead friend, Alan Porter, in 1920, but it's not quite so simple. I'm glad you mentioned him because I should like to say how much I feel the beauty of Symons' work. He himself was a little out of his mind, I think, latterly, which makes the pathos of his editing John Clare all the more.

PRESS: You have lived abroad a great deal. Has your poetry been affected very much by these long spells overseas?

BLUNDEN: I think living in Japan made a difference in even one's handwriting and perhaps one's manner. I don't go about 'as I should', bowing and making a faint hissing sound, but I'm sure my whole style of thought has been touched by Japanese experiences. For the poetry part, I suspect that I cut the corners a little finer than I used to do.

PRESS: Have you normally written in traditional stanza forms, metres, rhymes?

BLUNDEN: Generally, yes. Yet I daresay I could find free verses of mine before I was conscious of many modern free-verse writers. The First World War did something to shake us up on forms and metres, and generally on the music of verse.

PRESS: Do you read much contemporary verse?

BLUNDEN: I've read a great deal and just begun again. I don't ever neglect it altogether, but the busy way I have lived, teaching particularly, and lately for example in university expansion,—that has not let me read as much as I wanted. But much modern verse escapes me, as it does many people of my age. Whether it is our fault or the verse's fault, I wouldn't like to argue.

PRESS: Have you been much influenced by the other arts, by music or by painting?

BLUNDEN: I think painting more than music, although I was a choirboy for years. But painting, that has been much in my mind. I remember when writing my nature pieces, which I don't write so much now, the sense I had was of *painting* rather than describing. Perhaps it is a fault, but there it is. And yet, I think when I was told I was a rural writer I would rather have said rural painter, in my way. I don't know whether it is legitimate, though, for a poet to think he can paint in words. That's perhaps a fallacy.

PRESS: What kind of experience is likely to contain the germ of a poem?

BLUNDEN: I think something quite accidental disturbs something else. It's like digging in the sand and hitting a remaining land-mine or something. It's not quite so powerful a result in my case, but the tap at the window of a leaf on a wet day, or some echo in the house, or being alone in the house, or almost any unexpected little thing may disturb something inside one, I think. I have found, when I was younger, that if I went to the music hall (we haven't got enough of those), it might start up something quite irrelevant to the music hall, but what I had seen and heard did arouse or precipitate something. I made a few attempts to write on deliberately chosen subjects. And then, of course, I have often had to write because someone said you *must* write a poem on the passing of King George V, or whatever it was. However, I tried a scheme once for poems on famous trials and only one of them clearly survives, but that happens to be one of the poems which most of my readers like. It is called 'Incident in Hyde Park' and it's rather long. But it was one of those deliberate compositions which stayed.

PRESS: Do you normally write very fast and then correct later?

BLUNDEN: Yes, I think I must go pretty quickly and correct. Nowadays I correct more than I did. I may have learnt something in the course of seventy years almost. I used to be rather conceited that I could write a poem straight out and leave it at that. But I have noticed lately that, especially with my wife's eye on the matter, I feel obliged to take a good look at it. I often heard Robert Graves talk of the necessity of rewriting a poem, and I think somewhere I have got sixteen drafts of a poem of his, or I saw them. I don't know whether I could achieve any such records.

PRESS: Have there been long spells, of weeks or even months, when you have written no poems?

BLUNDEN: It's beginning to work a little like that now, but it hasn't exactly got there. The worst year I remember in this history, a personal one, was the last year of War One, 1918. I'd been keeping it up in the trenches and so on, then suddenly 1918 seemed to me almost the blackest of the lot. (And yet we won the war!) I found the whole military business suddenly too dull for poetry.

PRESS: You knew many of the First World War poets. Have you changed your views about their relative merits as poets?

BLUNDEN: I don't think very much, and indeed I remember with gratitude a number who aren't generally spoken of now. But the best, I think, are those who are accounted best at the present time. We didn't know Owen at the end of the First World War. I don't mean we didn't know him, the man, but his work hadn't yet appeared. When it did, it was edited by Sassoon first. I don't know even yet how to rate those two, whether to give Siegfried the benefit of the origin-ality which he displayed, because I don't think anybody, even Owen, had quite got to that point of view then. We learnt by some of Sieg-fried's early pieces or early war pieces. All of us tried a bit on our own without having quite his vivacity at that time and he seemed to be so purposeful in his anti-war pieces. But Owen now, it seems to me, if Siegfried doesn't object, has some Dante-like quality in tone which is not always in S.S. Yet we haven't heard the last of Sassoon yet. His religious verses are still being written and one day there may come up a pretty powerful one.

PRESS: Have you any particular audience in mind when you write poetry?

BLUNDEN: I wish I could tell myself about this. I don't think I have ever written for anybody except the other one in oneself. How there are two of us, I don't know, but I suppose all artists do maintain their own critical squad in their craniums. I wish I could answer it. I have a notion that a lot of people are poetic and to that extent what is called being poetical is allowable. And I don't really want to be too brilliant about anything; merely to detect something in life which somebody else would like to have noted in words. But 'I pipe to please myself': John Clare uses that as a motto on his first book—I think, from Spenser.

PRESS: Have you ever felt the desire to attempt a large-scale work such as an epic poem or drama or a long narrative poem?

BLUNDEN: It's come and gone and sometimes I was determined I was going to do it, but indolence and overwork and failure to have really enough in mind, I would suspect, prevented. In a way, the only sustained thing I have done was the *Undertones of War*, mainly in prose, but there is an extension of it in verse. That adds up, as I meant, to a sort of long poem. It varies, of course, in topics, but the uniting argument, if there is one, is that war is like that and ought not to happen.

PRESS: The audience has grown enormously for music in this country in the last forty years. Do you think that there could be a large audience for verse?

BLUNDEN: I think you are giving me a good cue here. I was at a sort of summer school lately of teachers, and they were assembled for a week solely for poetry. We had several poets whose names and work you know, like R. S. Thomas and Laurie Lee and Vernon Watkins, and Leonard Clark was running the course. But you know, it was fascinating to be among these teachers and to have their company, morning and evening, all for poetry, genuine, and they didn't seem to be in any doubt about the popularity of poetry at all. I mean, their own lives as teachers were full of it, and most accurate in reference to new poetry and so on, and if questions were raised they were of a subtle and often valuable kind. So I shouldn't be surprised if we don't have even more tastes in poetry than must have been with us in the eighteenth century or when the poems of Sir Walter Scott were being read in every home, read aloud. I think that's one answer also to the question, for whom do you write. It may be for that sort of domestic audience which formerly, as I say, used to listen to Scott read aloud by one of their number or the same audience which would have Coleridge calling to read his 'Kubla Khan' or Wordsworth his 'Prelude'. That is a hope, anyway.

PRESS: You think that this revival of reading aloud is a hopeful sign?

BLUNDEN: I think it is. It's bound to win if it goes on a bit longer. The world seems, on the face of it, so darkened with crime and idiocy at the moment that the other faction, the angels, are working hard too, and I think in the end they will probably get ahead.

3rd September, 1964.

Ronald Bottrall

RONALD BOTTRALL was born in 1906 in Camborne, Cornwall, and educated
at Redruth County School and Pembroke College, Cambridge. He held
academic posts overseas between 1929 and 1938, and during this period he
was Johore Professor of English at Raffles College, Singapore, and Professor
of English at the British Institute, Florence. He served as British Council
Representative in Sweden, Italy, Brazil, Greece, Japan and was Controller
of Education Division 1950–54. Since 1963 he has been the Chief of the
Fellowships and Training Branch, United Nations Food and Agriculture
Organization. He was awarded the O.B.E. in 1949. He won the Syracuse
International Poetry Prize in 1954. F.R.S.L. 1955.

His publications include *The Loosening and other Poems* (1931), *Festivals
of Fire* (1934), *The Turning Path* (1939), *Farewell and Welcome* (1945),
Selected Poems (1946), *The Palisades of Fear* (1949), *Adam Unparadised* (1954),
Collected Poems (1961).

ORR: Mr. Bottrall, when did you start writing poetry?

BOTTRALL: Well, I started writing something that perhaps had better
be described as verse when I was at school, and it seemed to me to be
so bad that I took great care, when I was an undergraduate at Cambridge, during the four years, to write no poetry at all, except one
poem of eight lines, which was published in *Cambridge Poetry 1929*.
I only started to write poetry seriously when I had left Cambridge
and when I was teaching in Finland. Whether this was due to being
alone in a strange country and having to fall back on my own
resources, I don't know; but that's how I started.

ORR: Let's explore this a little further. What are the motives, what are
the main springs, that set the poetic action in motion?

BOTTRALL: I rather think that it was a somewhat precarious and unhappy love affair that started me off.

ORR: But this didn't keep you writing poetry, did it?

BOTTRALL: No, I cannot pretend that I have gone through life with a series of unhappy love affairs, which would be too tragic! But, having got the impetus, I began to be interested in the writing of poetry and, as I suppose happens at the beginning, one has heaps of ideas and the problem is how you get them into some form of poetry, how you acquire some sort of technique. That interested me very much at that time.

ORR: What about subjects, themes for your poems? Do they present themselves to you or do you have to look for them?

BOTTRALL: I think that when one begins to write, themes present themselves with remarkable facility, situations and so on, which seem to be suitable for poetry and one hasn't got the technique always to deal with them. Then one arrives in mid career, at a point where these things coalesce and when one has a variety of themes and situations and the technique to deal with them. Then, as one goes on, I find, myself, that the technique is there and the themes get rarer and the situations do not seem to crop up.

ORR: What about the imagery in your poems? Can you identify it as coming from a positive source: something to do with your environment, your upbringing?

BOTTRALL: I think that one can trace in my poetry quite a lot of references to my childhood in Cornwall. Principally references to the sea, I think, and the coast of Cornwall and to some extent also to farms and farmland, as I lived more or less on a farm and within two or three miles from the sea. I think that that imagery does persist through my poetry. But, of course, also must be added an awful lot of impressions from constant travelling round the world, which often, I think, appears rather too esoteric and too foreign. I mean, it makes, perhaps, readers of my poetry feel like Kingsley Amis, that they don't like 'abroad'.

ORR: Do you find, then, that your poetry is constantly changing in flavour as you travel from one part of the world to the other?

BOTTRALL: To a certain extent, I think, yes. Strange countries, very different from ours, always make a great impact. Italy made a great impression on me as a young man and any country, for instance, like China or Japan always makes a great impression, because the way of living and the way of thinking, the way of dressing, everything is so different. You can't help being, unconsciously almost, *forced* to change your imagery somewhat.

ORR: Are there any writers who—I hesitate to say, influenced you, because this is a current train of thought, to examine the influence of certain people on certain other people—but are there any writers who have particularly impressed you in a way that has indirectly affected your writing?

BOTTRALL: Yes, certainly, as I think is pretty evident from my earlier work. The two writers of poetry who particularly influenced me (and I can say that without hesitation, I can use the word *influence*) were Ezra Pound and T. S. Eliot. I read Eliot first, but I didn't see a great deal of possibility in Eliot as a model, but when I read Ezra Pound, and in particular 'Hugh Selwyn Mauberley', I thought I saw how you did it: how I thought contemporary poetry ought to be written, how it could be written. And I owe a great debt to 'Hugh Selwyn Mauberley' and to Dr. Leavis who, when I was in Finland, suggested to me that I should read and study that poem.

ORR: This is something, perhaps, which you may like to talk about, since it is a field in which you have had a great deal of experience: the influence of poetry on people, the ordinary reading public, and its importance to them. Do you think poetry is important today?

BOTTRALL: As far as England is concerned, I am afraid that I do not believe that the poet is an important person in society or that poetry has much influence on the minds or imagination of people. To change to a totally different country, Japan is almost poetry-ridden. A poet is a great person, he is respected and revered. There are millions of poets in Japan: I don't know how many million, but several millions. Of course, when I say that a poet is revered in Japan, I mean a poet of standing and distinction. But in Japan poetry means something. It affects the minds of people and the imagery of poetry is something which is in their speech, and I don't find that in England.

ORR: Is this something you feel, though, that should happen to a poet, that he should be respected and revered and not treated, perhaps, like a postman or milkman?

BOTTRALL: I don't know. It's not a thing which worries me very much, because I have always written (if I may put it this way) to please myself and I have never published a line that I didn't want to publish and I have never written for money. But I don't think it is necessary that a poet should be revered and respected in the Japanese sense. In England it's simply that poetry now is unread and the poets are unknown. It's as bad as that, I think.

ORR: Turning again to your own work, do you find your interest in

41

the other arts, in drama, in painting, let us say, or music, have any influence on your work as a poet?

BOTTRALL: Oh certainly! My interests in the other arts are in this order: music, painting, architecture, sculpture, and drama, and it is music in which I am most interested and it is music about which I know most. That is in a way unfortunate because, while poetry is supposed to have some connection with music (I mean it is the art most closely, I suppose, allied to music), at the same time the notation of music being an abstract notation, one cannot make the same use of it, perhaps, in writing, as one can of painting and architecture and sculpture and certainly the drama.

ORR: Do you find yourself thrown into the company of other poets and other writers? Is there a sort of cultural creative milieu where people meet and discuss and throw about ideas as there used to be, let us say, fifty years ago?

BOTTRALL: Well, much less. In my early visits to Italy, for instance, there were certain cafés in Florence and Rome where poets and writers used to gather together, and they do it much less today. There used to be, of course, in London certain pubs (there still are one or two) but I think, there again, getting back to the family and helping to cook the dinner and wash up and all that sort of thing does put a stop to this sitting around and talking into the middle of the night, which used to happen thirty or forty years ago.

ORR: Do you think, then, poets today are much more of the people, if I can use such a term, than, let us say, the Lake Poets were?

BOTTRALL: Well, yes. I think one of the main reasons for this is that while it always was very difficult to live and be a poet and not earn some money elsewhere, today it is pretty well impossible. A poet has got to earn some money somehow. He has got to work in an office or even be in the British Council or the B.B.C.: all the places where T. S. Eliot said he shouldn't be, because Eliot's view is that a poet should not have anything to do with work which is like writing poetry. I don't know how he justifies his own case of being director of a firm which publishes poetry, but, at any rate, that is what he believes. I mean, he worked in a bank and he would have doubtless been a better poet if he had stayed in a bank, by his own theory.

ORR: Now this is something which you may be able to comment on, because your work, in fact, is connected with poetry. Is this a view you support?

BOTTRALL: Well, not exactly. I spent ten years of my life in university teaching and I felt that it got into my way a very great deal more than, for instance, being a British Council Representative; because when you are teaching poetry, you are using very much the same kind of energy that you use in writing poetry, whereas if you are, shall I say, putting over British culture, you are doing it in a more abstract and impersonal way and it does not take, at least to me, the same kind of effort as teaching literature, teaching poetry in particular, takes out of you. I found it easier, to put it this way, to write poetry when I was working from nine to five in an office than when I was a university professor with five months of the year with nothing to do much.

ORR: Now, I am not asking you here to produce a chapter from a do-it-yourself book, but can you describe, in as brief terms as possible, how a poem takes shape, how it happens in your mind and the process which transmits it from your mind on to the paper? This is a very difficult question, I know.

BOTTRALL: This *is* a very difficult question and takes with different writers very different forms. In my own case, it quite certainly takes two or even three different forms. Sometimes I have an idea at the back of my mind of what I want to write about, but I cannot get going at all. There is a poem called 'Natural Order' in my last book *Adam Unparadised*. That poem, 'Natural Order', is the result of a wish to contrast the artificial life of the Italian city states—artificial, but yet extremely regulated and cultured—with the sprawling, shapeless form of modern cities, metropolitan areas like London, and I could not get going at all, until I began to write a poem which starts off in a way that has nothing whatever to do with the matter. It starts off:

> Chemistry moves in a man
> And the retort bubbles over.
> Seed, lost by the million,
> Swimming, drowning, gone,
> Sought my mother's womb
> And one was the lover,
> The salmon that leaped the boom.

Immediately I got that far, I saw that this was the poem, though there is nothing in that opening passage which has anything to do with the idea that I first had. What I had missed, and why I could not write the poem was that, as well as the artificial order and the artificial disorder, I had missed the basic thing, natural order, which can make the poem possible. Now that is one way. The thing comes along and you don't even know that it is the poem at all. Another way is that you somehow start writing and the poem comes out. Then, of course, the third way, if you are writing in *terza rima* or sonnet form or something like that, you must have a pretty good idea of what you are writing about before you start; or, if you are writing a poem of any considerable length, you must have a moderately accurate conception of what you are aiming at. Then you have got to think it out to a certain extent—that is unavoidable—in the same way as you cannot write a fugue without observing the rules.

ORR: Do you find the conventional disciplines of poetry, the sonnet form, rhyme schemes, *terza rima* and so on are valuable to you as a poet?

BOTTRALL: Very. In the course of my work I have used almost every known metrical form. I think it is very valuable and if you cannot do that, I think that you are technically inferior and handicapped to that extent, however good a poet you are.

3rd October, 1962.

Robert Conquest

ROBERT CONQUEST was born in 1917, and educated at Winchester and Magdalen College, Oxford. He served in the Army and the Foreign Office. Research Fellow London School of Economics 1956–58, Lecturer in English University of Buffalo 1959–60. Literary Editor *Spectator* 1962–63. Senior Fellow Columbia University 1964–65. He is married and has two sons.

His published works include two books of verse, *Poems* (1955) and *Between Mars and Venus* (1962), and a study of Pasternak, *Courage of Genius* (1961). He edited the *New Lines* anthologies and *Back to Life*, an anthology of Soviet bloc 'thaw' poetry. His other work includes science fiction, criticism, and a number of books on Soviet politics.

MORRISH: Mr. Conquest, your first volume of poems was published in 1955. When did you start writing poetry?

CONQUEST: I never remember not writing it, really. I think it is said that poets can be divided between those who have written, when children, some sort of pastiche, comic poetry to amuse themselves and their friends, and those who have started off simply out of an emotional feeling of some sort when they were older, when they were eighteen or twenty. I only gradually started to write my own stuff, writing childish stuff first, as it were.

MORRISH: What twentieth-century poets would you say had influenced you most?

CONQUEST: I am rather against being influenced, particularly by contemporary poets. I think that no influence is worthwhile unless it is assimilated at some level which one is not conscious of, and that can apply as much to contemporary as to other poetry. I have been accused by friends of putting in too much Auden, in having assimilated Auden at possibly the wrong level when young; he was the sort of poet around. This, I am sure, was true and I do try to keep it out a bit. On the other hand, one is influenced by people younger than one's self. I find Thom Gunn influences me in curious ways.

MORRISH: You seem unlike most contemporary poets in that your work and experience have carried you outside the fields of literary and educational work. You have had experience in the world of international diplomacy and affairs. You have also written in an essay on Pound, published in the *London Magazine* not very long ago, that most of today's poets are exclusively interested in individuals and in human relationships. Would you say this was true of you, with your background?

CONQUEST: Well, I think what I meant is that thirty years ago people had their theories: you were a Marxist or a Freudian and all that, and you therefore had your frameworks when you were twenty, twenty-one or twenty-two, and could write poetry round that structure. Again, in the forties, you did not have to have any ballast of theories or thought at all: you could just bash away at whatever came into your head. But now it is again realized that a poem should be to some extent an intellectual structure. As well as everything else, it should have a shape, a form and a sense. Yet nobody really believes any more in any great metaphysical theories, any large, all-inclusive theories. We are all rather short-term seekers. And so there is only meditated reality, experience, to provide solidity.

MORRISH: Are you aware, in yourself, of a fear of the irrational, of the transcendental?

CONQUEST: No, I don't fear it particularly. I was not trying to knock the irrational or transcendental so much as to say, in fact, the opposite: that people who have strong systematic views are the ones who are frightened of the unknown; that they ward it off or channel it into moulds which it doesn't really fit. Anybody who thinks he has found out the truth about everything is very unlikely ever to make a poet. Even Hopkins is clearly writing about what he doesn't think he has got wholly under control. Although he is a Catholic and, you might say, has his system, the material he is interested in is precisely the stuff that is not covered by his system. I think that with any poet or almost any creative man, I mean artist, scientist or anybody else, the interest is on the frontier between what he knows and what he doesn't know, rather than in organizing what is known. Only the empirical view, the scientific method, if you like, though *scientific* is a narrow word, can cope. No 'system' can: it can only fake it up.

46

That doesn't mean that I do not have opinions. Of course I do.

MORRISH: Are you influenced by the scientific, technological developments of the twentieth century?

CONQUEST: I am deeply interested in them. I would read a magazine like *The Scientific American* in preference to literary magazines, if I had to choose, any time.

MORRISH: Do you feel that the influence of Freud and his successors has had an inhibiting influence on the writing of poetry?

CONQUEST: I don't know about 'inhibiting'. It has obviously changed it to some extent, hasn't it? But the theory that there was an entirely scientific psychology, which was believed about thirty years ago, has now rather petered out. People no longer believe that the Freudian system is a complete and general answer to everything, but simply that it provides a *few* answers to a *few* things. I think this applies to a lot of other things like sociology and even more to literary criticism.

MORRISH: Do you, in fact, have a low opinion of modern criticism?

CONQUEST: I would say that the real horror of modern criticism is this notion that they have found out all that is worth knowing, how to talk about and how to analyse literature, whereas, in fact, they have only touched a very narrow superficial layer. No critical system I have seen is capable of distinguishing between a good and a bad poem. It can say what it is about to some extent and very often puts in bits it isn't about. I remember Philip Larkin writing somewhere that originally critics liked difficult poems and put out propaganda that difficult poems are better than simple poems, because there is more to talk about and more to think about in them, but that now we have reached the stage where quite simple poems are proven to be difficult after all!

MORRISH: How, in fact, do you think you can tell the difference between a good and a bad poem?

CONQUEST: I think it's a matter of judgement.

MORRISH: Do you write for any specific audience that you have in your mind's eye or do you write just for yourself?

CONQUEST: Neither, really. I think that is a very important question, and again it is one that seems to be answered in a very superficial way by most critics and, indeed, sociologists. Everyone is always talking about larger audiences, as if this worries the writer. It doesn't worry me at all. But there is also the question of a 'public voice'. This is what I miss in a very great deal of American poetry. In English poetry, even obscure English poetry like Dylan Thomas or Empson, there is a touch of a public voice. There is *some* public you are writing for. A lot of American stuff seems to be written privately, not for themselves alone, but for themselves and a friend they have taken the bother to explain it all to first. You get that with Wallace Stevens, for instance. But I get the impression that one writes for what one thinks (partly judging from one's self) to be the ordinary educated audience. This is not quite sound, because a lot of educated people do not, in fact, read, or want to read poetry.

MORRISH: In your poem 'Galatea', the last few lines, you speak of the whole intent of art being passion and reserve. Why reserve, rather than, say, discipline? Reserve seems very introspective.

CONQUEST: I don't think you put *everything* down. If you put everything down, you would not have a poem. Discipline would imply letting it all out and then hacking it into shape when it is there. Reserve means only letting forward that which is the subject, the emotional subject matter of a poem. You obviously can't always write the poem you think you could write. The subject that excites you is not necessarily the thing you can write about. The poetic imagination, whatever that is, is not the same as one's conscience, one's general imagination or anything else. One might be deeply moved by the Hungarian Revolution, and a lot of people were—I was—but I could not write a poem about it. It did not even occur to me that I could. I suppose George Fraser wrote quite a good one. Very, very few others did, perhaps two.

MORRISH: Can we turn to *New Lines* now? This is successor to a very famous anthology which appeared in 1956. Now, in the blurb of the second one you have put out, you are quoted as having written: 'Like its predecessor, it represents a vigorous defence of the principles of poetry against the various fads and fanaticisms which continue to usurp, constrict and distort the art.' Well, this begs certain questions, the first of which is, what do you think are the *principles* of poetry?

CONQUEST: What I mean there is this: that a taste has been induced, partly by critics, for something which is not poetry, through feelings which are not aesthetic. I talked about people who liked puzzles: it may be admirable liking puzzles, but it is when you try and say *all* poems should be puzzles because we like puzzles—no, no! Stick to puzzles: leave the poems to people who like poems. Secondly, there is this notion that the appearance of sophistication is the thing to put over, the notion that a poem is something that the reader and the poet can smile about, feeling one up on you hicks. The feeling that if you say something in an oblique fashion, it is better than saying it straight, is a definite highly-established fad, partly tying up with the old academics, because if you say it straight, there is nothing for them to sit and interpret for you—so their jobs are involved. It always reminds me of that Irish folk poem 'The night before Larry was stretched': you remember the bit where he is asked whether he can die without having 'repinted' and he says,

> That's all my eye,
> And was first by the clergy invinted
> To get a fat bit for themselves.

I feel that about eighty per cent of criticism: it is by the *critics* invented, to get a fat bit for themselves. You can see their point. It would be much better if they had sinecures, and did not have to do any work. It is their *work* that's the trouble.

MORRISH: Going on to *New Lines* as a collection of the works of various poets living today, do you foresee the launching of something like the *Movement* with which you were credited on the first *New Lines* anthology?

CONQUEST: Well, I was never intending to launch a movement, although everybody who criticized it said, 'Oh! So this is a "movement" anthology, but it includes so-and-so. He isn't "movement" at all!' (usually referring to Dennis Enright) 'What do you mean, putting him in? He's not like the others.' The answer is, I was not trying to assemble a movement. I think that all the resemblances between the poets in the first *New Lines* and the poets in the second *New Lines* are resemblances which would apply between all English poets up to about forty years ago—between Chaucer and Kipling and Tennyson and Pope. They only *seem* to resemble each other. But it seems to me like this. It is like being in a city where you are in a room, three or four of you. You do not look in the least alike, but you go out into the street and, owing to an unfavourable mutation, everybody else has two heads. You then say, 'Look! We are all rather alike, aren't we?' You *are*, compared with them. Well, this unfortunate, unfavourable mutation took place about twenty or thirty years ago, and there are too many poets around with two heads. We do not really resemble each other. It is just that the ambience provides a contrast, as it were, and makes us look rather alike. The movement simply comes of assembling people who have managed to not have their genetic structure altered by this unfortunate blast.

49

MORRISH: Why did you choose the particular poets you have chosen for *New Lines No. 2*?

CONQUEST: Well, as any honest anthologist with any sense must, because I like them!

MORRISH: *New Lines No. 1* stimulated the publication of another anthology called *Mavericks*, which was edited by Howard Sergeant and Dannie Abse, because they said they felt the Movement was too concerned with problems of technique. Do you foresee a counterblast this time?

CONQUEST: I have no idea. One of the *Mavericks* is actually in the new *New Lines*. I found that the good *Mavericks* were just like, more or less, *New Lines*. There wasn't all that distinction. The bad ones were just bad. I mean, there were two or three excellent poets in that, Michael Hamburger and Vernon Scannell and John Hall: writers who were equally concerned with technique, I should have thought.

MORRISH: Do you see any common factor at all?

CONQUEST: Well, just this common factor: that they all write what I take to be English poetry, whereas a lot of people who are getting a good deal of support from semi-professional critics are not writing English poetry. They are doing something with words, but *what*, it is not clear to me: at least, it is clear to me, but it isn't interesting to me. It is like the difference between architects and chaps who pile bricks on top of each other. There is a certain distinction!

MORRISH: Do you regard this as a good time to be writing poetry?

CONQUEST: I should have thought it was as good as any other.

MORRISH: Do you feel today, perhaps, we are so self-conscious about art that the impact of any art, poetry in this case, is somewhat deadened?

CONQUEST: I agree, and I think self-consciousness about art has always been taken to be a sign of decadence in any civilization. I do not know how true that has been in the past, and I do not think it is true of our whole civilization as such, particularly. But I think it *is* certainly bad for the arts and deadens the effect. Well, yes, what sort of effect is this anthology going to have? A few thousand people will read it, and it might have an effect on some readers and some poets. I do not regard it as earth-shaking in any way. It would shake a very small asteroid indeed. It may conceivably encourage some good, or potentially good poets. It may discourage, or at any rate show that there is an opposition to, some destructive and parasitical critics.

16th July, 1963.

Hilary Corke

HILARY CORKE was born in 1921 in Malvern, Worcestershire and educated at Charterhouse and Christ Church, Oxford. He was a captain in the Royal Artillery 1940–45. Lecturer in English, University of Cairo, 1948–50. Lecturer Mediaeval English Studies, University of Edinburgh, 1952–56. He is married and has four children.

He has contributed poems, reviews, essays and short stories to most leading periodicals on both sides of the Atlantic. He published a collection of poems, *The Early Drowned*, in 1961.

ORR: Mr. Corke, do you remember the first poem you ever wrote?

CORKE: Funnily enough I do. I forgot it for many years and then I found it in one of my mother's drawers. I wrote it when I was three-and-a-half and it had a very nice drawing of a daffodil on it, and the text ran:

> The dafordils gro in the garden
> Wen the worm winds blo
> In there goldone and yelow
> And a-noding.

ORR: And what happened after this? Did you go on writing poems of this sort, or did a change take place?

CORKE: I think there were no more successes for ten years or so! But then, like everybody else, I started to write when I was fourteen or fifteen at school and I have written since then continuously.

ORR: Can you analyse why it is that you write poetry now?

CORKE: That is a very difficult question, isn't it? But I think of it as seeing a gap, so to speak, where a poem ought to be: and the feeling that there might be a sort of shape that would fill itself out and that would fit into it: a shape that is something presumably inside one's self, if one could get it out properly without damaging it in the process, and it would belong to this gap, which you can call a gap in the whole body of all the poems that ever were written.

ORR: Do you find that poems are dictated to you, that themes present themselves to you?

CORKE: I don't have any one way of beginning, really. Sometimes I think of an idea and think, 'Oh yes, that is something a poem should be written about.' Sometimes it may be, like everybody else, even a single word, or a line, a phrase comes into one's mind and then one wonders to what poem this phrase could belong, and, in fact, one's first guesses may often be very wide of the mark.

ORR: Are you very self-critical? Do you apply harsh and stringent judgements to your own poetry?

CORKE: I certainly try to when they are written, rather than when I am writing them. I think that, when you are writing them you have got to be a fool, really try to be a holy fool if you can: but, at any rate, be as stupid as you like and let the poem pull you in whatever direction you feel it is going. This is a very difficult thing to do because you think: 'Well, this is getting worse and worse and I really can't commit myself to this nonsense I am writing now.' But I think one should because, after all, one doesn't have to let it see the light of day afterwards.

ORR: Is it important to you to have an audience?

CORKE: It varies. It depends on the sort of poem. Sometimes one does think of the audience very much. One says: 'I wish I could get this through to them.' At other times one is spinning things for oneself and the audience can look over one's shoulder, if it likes, but they aren't really there.

ORR: Does it depress you that there is such a small audience for contemporary poetry today?

CORKE: Yes, immensely, if it is that small. I suppose it is tremendously small. But I don't think the actual statistics of it would worry me particularly. It would depend on the sort of people it affected. It would depress me much more to find one intelligent nice person who did not take any interest in poetry at all, than to think of one hundred thousand people who didn't engage me anyway also not being interested in it.

ORR: Your poems have appeared in collections along with the poems of other writers. Do you consider yourself in any way part of a movement in poetry, or do you consider yourself simply as the isolated poet writing for himself and for his public?

CORKE: I think of myself as isolated. I don't particularly like that. It would be nice to be in a movement, in one sense. It is always nice doing things with other people who think along the same lines as yourself. Probably as a historical accident I find myself isolated.

ORR: Does your appreciation of other arts, let us say music, painting, sculpture, play much part in your composition of poetry?

CORKE: Yes, music particularly.

ORR: How does this work? Can you explain a little?

CORKE: Well, in the basic sense of what is tiresomely called the music of words and that sort of thing. Certainly poetry, in any language, produces effects which are analogous to those of music, mainly rhythmical effects which are, in fact, very much more subtle than those which one gets in music, because there is no strict time scheme behind them. But also I think musical forms—although it would be difficult to make it very plain how this happens—but musical forms, if one is used to them, do have an effect on the writing of verse.

ORR: Is form, is structure, an important part of your poetic composition?

CORKE: Yes, I try to let it be.

ORR: Do you place, for example, much importance on the stricter forms such as the sonnet, let us say?

CORKE: I have done, yes.

ORR: Does this liberate or enslave the poet, do you think?

CORKE: 'It is very much easier for him in one sense' is the standard answer, isn't it? Because the fact that you have the form and you don't have to think about finding the form, leaves you free to concentrate on other aspects of what you are doing.

ORR: But you haven't found, have you, that the imposition of a form means that you are trying to pour a quart of milk into a pint bottle?

CORKE: Then you have guessed wrong, haven't you? You have got the wrong form in that case. I think in quite comic ways, really—rhyme for example—the fact that, if you write one word at the end of a line there are only going to be twenty words in the language that have got to go in the next line but one, is often a very fruitful source of ideas you would not otherwise have had, because you run through a whole lot of words each of which seems equally ridiculous and to have nothing to do with the subject in hand, and you suddenly see that one of them *might* have something to do with the subject in hand in a way that you would never have guessed if you hadn't been bound in that particular manner. And I think that stanza forms have the same sort of effect, perhaps: you find that you are supposed to be filling up four lines and what you want to say is filling up five. Well then, you have got to cut out a line's-worth of stuff and find out which is weakest and what can go. In that case, it may be very valuable to you. But, of course, if it is the other way round and you are trying to pump up two-and-a-half lines into four, that is not so good.

ORR: Does the whole process of composition of a poem, let us say a short poem, take you a long time? Does it stretch over a period of weeks?

CORKE: It stretches over a long time, yes. If I added up the number of hours taken on the poem it might not be very great. In fact, I think on the whole I am probably more one of Nature's sprinters than a long-distance runner. But I would never send a poem out to a publisher in less than a year from when I began it. That, I think, would be the minimum. I usually try and get the whole of the first draft down in one sprint and then feel rather tired for the rest of the day, and then leave it, if possible, without thinking about it at all for two or three months at least, until I can look at it as if it were somebody else's poem to a certain extent, and then enter upon the brutal phase of my relations with it, when, as you suggested earlier, I try to be as critical and damning about it as I can.

ORR: Is there an influence on your work that you can detect of other writers, writers who have moved or led you?

CORKE: No particular writers. A general influence, I suppose, from the writers whom one happens to pick up first. I think it is very largely a question of accidents of education and that sort of thing, although some of those may be totally unfashionable and almost pointless from one's own present point of view. Nevertheless, because they have got in so soon and occupied so much territory in one's mind, they may have some sort of influence. Donne was the poet I liked most when I was in my teens. Blake got in. I don't think, though, he has had any influence at all. I read a tremendous amount of Blake, and then other people like Tennyson, and things that sound like terrible confessions. But I still enjoy reading Tennyson.

ORR: What about Yeats and Eliot? These are the names that crop up.

CORKE: Yes, Eliot I got early. Yeats I missed and therefore I think that I had, to a certain extent, hardened before I got Yeats. I think he is a marvellous poet. I enjoy reading him tremendously, but I don't think perhaps in my case that anybody I read after the age of twenty-five has influenced me in any sense.

ORR: You don't find, do you, that you consciously have to shake off an influence? That you write something and suddenly realize that this is strongly influenced by a cadence of somebody else?

CORKE: Yes, this does happen, indeed it does; and I think I can get rid of it, and it usually turns out to be the absolute crux of the whole poem. Terrible! Well then, I am just bold-faced about it and go ahead, because I think, I hope, that I have made it my own, even though I have stolen it in some way.

ORR: Do you feel that, as a person living in the middle of the twentieth century, you are at all bound to write about the larger themes which concern the world of the twentieth century?

CORKE: That begs the question of what the larger themes are: some are internal as well as external. No, I don't think that I am bound to write poems about 'Banning the Bomb' and that sort of thing, though I have done so. But I mean, as a person living in the twentieth century, these themes, should a number of them be present in my mind—*if* they are—then I should wish to write about them; but I don't feel a sense of social duty about it, no.

ORR: There isn't any particular recurrent theme that attracts you, is there?

CORKE: There are some to which I certainly return, and which I certainly try to steer clear of: such, for example, as drowning or poems about the sea and drowning. I tend to write a lot of poems about death.

ORR: Why?

CORKE: Well, I consider this one of the major themes of the twentieth century and every other century.

ORR: But is there any particular reason why you should write about the sea, for example?

CORKE: No, it might even be force of habit. It is a bad thing, I think, in one sense: because if one really writes a poem that has come out right, one should not wish to return to the subject, and I suppose it is continually attempting to do something that I feel I haven't quite succeeded in pulling off.

ORR: Have you ever felt that you wanted to express yourself in verse drama?

CORKE: Yes, I have. I should like to do that. It is largely a question of time and effort, I suppose, and also in that particular case, of course, the audience. There are so many other factors to get in which would be very much easier for somebody who did spend a lot of time amongst his contemporaries discussing literature, the stage, and what should be done next and so on. It is a very impure form compared with the sort of verse that I find myself confined to, not necessarily to my own pleasure.

ORR: One could perhaps say (if one can make an analogy with music) that verse drama was the operatic scene and the poems which you are writing are the chamber music.

CORKE: Yes, something of that sort. But I should like, for example, to write the libretto of an opera. You know, you said about being in a movement and working with other people. That is the sort of way in which I should like to work with people, I think: that is, to contribute one side of something and to have somebody else contribute something different and to work with them in that way, rather than getting in a gang with six other poets and writing each other's poems.

10th July, 1963.

Julian Ennis

JULIAN ENNIS was born in 1915, and read English at Merton College, Oxford, 1934-7, under Edmund Blunden. He has been Senior English Master at a boys' grammar school for many years. He has edited school textbooks under another name and made contributions to educational controversy and research.

His poems have been published in periodicals and have also appeared in P.E.N. volumes and other anthologies. Amateur groups have produced his plays, notably *Just About Enough*, a 'tetralogy of miniature moralities'.

ORR: Mr. Ennis, is there a particular set or pattern of themes which appeals to you and draws you to form them into poems?

ENNIS: I think all the poems that I have written, with the exception possibly of certain lighter ones, are on only one theme. And I like to think it is the one theme of all writing and of all art.

ORR: Could you define this theme?

ENNIS: Every poem, I think, no matter how big or small, is a shape, a movement around some silence, and I think the poem, therefore, is about innocence. We are trying not to be 'fallen men'. We are expressing our wish to be Adam, our horror of being Fallen Adam.

ORR: I notice you use the word 'we' the whole time. This is rather interesting. Do you consider yourself, then, as part of a flowing forward movement of English literature and not simply as a poet in isolation at one particular time?

ENNIS: Yes, and I wouldn't have necessarily restricted it to England, either. There is no point in writing these things if one doesn't find that the very greatest, as well as the little people like myself, are doing the same thing. I can't see any point in it otherwise. I find that the very greatest poetry that has ever been written (and I can only

speak about English poetry really, of course), does what I am
trying so hard to do. The very, very greatest lines of English verse—
and there are only a few of them, aren't there?—occur in, I suppose,
the fifth acts of Shakespeare's tragedies. Something absolutely still,
absolutely pure, absolutely innocent, kind of pre-Fall language. When
Macbeth hears that Lady Macbeth has died, he says, 'She should have
died hereafter. There would have been a time for such a word.'
Every word in this is a monosyllable, you notice, except 'hereafter'.
But even Shakespeare cannot hold it, and then he goes on about
'brief candle', you know, and 'Life's but a walking shadow'. Out
come all the images and grand stuff. He could only, himself, write a
line or two like that perhaps once or twice in the whole of a tragedy.
That's what we are all trying to do, to write a line which says everything and nothing. It's almost silent. There is no 'poetry' there at
all: it is almost nothing, on the brink of nothing. And these little
poems of mine, I regard as shapes and movements. I must try to hear,
as it were, a silence and a nothingness at the very core of them. And
that is why I think the subjects are what they are. I mean, I am haunted
by Jesus, for instance, I am haunted by Christ—and by animals, too.
I think we have a tremendous feeling, in modern man especially, of
guilt towards Christ, of guilt towards animals, because we feel that
they are so inartistic, unpoetic.

ORR: Do you incline, then, to accept the Johnsonian view that there
should be a moral, a didactic purpose in poetry?

ENNIS: I am not concerned with telling man, telling myself, telling
anybody that this is the state we are in. Everybody knows it, if he
only knows it in his blood. I can't as an artist wish that it wasn't so
because if it weren't so there wouldn't be any art, in my view anyway. There would be no point in writing.

ORR: But communication is important to you? It isn't just a selfish act,
the composition of poetry?

ENNIS: I never think of anybody else at all when I write, because I can
only say, 'Well, that seems to me to have shaped it and said it.'
I can't do any more. I must leave it.

ORR: But you are not inclined to regard the writing of poetry as
auto-therapy, are you?

ENNIS: Only in the sense that I am a man, and perhaps if I cure myself I
may be helping to cure everybody else. On the other hand, I want
the poems to be immediate, in a sense. I know there are all sorts of
things, even in these little poems, which perhaps need some explain-

ing, some thinking about (I hope so, in a way) but I want them to be really very simple, immediately intelligible.

ORR: But if I may say this of your poems, you have achieved what I think is still a comparatively rare feat in contemporary poetry: you have produced poems which do make an immediate impact upon the listener and upon a reader at the first time of hearing or reading. Does this necessarily add to the value of a poem?

ENNIS: Oh yes. The very greatest poetry, like that I referred to, makes an immediate impact. It is the same with the very greatest art of all kinds. One walks into some of the places where the Giotto frescoes are preserved in Italy, and the impact is colossal, isn't it? Well, we are talking of the very highest painting now. One ought to spend weeks and weeks just looking at them. But there's an immediate impact of tremendous, overwhelming simplicity and clarity, and I think it is very important. And this is what I try to do, but I must make it clear to myself, you see. Perhaps I am extremely naïve and must eschew complexity as far as possible.

ORR: But do you think this is the zenith of artistic achievement in any art: the supreme, sublime simplicity?

ENNIS: Absolutely, yes. I believe that all music, all painting, all sculpture, all forms of art are struggling to it, and if they get there, and when they get there, we know it. Take another obvious example from music, in the Beethoven Violin Concerto. I don't know why this is: musicians would know, but after the cadenza in the first movement where there is the complexity of all the themes that have gone before, the violin plays a tune which you could hear the errand-boy whistling down the street. It seems as if this is the point of the whole thing.

ORR: Do you think there is a correlation between the various arts, then?

ENNIS: I think they are all doing the same thing. I think that man as an artist is doing the same thing, performing the same function, struggling back to something.

ORR: You mean you could just as well have been a composer, let us say, or a sculptor?

ENNIS: Oh yes!

ORR: But the element of choice does come in, doesn't it? After all, you could perhaps choose to write a novel or a play?

ENNIS: Oh yes. I didn't wish necessarily to separate the writing of verse. If you are writing, something is compelling you towards verse all the time because it is the highest point of writing. The lines, such as

the ones I quoted from *Macbeth*, I mean, these are just by their very
nature verse, they can't be prose. But I didn't mean to imply that I
don't struggle with these other forms. I very much like writing plays,
but I find that my plays are not intelligible, by comparison. Of course,
one doesn't have to struggle with the form quite so much. It is this
tremendous fight—take a small form like the sonnet—this tremendous struggle which produces the *clarity*, if you ever get it, of course.

ORR: Are the conventional forms of poetry important to you, then—
sonnets, rhyme-schemes, regular metres?

ENNIS: Oh yes, because we have at last moved out of the 'modern'
experiments. They had to come, and I myself used to try to write
in free verse, but the writing of free verse is less difficult, of course,
than writing in forms. And yet, paradoxically, very few men have
ever succeeded in it like Lawrence. But that is all gone, I'm sure, gone
already.

ORR: Let's look a little more closely at your poems. I notice that you
use consciously a great number of literary echoes, particularly
Shakespearean ones. Is this an attempt at enrichment of an image or
of an impression in the poem?

ENNIS: You see, I spend a lot of time with literature and my memory is
soaked in quotations, and when I am writing these things come
welling up. In, for instance, 'Houseproud',

> Cobwebs shall possess my house merely. . . .

of course is an echo from *Hamlet*, is adapted there because of the
symbolism of the house. I wanted to say to myself: 'In a sense,
Hamlet might have written this poem much better than I have and
so I must pay some kind of tribute, as it were, to the way he put it
originally.'

ORR: I don't know if you have ever tried to analyse consciously this
business of inspiration, but would you say that the majority of your
inspiration is drawn through a filter, a filter of, let us say, literature
or art or music, or that a great proportion of it comes to you direct
through your own senses?

ENNIS: Always one of two ways. Either from some word or phrase,
just as a composer might hear an errand-boy whistling something
and say, 'By Jove! that must become a symphony.' That is one way:
that, if you like, is the literary way. The second way is experience.
The 'Elegy on Two Pets' is real, you see. That cat did come back one
day with its lower jaw practically smashed to pieces and hanging on

by little bits of skin. Something must have happened down inside me because that poem wasn't written for quite a long time afterwards, as a matter of fact. I used to dream about the cat, you know. Therefore I had to write this poem eventually, in a sense, to get rid of the cat which was haunting me. But the cat is meant to be a symbol, of course, of other things.

ORR: But it has to reach the Wordsworthian stage of being recollected in tranquillity, does it?

ENNIS: Well, I have never understood what this famous phrase means.

ORR: Doesn't it mean, surely, that something happens to one and then one goes away and thinks about it for twenty years, and then one remembers it afresh?

ENNIS: Yes, but then, doesn't Wordsworth go on to make the point that in the tranquil recollection you work yourself up into a new and now poetic state of ecstasy, or whatever it may be? I don't think this is right. I think that the original experience can be awful, but that later you are very cold about it, very detached in a queer sort of a way and don't get worked back up to anything of the original. In fact, you are then an artist, you are a craftsman. It is then the poem that matters.

ORR: Do you find afterwards that you can look on this poem almost as if it were somebody else's creation? Can you evaluate it dispassionately?

ENNIS: No, I don't think one ever can. And, in fact, I don't, because if I do, then I am being a critic. You remember what Beckett said about critics in *Waiting for Godot*. He puts them as the worst of all enemies. I think we are all the enemies of other people's writing. I don't object to being a critic of everybody else, the greatest and the smallest, but if I am going to start to be a critic of myself then I shall probably stop writing.

ORR: Do you find yourself much in the company of other poets, of other writers?

ENNIS: I have never cared very much for some kind of club atmosphere or coterie. I much prefer, say, just Wordsworth and Coleridge reading their poems to each other like that. But Browning sitting around with a lot of people listening to him and so on, even if they're poets, it has just never appealed to me. There seems to me something morbid about it.

ORR: But do you believe there is value in the interchange of ideas between poets?

ENNIS: Very great danger. If one began to discuss a poem one was writing with another poet, especially if he was a better writer, it might end it. I prefer Henry Miller's attitude: 'This is me. I am not to be interfered with and there is a great danger in being interfered with. I avoid the literary world.' I think I like that attitude.

ORR: But you do read, I expect, products of the present-day literary world?

ENNIS: I do, indeed!

ORR: Are they important to you, and in what way?

ENNIS: They are important because they've shown me the way to go. I think one's got to be, in all one's artistic life, *contemporary* and one must never write like the poets of the thirties, like the Georgians, like the Elizabethans, like anybody else at all except one's own contemporaries, and I read them not only because they are good, so many of them, but to see what is the current idiom, to find out whether I am using it. I'm a modernist in this sense, and I think in all teaching, for instance, it should always be the current, contemporary language which is used and taught.

ORR: Is the writing of poetry your most important occupation?

ENNIS: Oh, yes, it is the most important kind of writing, the most difficult. And these poems are prayers, aren't they, in a way? They are my prayers and that is easily the most important thing until I give them up and pray properly, I suppose.

30th August, 1963.

Roy Fuller

ROY FULLER was born in 1912, qualified as a solicitor in 1933, and has practised that profession ever since. During the war he served in the Royal Navy. Since the war he has divided his spare time between poetry and fiction.

His *Collected Poems* appeared in 1962, and a new book of verse, *Buff*, was published early in 1965.

ORR: Mr Fuller, did you start writing poetry when you were very young?

FULLER: Not very young. I always thought of myself as a prose writer at school. I don't suppose I started writing verse until I was seventeen,

ORR: What sort of things did you write when you were young?

FULLER: Poems? Very bad ones. I was influenced as a very young man by all the wrong people, or all the people I consider to be wrong now, and it wasn't until I was really quite elderly, I suppose twenty-one or twenty-two, that I even discovered the kind of things that were being written in my own time, that I now consider the valid tradition of writing poetry.

ORR: So the poems you wrote at an early age don't bear very much relation in style or content to the poems you are writing now?

FULLER: No, I was a very slow developer.

ORR: Do you find that the more rigid of poetic forms, forms like the sonnet, which I know you use in your writing, impose a *restriction* on the poet, or are they a helpful means of expression?

FULLER: Helpful: they always seem to me to encourage my own writing, and therefore I regard them as free forms. That is to say, it is free verse which to me is the constricting form and the one which I find difficult; so that if I were attempting a poem in free verse, I should find it very much more difficult to get to the end of it than I would a sonnet.

ORR: You find the rigid discipline that a sonnet imposes helpful to your expression and thought?

FULLER: I think it's helpful to getting the thought out in a form which is going to communicate itself to the reader, and it's also helpful to me as a writer, because I feel that I am much more likely to have got it right when I have got the form right than messing about with free verse, which obviously depends on a very acute ear, which I don't think I've got.

ORR: When you are writing a poem, do you have any particular type of reader in mind?

FULLER: No, I don't think I think of the reader. I was always brought up to believe that poetry should try to widen its audience. That is to say, that the poem shouldn't address itself to a clique. The idea is that one is really speaking to a big audience, although one knows, in effect, one isn't reaching a big audience. Of course, I personally do pre-suppose that the reader is acquainted with, for example, the works of Freud and the works of Marx and the works of Burckhardt and so on. My poetry is, I suppose, intellectual. In that sense, I suppose the people who are going to get the most out of the poems are the people who have read fairly widely.

ORR: You don't feel it necessary, as Mr. Eliot has done on occasion, to add a series of explanatory notes on your poems for the benefit of the reader who hasn't read these works?

FULLER: I don't feel it necessary. But I think if, for example, I were reading my poems to a live audience, it would be very helpful for them and probably for me, and not really giving the poem away at all, to explain some of the sources that led to the poem being written.

ORR: Do you write your poems with the idea of having them read aloud, or reading them aloud yourself?

FULLER: No, I don't. I really write them for their look on the printed page.

ORR: What do you think can be the impact of a poem at first reading on an audience which hasn't had the opportunity to study it before?

FULLER: Well, I think there are two kinds of poem, probably more. There is a certain kind of poem which does make an impact on first hearing, and then there's a kind of poem which doesn't make any impact at all on first hearing.

ORR: Where do your poems fall in this?

FULLER: There again, I think there are two classes. I believe that some do make an impact on first hearing, but I think there are more that do require a bit of homework.

ORR: Can you remember any of the poets who influenced you most?

FULLER: My great influence has been Auden, and that was a continuing influence, I suppose, right up to the war, and probably still is.

ORR: But you think that influence is now lessening, as your own style matures and hardens?

FULLER: Yes, and also as Auden's style has matured and hardened: that is to say, I don't find him as congenial a poet now as I did in the thirties.

ORR: And do you find in your writing that you take into account any of the other arts: music, painting, prose literature, and so on?

FULLER: I think I take into account more the non-artistic prose works. That is to say, I'm influenced more by works of archaeology, anthropology, psychology, than I am by artistic works, though I have been influenced by books about art and I usually compose my poems to the sound of music.

ORR: You have written, I think, three novels?

FULLER: More: I have written six, counting novels for children, and the seventh is just about to be published.

ORR: And do these novels bear any relation in style or thought to your poetry, or are they something of a completely different *genre*?

FULLER: I think they started off by being completely different, but as they've gone on I've found them really rather closely allied to writing poetry, and, in a way, I think they're a substitute for the long poems that I would really like to have written and never have, and which I think are terribly difficult to do these days. But a book I wrote about a school, called *The Ruined Boys*, although it's perfectly realistic and so on, in a sense is a poetical novel, that is to say, the language bears some of the hall-marks of poetry, I think.

ORR: What impact do you think poetry has on the present-day reader, in this age of television and the cinema?

FULLER: I don't think it has very much impact, and I don't think it's had very much during my lifetime, except in retrospect. That is to say, I think poets who were at first neglected eventually become part of modern life. Eliot is a splendid example. Eliot in the nineteen-twenties was a poet for a minority, whereas Eliot in the nineteen-fifties really entered into the consciousness of most cultured people.

ORR: Do you think this has anything to do with his dramatic work?

FULLER: Yes, I think it has. I think the process of Eliot becoming available to a wider readership is probably helped by his becoming a playwright. But I think the general process is really a part of the very gradual assimilation by a wide readership of cultural experiments today, which is a typical process of the art of our time.

ORR: Have you ever had any desire to write a poetic drama?

FULLER: Yes, I have, but I have come to the conclusion that writing a prose drama would be hard enough for me, and therefore writing a poetic drama would be far too hard. I don't think I ever should.

ORR: Do you think poetic drama has any place on the stage of today?

FULLER: I can't think that it has, with the available talent. But I think it's perfectly possible for a group of poets to arise who would express themselves in poetic drama.

ORR: Do you think, as a rule, that it takes a certain amount of time for a writer's works to become assimilated into the general mass of culture?

FULLER: Yes, and it's taken longer as the years have gone by.

ORR: So a writer has less and less chance, then, of being acknowledged in his own lifetime?

FULLER: No, I think that the truly great writer must, on the whole, get acknowledged. It is the less great figure who probably goes on existing on the periphery of general consciousness, which is a great pity.

ORR: And do you think there are many of our contemporary poets who will be read in, let us say, two hundred years?

FULLER: No, I don't think there are very many: no more, probably, than at any other time. And yet sometimes I do think that in general the poem today is very much more clever, expert, closely observed than perhaps at any time in the past. Somebody once said that the typical twentieth-century poem was part of a collective poetry, written, as it were, by one collective poet, and I think, in a sense, that is true. I think if one looks at the short lyric of the past compared with the best lyric of today, it's very much less well-observed, much less clever, and in that sense it may be that our poetry will survive as a sort of great anthology of the first part of the twentieth century.

ORR: Does poetry reflect, do you think, the age in which it was written?

FULLER: I think it must, and must depend on the age for its validity. I mean, in a sense, the poet by temperament and training and desire and so on has poetry in him. What he very often hasn't got in him is the subject matter and a close enough feeling for the common emotions. One sees this, I think, in the poetry written during the war. The fact that one had to write about being trained as a soldier, the fact that one had to write about the things that other people were writing about, didn't really lessen the amount of poetry at all.

ORR: To get back to your own poems. Do most of your poems arise directly out of a deeply-felt personal experience of your own?

FULLER: I think less and less as one gets older. Most of my poems now really arise out of a more general situation of the poet at a particular age, the general emotional situation; and I think more and more I rather assume a personality, than write about my own experiences directly. In the latest sequence I have written, I have assumed the character of various people in the Faust legend: that is to say, in some of the poems I am writing as Faust, in some as Mephistopheles. That probably happens to most poets as they grow older, that their personal experiences are less immediate and varied, and therefore they are inclined to assume *personae* which don't really properly belong to them.

ORR: But don't personal experiences of your own creep in?

FULLER: Oh yes, they must do, yes indeed, and indeed one wouldn't assume the mask of Mephistopheles unless one personally felt that this was an appropriate mask to put on.

ORR: Is the writing of poetry your main occupation?

FULLER: Well, so far as time is concerned it has to take third place to writing novels and being a solicitor.

17th October, 1960.

Michael Harnett

MICHAEL HARNETT was born in 1941 in Newcastle West, Co. Limerick, Ireland. He is editor of *Arena*.

His poems have been published in several Irish magazines.

ORR: Michael, how old were you when you began writing poetry?

HARNETT: I was almost fourteen.

ORR: What sort of things did you write about in your first poems?

HARNETT: About what I was surrounded by: nature, mostly, in the beginning.

ORR: Where do you come from?

HARNETT: A town called Newcastle West, in County Limerick.

ORR: And what sort of country is there around there?

HARNETT: It's very soft, gentle country. There's nothing spectacular about it at all. No hill reaches a thousand feet down there, I'd say, and the rivers are very, very shallow. But there's lovely country; it's very woody and very green.

ORR: And you were telling me that when you began writing poetry you hadn't read much yourself.

HARNETT: I had read nothing at all outside the poems that were on the national school-books.

ORR: You don't feel that a poet has to read and absorb a lot of poetry before he begins writing, do you?

HARNETT: No, but I think ancestry has a lot to do with it: I mean, *heritage*.

ORR: And what was your heritage in this respect?

HARNETT: Well, there's a river in County Limerick called The Maigue. I think in the seventeenth century there was a group of poets called the Maigue Poets, and they really set the foundations. They were very good Gaelic poets then. They started writing and they spread the whole craft. It was a real craft around there, and in North Kerry. But it wasn't poetry, it was just verse, good rhyming doggerel.

ORR: What made you want to write poems? Why did you want to write poetry instead of, let us say, making model ships or doing crossword puzzles?

HARNETT: It's so long ago, I don't remember the reason. I just sat down one day and I remember saying distinctly to my sister, who was, I suppose, nine at that time, 'I am going to write a song.' That's what it was, a song and no more: it was a simple little lyric.

ORR: Well, let's take it to the present day. Have you ever thought why you go on writing poetry now?

HARNETT: I think confession is the reason. I think every man has to confess.

ORR: Is this, then, a sort of religious act for you, the writing of poetry?

HARNETT: It's not so much religious as deeply psychological. I have to tell everything that happens to me, regardless how intimate it is, always.

ORR: But is this addressed to an audience or is this just something that you have to write for yourself, for your own satisfaction, for your own catharsis?

HARNETT: Oh no, no. It is confession in the full sense. I must have a confessor, there must be somebody to whom I can speak. I must have a friend, a lover, a man or a woman, to whom I can speak frankly about anything, about everything that happens to me.

ORR: Do you write your poems with the sound of them very prominent in your mind: the idea of having them spoken?

HARNETT: Oh well, yes, being Irish, I do. I mean, the sound is very important, but clarity is very important too.

ORR: Well, of course, don't you agree that a poem in order to make an effect as a piece of sound must also have, not perhaps absolute clarity, but quite a degree of clarity, in that the listener can grasp a proportion of it at a hearing?

HARNETT: This might be egotistical, but I think if you are Irish you can speak beautifully and be understood at the same time. *Musically*, I mean, not necessarily beautifully. But it is the same thing, I suppose.

ORR: You think the fact of your being Irish as distinct from English, though you are writing poetry in a language which is known as English, this makes a great difference to you?

HARNETT: Oh yes, it does. There is no division between my poetry and the poetry of Langland. I am not comparing myself to Langland, but my poetry is almost totally Anglo-Saxon. There are very few Latinisms in it at all, very few. It's almost purely Anglo-Saxon with a few Gaelic turns of syntax: not Gaelic words, but grammatical acrobatics, if you like.

ORR: Is there a degree of conscious construction in your poems? Do you plan a poem like an architect plans a building, or does some of it just come willy-nilly?

HARNETT: It varies from poem to poem. I have written some long sequences of poems, like a novel, with a beginning, a middle and an end. I know what is going to happen and what should happen and I do my best to achieve that. But otherwise, I mean, I am just walking along the street and there's a line, and there's another line, and that's the beginning, and then, inevitably, the middle and the end come in. And they conform. I mean they're not equal, but in proportion, in a rhythmical sense, in the first place. There's a certain type of pattern. There's no sentence in English that is not poetical, because if you take any spoken sentence and you use that rhythm or re-use that rhythm again you have a poem.

ORR: Do you work very conscientiously at the polishing, the finishing of your poetry, though?

HARNETT: No, no.

ORR: You like to dash it off, do you?

HARNETT: I just write it: it's finished! There's only one poem I ever wrote which I revised and that was a long poem; that was three drafts, and that only took me a week, which I consider very, very long for a poem.

ORR: But most of your poetry which we hear and read is exactly as it was first written on paper, is it?

HARNETT: Yes, except maybe for a word or two. I very rarely revise, very rarely.

ORR: Do you throw your poems away?

HARNETT: Well, before my poems get to the eyes and the ears of other people, I am very ruthless myself. I usually write poems in a sequence. I mean I never—very seldom—write one poem. I write, maybe, twenty poems on a theme, enlarging it in variations, and developing and clarifying, and then maybe eighty per cent of that is torn up and burnt and thrown away. It never reaches the audience and the public or the reader, or anybody.

ORR: Do you find yourself drawn, Michael, to particular themes or sets of themes, as ideas for poetry? I mean are there a dozen, or half a dozen, or a hundred things in this world around you about which you feel 'That is the sort of thing I would like to write about'?

HARNETT: Well, there are not a hundred, there are only two things, I think, about which I write.

ORR: And what are those?

HARNETT: One is a wife, a woman: I am very orthodox about marriage and a wife. And the second one is death, about which I am very much afraid.

ORR: And this is something which you are constantly trying to work out in your poems, is it?

HARNETT: Well, I know there is no solution. There is no solution at all to the death part of it, but I believe there is no solution to the wife part of it. I may get a wife, but I know 'Into every life a little rain must fall.' Well, I know an awful lot of rain is going to fall into my life, anyway!

ORR: Are there any writers, poets or prose writers, whom you particularly admire, or even writers who have had an influence on you?

HARNETT: A lot of writers influenced me because I did all my reading within a year, 1961–62, when I read most of the writers and the poets that matter. But I think the writers who influenced me most were Lorca and Pasternak.

ORR: How did they influence you? Did you find that there were influences of their style creeping into yours, or that you wanted to write about things which they had treated?

HARNETT: No, no. I could say influence of style, all right, and of theme in a little way. It could have been anybody else, I mean any other great poet. It's *humanity*, that's all, like Shakespeare has.

ORR: Do you feel at all drawn to write about problems which afflict the contemporary world?

HARNETT: Well, there is one great thing which I dream about and have nightmares about and which I never experienced. It was Nazism, and the extermination of the Jews, which upsets me very much. I mean even now, when it's all over and done with. But it's about the only political (but of course it's more than political) thing that I brood upon which is not within myself. Otherwise I am completely egotistical.

ORR: As a poet, Michael, are you firmly rooted in Ireland?

HARNETT: Well, I believe that Ireland is my native soil. I wouldn't be lost in London, but I would be very unhappy. I was very unhappy when I was in London in 1961.

ORR: You feel that you're happiest and you're most creative in Ireland, do you?

HARNETT: Yes, well now, 'happiest' is too strong a word to use to me because I never reach the superlative of that adjective. But I would say that I am at my happiest in Ireland, yes: in Dublin, even though I am sure the literary world in Dublin is much like the literary world in London. I mean everybody knows everybody else.

ORR: Is writing poetry something which has brought you satisfaction? I know you speak of it as a sort of confession, but is it something which has brought you, personally, satisfaction?

HARNETT: Well, no more satisfaction than defecation would or bleeding. Of course, not bleeding, that would be a masochistic satisfaction, I know. But defecation, I'd say, would be the parallel; or breathing.

ORR: It's just something that you have to go on doing?

HARNETT: No, I wouldn't say 'have to go on doing' because I know I will end sometime within a few years, I am sure. At the moment, it is a part of me. When a poem is written, it is put aside. I mean, if you like, I forsake all my children.

ORR: Do you want large numbers of people, though, to read and appreciate your poetry?

HARNETT: Well, I think it contains a sufficient message of love. I do want a large audience: I think it would be good for people. That sounds egotistical, too. My dream of a perfect poem is a kind of a hypnotic formula, it's like brain-washing. I would instil love (what Christ talked about) into the reader's mind: a kind of psychological trick by which the reader reads a poem and he can never forget it afterwards.

ORR: You talk about a hypnotic effect: this means the exercise of power over a large number of people by the poet. Do you have a desire to exercise power over people?

HARNETT: No, no. I have the desire that my *poetry* should exercise power over people.

ORR: Well, isn't this the same thing? After all, you are the creator of the poetry.

HARNETT: Oh no, I am not as perfect as my poetry is at all. I mean, I don't love as much as my poetry does or suggests or wants. I cannot.

ORR: This is a difficult question, asking you to look at yourself, but is

73

there, as you see it, an element of vanity in your nature that you want to be applauded as a popular or famous poet?

HARNETT: Yes, there is.

ORR: You like to be admired?

HARNETT: I draw a very definite line between myself and my poetry. I like my poetry to be admired because I believe it's good, and I believe it contains what's known as a message. But as for myself I don't care. But, of course, one inevitably follows the other; if my poetry is popular, my name is going to be popular, anyway.

ORR: Is the writing of poetry, Michael, your main occupation in life?

HARNETT: Yes.

ORR: Do you ever have feelings at any time that there is anything else that you would rather have done, which would have taken up a similar proportion of your life?

HARNETT: Well, yes. I would like to be a musical composer, and I know nothing about it, nothing at all. I'm even a bad listener.

ORR: You feel this is on an even higher plane than poetry?

HARNETT: Yes. I feel that there is no poet as good as Beethoven or Bach or Mozart. That might not seem like a fair comparison, but that's the way I feel, as regards expression.

ORR: Not even Shakespeare?

HARNETT: No, not even Shakespeare.

ORR: Do you have a favourite poet in the English language?

HARNETT: I don't think so, no, not a favourite poet. But at a guess I should say Shakespeare, because the reason is I read more of Shakespeare than I read of any other poet. I was so interested in my own development that I didn't bother. A poem had to be really, really very good to attract my attention. I never read beyond the first or second line of a poem. Hopkins is about the only poet that attracted me because of his eccentricity and experimentation, and Joyce. I think he's a great poet. I think *Ulysses* a very good poem. I mean, more than half of it is a very good poem, anyway.

17th October, 1963.

Hamish Henderson

HAMISH HENDERSON was born in 1919 in Blairgowrie, Scotland, and educated at Blairgowrie, Dulwich, and Downing College, Cambridge. During the war he was an intelligence officer with the 51st Highland Division and other infantry divisions, and served in Africa and Italy. He has been a folklorist in the School of Scottish Studies, Edinburgh University, since 1951. He won the Somerset Maugham Award for Literature in 1949.

His published works include *Ballads of World War II* (1947), a collection of songs with items by the editor, and *Elegies for the Dead in Cyrenaica* (1948).

ORR: Mr. Henderson, let me start by asking you about your upbringing. You are a pure Scot, aren't you?

HENDERSON: Yes. I am a Scot on both sides. I was born in Perthshire, in the little burgh of Blairgowrie, and I spent my childhood years there. I was educated at Blairgowrie High School, and without any doubt my poetry and my songs owe a good deal to the speech habits, and the singing habits, of the people in that part.

ORR: How early did you come to poetry?

HENDERSON: Well, I was always very interested in folk poetry, without knowing that it was folk poetry or balladry or anything like that. Lots of people in the area were singers: 'The Bonnie Hoose o'Airlie' and 'Lord Randal' and the big ballads like that were sung by a whole lot of people in and around Blairgowrie, and up in Glenshee where I spent part of my childhood too. Without a doubt they did play a very big part in my feeling for poetry, and most of my life has been devoted to an interest in them and research work about them. For the last fifteen years, nearly, I have been working in Scotland on the Scots folk poetry, and this is the sort of poetry that I like best.

ORR: Tell me, do you find this an advantage or a handicap, being a poet yourself and also having an occupation which has to do with poetry? Do you believe, as Mr. Eliot has advised, that young poets should not have anything to do with poetry in their daily lives, that they should go out and be postmen and milkmen and butchers and things like that?

HENDERSON: Well, I think that the job that I have isn't the sort of job that Eliot means when he says that people should go out and do something else. He is thinking there of the sort of intermediate or hermaphroditic jobs with literature like Autumn Supplement critics, and that sort of thing, whereas I think that my own work in the School is not this same sort of job at all. Most of what I am doing is, in so far as I am capable of it, pretty hard intellectual analysis of what goes to the ticking of this particular thing. I have got to find out, for example, how it fits into the mental climate of the places that make it, and I have got to analyse all sorts of intricate variants between one ballad and another, one version and another, and this is an academic work which is far removed from the light industry of poetry or literature.

ORR: Now, whom do you regard as your poetic ancestors? Since you are a Scots poet, presumably your poetic ancestors would be the Scottish Chaucerians, Dunbar, perhaps Burns, rather than Shakespeare, Wordsworth and Tennyson?

HENDERSON: That's true, but no Scottish poet, of course, has ever been able to ignore, even if he wanted to, the enormous literature lying over against him. The Scots Chaucerians, so called, couldn't do it; they knew perfectly well who had preceded them, and Scottish literature, therefore, has always been under the shadow of this big ben, as you might say, across the way. And needless to say, like every other Scottish poet, I have read the great English poets, and it would be idle and stupid and ridiculous of me to deny that all the major English poets that I have read have to a certain extent influenced me.

ORR: Which have been the strongest influences?

HENDERSON: Well, I think in many ways the modern English poets. Without any doubt as far as the *Elegies* are concerned, Wilfred Owen influenced me greatly. I read him when I was a schoolboy, and I have gone on reading his poetry ever since. I think it is the most wonderful English poetry of this century. Eliot, too, has undoubtedly influenced me very greatly. And I love the later poetry of Yeats. I carried with me, throughout the war, the little Cuala Press *Last Poems* of Yeats that was published in 1939, and I was continually reading poems like

76

'The Circus Animals' Desertion' and 'Under Bare Ben Bulben's Head' and the two plays, *Purgatory* and *The Death of Cuchulain*.

ORR: Can we try and define, before you go on, just what we mean when we say you are influenced by a poet. Does this mean you are influenced in terms of what the poet thinks about, what he has to say, or the mechanics of how he sets it down on paper? How does an influence really work?

HENDERSON: Well, that is one of the almost unanswerable questions. I mean, a poet and the influence of a poet works at every level, surely. One can't possibly listen to what he has got to say without taking some account of how he says it, and I should imagine that if one were to isolate, for example, the influence of Eliot in my poems, 'the way he says it' is undoubtedly there. 'The way he says it' is more important, in this case, I suppose, than what he had to say. I don't think that my poems, these *Elegies* anyway, are really *like* Eliot's poetry, though I know one or two critics have said so. I think the intellectual background is completely different, and also the influences upon the *Elegies* that I think most important are the ones which, to a certain extent, liberated me from too great a bondage to Eliot. I read a tremendous amount of German poetry, and I was absolutely dumbfounded when I read the poems of Friedrich Hölderlin. If any poems have directly influenced my *Elegies*, I think it is the poems of Hölderlin, and especially the later poems, the poems of his madness. In a time of tremendous suffering and war, small wonder that poems of a poet's personal suffering, horror, ecstasy and extreme agony should influence another poet. The last poems of Hölderlin are amazingly modern too, as Michael Hamburger was pointing out in a recent number of *Stand* I was reading the other day. I was reading the originals of Hölderlin's later poetry and these translations of Michael Hamburger, some of which are quite good, but I was more interested in what he had to say about them. And there is no doubt in my mind whatsoever that Hölderlin is one of those poets whose influence has never completely come to the fore as far as the thirties and indeed the forties are concerned in English or Scots poetry, for the obvious reason that he is a foreign poet, and the number of people who really can appreciate his influence is going to be smaller than in the case of an English poet.

ORR: Let's look now at the themes which attract you in poetry. You've mentioned suffering: is this the one all-pervasive theme that you feel driven to write about?

HENDERSON: Oh no. It certainly is a main theme in my *Elegies*. They are poems of passive suffering. They are poems of stoicism, which is undoubtedly a virtue in the times that we have gone through, and to a certain extent I think my own *Elegies* prefigure the greater threat of annihilation which stands over everybody now. And not to think of suffering in such a period would condemn one, I think; at any rate would condemn me, because of the sort of person I am.

ORR: What other themes do you feel drawn to write about, then?

HENDERSON: Well, in many Scottish writers you get the strong swing of the pendulum between the strong, deep heavy notes of the lament as, for example, in Dunbar's 'Lament for the Makars', and something different altogether, which can be the wildest ecstasy of the dance. This always seems to me to be much more possible for a Scottish poet in music than in poetry. Well, I don't say for every poet, but when I swing to the other extreme I move into music, and because I love Scottish folk-music generally, I find that when I begin writing in a 'Crazy Jane' mood, not only the words but the tunes suggest themselves to me, and I finish up by not publishing the poem in a magazine but singing it in a folk song club. And then people begin listening to it and they begin repeating it. For example, my song, 'Farewell to Sicily', The Highland Division's farewell to Sicily, was beginning to get sung by people here and there almost as soon as I had written it. And only today I got an airmail letter from the States giving me the text of a version of this particular song which is quite a distance away from the way I wrote it, sung by a group in the States.

ORR: Do you see yourself then more nearly as a troubadour, a minstrel, than an intellectual poet sitting down and wanting to have his words regarded on the printed page?

HENDERSON: I think that is a false antithesis. They talk of the 'Scottish Schizophrenia', but I don't think it is possible for a Scottish poet to make this sort of schizophrenic split. I don't think of myself as a troubadour or anything as airy-fairy as that: I think of myself as a lyric poet, a satiric poet, a ribald poet, at times a bawdy poet, who thinks not only in terms of words but in terms of music. If at the present moment lyricism, ribaldry, bawdry have been separated from music, it is a passing phenomenon. We are in the preliminary stages of an enormous revival of oral tradition. Everyone knows that. A lot of people don't *like* it, but everyone can see it, and in so far as my poems are part of the beginning of this, I am pleased at the idea.

78

ORR: Do you feel attracted to writing poetic drama?

HENDERSON: I have written poetic drama, but I am not very sure if I have been successful. Years ago when Joan Littlewood used to come to Scotland with Theatre Workshop I worked for a time upon a play which was mainly in prose, but the sort of O'Casey prose that was, as you might say, a half-way house between prose and poetry. I was immensely attracted to it, but I eventually decided that I would not permit it to go forward. I didn't think that I had been successful with it. I may have a go at it again.

ORR: Do you want to write novels and essays?

HENDERSON: Essays yes, but essays about my own subject of folk poetry and of folk tales. I have written one which has got certain, I think, literary merits, apart from the purely academic merits. On the academic side it has not been challenged yet: I don't know whether it will be, although it contains a whole lot of different ideas in it. It's a long note upon a particular folk tale in Scots, 'The Green Man of Knowledge,' a version of an international folk tale, Aarne-Thompson Märchen-type 313, 'The Magic Flight'—the tale of which the Jason and Medea legend is the archetype—which I recorded in Aberdeenshire in 1954. It brings together the Irish and the Scottish Gaelic versions of the 313 tale-type, a gypsy version from Wales, and many of the other versions. It is one of the basic folk tales that you find in nearly every country under the sun, and consequently, one of the perennially fascinating folk tales. I have also brought in *Sir Gawain and the Green Knight*, this puzzling, wonderful and beautiful Arthurian poem which so many people have barked their shins on, and no doubt I have barked mine. As I say, it is a literary essay as well as an academic one.

ORR: Do you feel drawn to writing about contemporary problems about the world as it is around us today?

HENDERSON: Well, in so far as I have written about the most pressing problems of all, namely those of continuing existence and the bomb or what have you, I have felt in this case too that song is the thing that expresses my feeling best. I have written, for example, a song which I call 'The Freedom Come-All-Ye' which is written under this tremendous shadow of the bomb. It's a song which tries to gather together a number of the problems that face us in Scotland and the world. It faces the tremendous problem of race, for example, and it faces the tremendous problem of human brotherhood and the threat of annihilation and as I say, I don't make any barrier at all between poetry and song now. I think that the two have got to go together. I intend to go on writing in this way. To a certain extent, the poem 'The Cell' is already a sort of appendix; something that no longer really has much point in my own creation. I hope to complete the long poem. I think it has got some passages that are of merit, and I would like to complete it.

ORR: Do you feel yourself cut off from, or do you feel very strongly part of English contemporary poetry, the poetry of the nineteen-sixties? I am thinking of people like Ted Hughes and Thom Gunn, Edward Lucie-Smith, Peter Porter and so on.

HENDERSON: Oh, I should suppose I am undoubtedly cut off from them. I like their stuff; I mean, I still read poetry for pleasure, which is a thing that I know not all poets do. But I think that I am doing something different, and it is this thing which I'm trying to describe. As far as Scottish poets are concerned, I think that the ones that are nearest me, at any rate in the attempt to heal the gap between song and poetry are Sydney Goodsir Smith, who is in many ways the most successful writer of poems in the folk idiom, an extraordinary poet; also MacDiarmid, when he was writing in Scots in his first two or three books, in *Sangschaw*, in *Penny Wheep*, in *A Drunk Man Looks at the Thistle*. He draws on this particular folk tradition in the most marvellous fashion. These are the poets that I feel are much closer to me than these modern English poets that you mention.

ORR: Are you a severe critic of your own work? Can you stand back and look at it quite dispassionately?

HENDERSON: Yes, I think I can. So dispassionately and so critically, in fact, that I have jettisoned a great deal of stuff that I might not have jettisoned, I suppose; but I went through a period of extreme critical strictness, especially in the early nineteen-fifties when I was working on the long poem that I have mentioned, and I ditched a great deal of it because I felt that in the long run it just didn't say what I wanted to say, and then I left it at that.

ORR: Is the satisfaction you get from writing poetry (presuming that there is a satisfaction) the satisfaction of actually *doing* the thing, of working it out like a crossword puzzle, if I can put it at that level, or is the satisfaction rather in having created a piece of work to look back on?

HENDERSON: Oh, that is a very difficult question indeed. I think that what Wilde wrote in *De Profundis* has got some bearing upon this question when he says that the object of love is to love. To feel itself in the joy of its own being. To a certain extent this is poetry too: one shouldn't divide it between the moment of creation and the created completed thing. Its joy is the joy of itself, to feel itself in being. I certainly have felt that, whether I have published a thing or not, or whether I have come in contact with people to whom I can read stuff or anything like that. Periods when one actually feels that one has got something and that it's moving. And that, I suppose, to every poet is the most important thing. To have this sensation of the thing moving and being and in existence, and not dead and failing.

ORR: And is the idea of communicating what you have to say to an audience important to you?

HENDERSON: It is, but of late, as I say, this has always with me taken the shape of direct communication, not so much communication via the printed page, although I have published things here and there. I have preferred to read poetry out, and if it is a song, to sing it. I am quite conscious of the fact that this immediate communication has got its own strong drawbacks. The audience cannot often grasp a thing immediately. But nevertheless, this immediate communication, this immediate aural communication, has been to me personally of enormous interest.

13th October, 1964.

David Holbrook

DAVID HOLBROOK was born in 1923 in Norwich, and read English at
Downing College, Cambridge, under F. R. Leavis. During the war he was
an officer in a tank regiment, and took part in the Normandy landings. He
has worked in publishing, adult education and school teaching. In 1961
he was made a Fellow of King's College, Cambridge, and this 'writing'
fellowship was extended in 1963. In 1964 he was awarded a Senior Lever-
hulme Research Grant. He is at present working on a book on the training
of English teachers, and another on psychoanalytical ideas and their
relevance to creativity and literary criticism. A book of verse and a novel
about war are in preparation.

He has published two volumes of poetry, *Imaginings* (1961) and *Against
the Cruel Frost* (1963), and a book of short stories, *Lights in the Sky Country*
(1962). He has also published books of literary criticism, *Llareggub Revisited*
(1962), *The Quest for Love* (1965); books on English in education, *English
for Maturity* (1961), *The Secret Places* (1964), *English for the Rejected* (1964),
and edited four anthologies for school use.

MORRISH: Mr. Holbrook, what do you think you can express in poetry
that you can't in any other literary form?

HOLBROOK: Well, I do a great deal of other writing, on literary criticism
and on education, and poetry seems a vigorous complement to this. I
feel that if I am going to be able to contribute anything to literary
criticism or to the teaching of English, I ought to go on exploring my
own inward problems, my own inward reality, in as creative a way
as I can. It seems to me that it can be of value to explore one's own
inward world metaphorically, in terms of symbolism, and that it
ought to be part of the educated person's apparatus—the capacity to
develop a habit of doing this, in such a way as to communicate
something of it to others. If one can communicate one's own states

83

of depression, one's own moments of gloating on experience, one's own moments of success, and one's own moments of failure accurately enough, and catch the rhythms and the quality of the mood, one may have something to offer.

MORRISH: Yes, but this doesn't explain why you don't write novels.

HOLBROOK: Well, I do write novels; at least, I've written one which I go on rewriting. This is a quite evident prose task because it is an attempt to deal with battle experience—what meaning did *this* have in one's life? In poems I find myself impelled to catch the fleeting moment, the various components of a transient mood, at a crux at which several things come together into a whole.

MORRISH: How do you guard against the sort of self-indulgence which self-expression in poetry can lead to?

HOLBROOK: Well, you do guard against it but, of course, one does sometimes fail, and this is part of the struggle. A very great friend of mine called Douglas Brown has recently died, a very sensitive person whom I always felt to be my ideal reader. He would read poems for me and would always try to distinguish whether each represented a man speaking to men, or whether a poem was simply the indulgence of a private mood. This, of course, brings up the question of the function of the poet. I am always searching for a more objective platform, the third ground where one is obliged to entertain, to provide something satisfying to an audience, rather than merely working on one's own private inward life to one's own satisfaction; where one is obliged ... well, to *sing*, to produce poems of a lyrical kind, within the compass of what the audience can take, and recreate in them the mood which you are exploring.

MORRISH: But this sounds as if you think the poem on its own is not sufficient, as if you need the strengthening influence of another art, for instance music, to give a greater impact?

HOLBROOK: I think some of my poems make an impact if I read them aloud to an audience, particularly the rather more extrovert poems like 'Cardoness Castle'. I don't enjoy reading to an audience a poem such as 'The Return' (the last of the series called *Out of This World*), which is an attempt to register a moment of very considerable suffering, and the way out of it. But I still feel that I want to explore the possibilities of poetry having more of a public function, an obvious, energetic, public function, than that represented by selling fifteen hundred copies of a small volume.

MORRISH: Your poetry is *autobiographical*, which could imply a certain

84

limitation of imagination because it is very closely fixed to facts of your own life. Do you feel this?

HOLBROOK: Yes, I do tend to write about my own experience. Perhaps this is simply a limitation in me. I have tried to write poetry in the context of a more 'invented' situation by writing with composers. I have done several pieces of work with Wilfred Mellers. He and I wrote two ballad operas which turned out to be unsuccessful in dramatic terms. I have also done some work with Elizabeth Poston who was a disciple of Vaughan Williams, and with Alan Ridout, a young composer who started off very stern and serial, but who has since mellowed.

MORRISH: How did you start writing poetry to be set to music? What stimulated you in the first place?

HOLBROOK: Originally with Wilfred Mellers. He and I did a great deal of work in adult education, lecturing, and we were both tremendously interested in opera and in masque and Shakespearean drama; and in conversations we gradually began to invent things which we thought we could do.

MORRISH: Did you find the discipline of writing poetry specifically to be set to music rather irksome?

HOLBROOK: No. This gives me a great deal of delight because I invent a rhythm—for instance, I invent something which has, shall we say, a light touch, and then I find it interpreted and it is sung back to me and I can see this created thing, away from me, in this public arena. For example, I have written some children's songs for Alan Ridout. He'd been asked to write five songs for children and asked if I would write the words. We were having a very cold spell at the moment so, in fact, they were written about a cold snap. I wanted poems that would make a direct impact on children. In one I wanted something that would suggest the evanescent quality of early spring wind—a very light touch, very direct. Such a need means you've got to work hard on your lyric to make it something which can be set in a musical scheme, which has got the right number of syllables, and which can suit its purpose. This song was called 'First Wind of Spring':

> Watch for it, early spring:
> It is a not-caught-easily thing!
> It is a small, brisk circling wind,
> Bringing the flowers behind!
> — River banks, in the sun,
> In the shy February one,

See it pluck your coat and then
Wreathe the water. Gone again!

I have tried other more operatic things, for example a ballad opera, again for Ridout, which turned out to contain a series of lyrics about depression in terms of natural imagery. The central character was a girl who was in a suicidal mood, having been jilted, and in order to get her out of this mood, characters in the little operetta take on very manic roles. So it was appropriate for them to sing rather Brecht-Weil kind of songs, expressing a kind of ironic wisdom about relationships: Ridout, working on the basis of my script, has explored a sort of 'pop-song' version of serial setting. Both of us regard this as experimental work, and we hope later we shall co-operate on something else.

MORRISH: Are you interested in communicating to as many people as possible, or do you envisage a certain *kind* of audience, a well-educated, rather middle-class audience in this country?

HOLBROOK: Well, in adult education, I've gained a good deal of insight into the sort of problems of adults living ordinary full lives, and got from them a tremendous sense of the value of the imaginative experience to living. For instance, a health visitor student once told me that one evening after we had been discussing Cleopatra's death in *Antony and Cleopatra*, when she got home she was asked by a neighbour to lay out a corpse. She said it was deeply moving, to have in mind the perspective of mortality that Shakespeare had given her, as she performed this terrible task. One finds too, with adult students, that they come in and talk about human relationship in literature with their daily life in mind. I feel that there is a tremendous need to foster that accurate use of language which poetry is, in exploring both the outer world and the inner world. And that it is a great loss in our society that people do talk so much in the clichés of the popular press and of advertising. I mean, immense damage is done to a word like 'love' by the advertising slogan that says 'People love Player's' for instance. I think one's got to work on the re-creation of the capacities to use language for the vital purposes of living. And this is why I concern myself with English teaching, and why I write books on education.

MORRISH: Would you say then that education, and indeed art, is a way to protect people against the society they live in?

HOLBROOK: Yes. I think that our society has simply become inefficient in terms of the inward life. I have found, teaching secondary modern

schoolchildren, that they are capable of the most marvellous creative
output in painting and drama and writing. It's small compared with
the output of more intelligent children, naturally. But they *can* use
their language, which means they are using their emotions and
thinking powers to explore experience, and when they do they really
do become much more efficient as persons. They are much more able
to carry on a conversation, to deal with other kinds of learning. From
this it seems to me that it isn't so much just a case of 'protecting'
people against their society but retraining people in using their poetic
functions, to look at life, as they do as children. Not simply to live
out the trivial fantasy that they see on television and the films, but
really to use language to look at human relationships and family life
and their own inward life and say, 'What can I make of it?'

MORRISH: This seems to me a rather more sophisticated attitude to what
one might have called 'Folk Culture'.

HOLBROOK: Yes. I think we have got to remake a popular culture which
has a content of its own. And therefore I see the audience beginning
to grow in the secondary modern schools and the grammar schools,
where the value of art and the creative purposes is understood, as it is
beginning to be, I think, at a tremendous pace; and in the training
colleges where young teachers are also taking much more of a creative
line about their subjects. They do read poetry with great interest,
very close attention. Some of the readings I have done have been to
university groups and training college groups where, to my surprise
and gratification, I found that the family poems, about domestic
problems and about children and so on, pleased the young men and
women more than anything. I thought they might have thought
this a bit fuddy-duddy, but not a bit of it.

MORRISH: How do you feel about the work of your contemporaries
against which criticisms of *obscurity* have been raised?

HOLBROOK: Well, I feel that there's a great deal of poetic fashion about.
It seems to me to lack definition and essential germinal content. I
think we have to be very careful about obscurity because Eliot is
obscure, and a lot of Pound is obscure, and you have to work hard at
what they're saying, but I think if you work hard at their obscure
poetry you can get rewards from it. With them it would seem to me
that the obscurity has a point because it's communicating something
very complex. In my own work certainly what I try to get is something simple and direct and which *will* communicate immediately.
Perhaps, at times, this has produced rather crass over-simplicity: but

what I want to try to do is to write a poem that can make an immediate and direct impact.

MORRISH: When did you start writing poetry?

HOLBROOK: I have always written poetry off and on.

MORRISH: You mean ever since you were a child?

HOLBROOK: Yes, in adolescence I wrote a great deal of poetry. I think the first poem which made me feel that I ought to work harder at writing was the one about a walk by the river with my daughter. One of the most flexible periods of one's life, when one's really beginning to work on one's life problems, is adolescence when, of course, we know people do pour out poetry privately. The other, I think, is the early years of a marriage when your children arrive and immediately begin to challenge all your own weaknesses and to show up your mortality, and Time becomes a reality. In my own case this challenge of a child's existence and the child's enquiring mind produced a sort of crisis which I have felt that I must try and solve—my own reconciliation to mutability and time and mortality—and try and grow up, as it were, so that I could be more adequate for them.

MORRISH: What development do you see in your work since you started publishing?

HOLBROOK: I think there are some rather journalistic poems in the first things I published which I would feel now not to be appropriate subjects for a poem. I try, I think, to control words more carefully.

MORRISH: You are more interested in technique?

HOLBROOK: Yes. The reviewers say in my poems that I don't have a technique, which annoys me because although I'm not explicitly very interested in technique I do struggle hard to define a mood, an attitude, by controlling the language. And sometimes, I think, in a poem like 'Winter Sunday' this does come off. It seems to me that technique is only of value in the service of saying, as accurately as one can, things about a complex experience, and trying to ensure that the reader can possess it as you mean him to possess it.

MORRISH: What do you still want to do? Do you want to try another form within your poetry or to find another platform?

HOLBROOK: Well, I still want to try and solve the problem of collaboration with music. I have just written an opera for youth which was commissioned by Middlesex County Council. This is with John Joubert. I would like to write school opera, campus opera, college opera, for that audience which I know reads my educational work; and from that I would like to try and write something in the nature of verse drama, with or without music. I have written one or two but nothing yet that works. But I think here the problem is to get an audience so much 'with' you that you can enter into the deeply serious areas of human feeling and relationship in a positive way, and, if I can use the word, a *tender* way. The problem is, how is it going to be possible to write verse drama which can say sincere and touching things to an audience in the context of so much that is untender and prurient in the theatre today. But this is something that I want to try and do.

17th November, 1964.

Elizabeth Jennings

ELIZABETH JENNINGS was born in 1926 in Oxfordshire and educated at Oxford High School and St. Anne's College, Oxford. She worked as a library assistant 1950–58 and a publisher's reader 1958–60. She won the Arts Council Prize for Poetry 1953, and the Somerset Maugham Award for Literature 1956. F.R.S.L. 1961.

Her publications include *Poems* (1953), *A Way of Looking* (1955), *A Sense of the World* (1958), *Let's Have Some Poetry* (1960), *Every Changing Shape* (1961), *Song for a Birth or a Death* (1961). She edited *The Batsford Book of Children's Verse* (1958), and published a translation of Michelangelo's *Sonnets* (1961).

PRESS: When you first began to make your reputation about ten years ago, people thought of you as being part of the Movement, the *New Lines* poets and so forth. Do you think this kind of grouping was helpful to you or justified?

JENNINGS: At the time I think it was positively unhelpful, because I tended to be grouped and criticized rather than be grouped and praised. I think now that the Movement has really broken up, and each of the members of this movement, such as Davie, Gunn, Amis and Larkin, have found their own styles and are really so different you could scarcely call them a movement any longer.

PRESS: Do you think that they had an affinity with one another at the time?

JENNINGS: I think so, yes, but I think like all true movements, it was not a contrived one.

PRESS: Did you yourself feel that you wanted to get into your poetry certain qualities which you didn't find in your contemporaries?

JENNINGS: Oh yes, certainly. Well, two big differences between myself and my contemporaries were that I was a woman and also a Roman Catholic, which meant that I wanted to write about subjects which were simply uninteresting to most Movement poets: at least uninteresting to them in the way they were interesting to me.

PRESS: Do you feel that being a woman and a poet in some way marks you off from men poets, that poetry is very largely a man's world.

JENNINGS: I think not, though, when one does, in fact, look back, or even look now at American and English poets (and I incidentally dislike the word 'poetesses', I was glad you didn't use that) there aren't many. So there must be perhaps something essentially masculine or virile about it, or it may be that in the past women have not had the time or they have not had the inclination or they have had other things to do; and it is also true that women have not usually been composers or even good painters, so the awful truth appears to be that women are not, on the whole, good or important artists. Yet I can't really agree with that. Certainly now we have people like Elizabeth Bishop and Marianne Moore, and we had Sylvia Plath, and I think in America it is possibly easier to be a woman poet, where it isn't so odd to write poetry, where one isn't called a 'poetess', and where to be an artist is not a question of sex.

PRESS: Do you feel that your religious beliefs very strongly influence the kind of poetry you write, not necessarily in a didactic way but in your attitude to the world?

JENNINGS: Yes, certainly, more and more. But another thing that I wanted to say is that I do have a feeling (and this may be because many people have told me about it) that I have been too formal in the past in my poetry, too strict, too rigid; I have even been called cold by people who don't like my verse, and sort of delicate and feminine and so on by people who do. But I want to loosen up my verse and this is a thing that you can't do consciously; but it seems in a way to be happening, I think, at the moment.

PRESS: Are your new prose poems part of this?

JENNINGS: I think they are a movement towards it, but now I am writing things which are even more free than those.

PRESS: Have you had any ambitions to write a long poem?

JENNINGS: Yes I have, often, but it will never come off yet. I have never got beyond writing a sequence of lyrics. In other words, a collection of a kind of short poems that I would write normally.

PRESS: Are you very much moved by music?

JENNINGS: Yes, but of the three great arts, painting comes next. I do a lot of experimental, amateurish painting.

PRESS: And have you wanted to experiment with other forms, such as the novel, the drama?

JENNINGS: Yes, I have a great ambition to write a libretto for an opera.

PRESS: Why do you want to write a libretto rather than a dramatic poem or play?

JENNINGS: Well, I think that I need the help of another form. I don't think I could do it alone, and maybe I have more feeling about music than I realize.

PRESS: Do you write swiftly and then revise a great deal, or do you write your poems slowly, painfully, carefully?

JENNINGS: I write swiftly and revise very little.

PRESS: And you've found that these strict forms for which you have been criticized are the natural media in which you write?

JENNINGS: Yes, certainly. They are not laboured and they don't go through many versions. The thing is, of course, that I have been writing since I was a child and therefore I have got accustomed to certain forms, and I think I have experimented within a range of forms but so far, but with some exceptions, I have stuck to formal verse. Not always rhymed verse.

PRESS: Were you very much influenced by either immediate contemporaries or by poets of earlier centuries?

JENNINGS: Well, when I first started writing I wasn't influenced by anybody because I hadn't read very much, and I was very young indeed. Then when I was about fifteen or sixteen I read Eliot, and I wrote long poems of sort of *vers libre* which I imagined were influenced by Eliot, and which were very personal, in fact. I was getting rid of a lot of things that I wanted to say and using what I thought were mostly early Eliot forms, but they weren't really like Eliot at all: they hadn't got his strictness, but I thought they had. I felt that I was being influenced by early Eliot and then later Auden, then very much Edwin Muir, and then much more formal poets like Yeats; and I still believe that Yeats is the greatest poet of the century.

PRESS: What about American verse?

JENNINGS: Yes, Wallace Stevens, but more for ideas than forms, because I was almost obsessed at one point with the idea of what one made of a thing and what was reality, with objectivity and subjectivity, and then one day I picked up an anthology and found some Wallace Stevens and I thought, 'Ah, this person has done it, but maybe one can do something else like this or take it further'; though not quite as ambitious as that, but he was a big influence at one period, yes.

PRESS: Do you feel that the necessity of earning a living is a check on your writing poetry?

JENNINGS: Sometimes it is a worry, but I like writing prose as well and obviously you can't just sit down and wait for a poem to arrive. I like reviewing and I like broadcasting, and I like the other odd jobs I get, and I think sometimes they help towards writing poems. I don't think one should sit about (I mean, if one had the money and was able to) waiting for a poem to come. And anyway, one must have all sorts of experiences, travel and people and so on.

PRESS: Are you very gregarious?

JENNINGS: I am shy but gregarious, yes.

PRESS: You like meeting people?

JENNINGS: Yes.

PRESS: And travel?

JENNINGS: Very much, especially to Italy.

PRESS: Do you feel that your liking for Italy and the Mediterranean in general is because these are the countries of the Catholic faith?

JENNINGS: Well that, certainly, and also the fact that you are accepted there as some kind of artist. I have quoted this often (I hope I haven't quoted it to you): I was having a Campari in a bar in Rome once, I was speaking pretty bad Italian, and I was asked by the barman what I was doing, and I somehow sensed that it was all right to tell him, and I said that I was in Rome because I had a prize and I was writing poems, and he said with the utmost delight and absolutely no self-consciousness, 'Ah, you are a poet.' This is very difficult, almost impossible to envisage in a pub in England, (possibly one or two in London)—one just would not say it, too many people would be embarrassed, and I think this is another reason why I find the Mediterranean countries very sympathetic.

PRESS: Do you think it harder now than ever to write poetry in this country?

JENNINGS: For me, no. It's hard for me to know what it would have been like, say, if I had been older. But what I do know is that the best audiences that I have given poetry readings to are teenagers. They are most attentive, most intelligent, and most probing as askers of questions, which I find rather cheering.

PRESS: Do you think that they will continue to be readers or that it is because they are young?

JENNINGS: Hard to say, but some of them certainly seemed as if they wanted to be poets themselves, and they would go on reading even if they only took the books out of the library and didn't buy them. No, I didn't get the feeling it was just because they were young.

PRESS: Did you think that this revival of reading aloud is helpful to poets?

JENNINGS: Certainly, yes.

PRESS: Do you write any poems which you consciously design to be read aloud?

JENNINGS: No. The only things I have ever consciously written for a purpose have been when I have collaborated. I collaborated with a Spanish scholar on a translation of a Spanish play: I don't know Spanish and I sort of versified it, and it was broadcast on the Home Service which delighted us because we didn't want an egg-head audience. We also collaborated on a translation of Michelangelo's *Sonnets*, but I do know a bit of Italian, of course.

PRESS: Are you much affected by reviews, whether good or bad?

JENNINGS: Yes, terribly.

PRESS: Do the good encourage you?

JENNINGS: They encourage me, and then after a bit I look at them and wonder if they are true. The bad always make me feel doleful, and I feel *sure* they are true. And sometimes I learn from them. I learn from the bad more than the good.

PRESS: What kind of things do you learn, specific points of technique?

JENNINGS: Yes, or when I am repeating myself, that kind of thing.

PRESS: Do you think reviews are important in the sense that they help to make a reputation?

JENNINGS: Yes, I suppose so, but what I am quite certain is that they don't help to sell a book. I remember once doing a very short thing on a broadcast programme and imagining that thousands of people (because it was quite a flattering review) would then go and buy the book, but I don't think it made any difference. Whereas if my book had been a novel, I am sure it would have made a difference. Perhaps it is a good thing in a way. One might start writing things simply for a certain audience. That would be a great temptation, possibly, I don't know. But certainly one doesn't have it now.

PRESS: Does the writing of poetry give you intense pleasure or is it more an absolute emotional necessity?

JENNINGS: It's both. About halfway through the writing of a poem I think I know if it is going to come off and be any good, and there is intense pleasure. And there is emotional necessity about it, yes. I mean, I can never pick up a piece of paper (by the way, I must always have a piece of paper and pencil; I can't memorize, as some people can, a poem on my own that I am making at the time) and decide that I have just *got* to write a poem and now I will do it. It starts with a peculiar feeling of excitement. It must satisfy some emotional need and it also gives pleasure, yes.

PRESS: Do you find there are long periods of silence when no poems come?

JENNINGS: Well, when there is a period of more than about two months and no poems come I begin to get very worried indeed, yes. I think it is all gone for good.

PRESS: I think Auden said that no poet knows whether he will ever write another poem.

JENNINGS: Yes, yes, I so agree with that. He said other people regard a poet as a poet if he's written a book, whereas a poet only feels he is one when he has just written a new poem, and I absolutely agree with him.

PRESS: One never knows when the visitations will come?

JENNINGS: No.

24th September, 1964.

David Jones

DAVID JONES was born in 1895 in Kent. His father was Welsh, his mother
English of partly Italian descent. He started to draw at a very early age and
his drawings were first exhibited in 1903–4 at the Royal Drawing Society
for the Encouragement of Youthful Art. He served with the Royal Welch
Fusiliers on the Western Front 1915–18. He then studied at the Westminster
School of Art 1919–21. He began to engrave and a number of his engravings
were commissioned as book illustrations; in 1928–29 he made a set of
copper-engravings for *The Ancient Mariner*, published by Douglas Clever-
don in 1929. His paintings have been exhibited in a number of galleries,
including the National Gallery and Burlington House, and in numerous
exhibitions abroad. The Arts Council arranged a retrospective exhibition
of his work which was shown at the Tate Gallery 1954–55. A link between
his painting and writing can be found in his inscriptions, mainly in Latin,
sometimes with some Welsh and occasionally English, on an opaque
chinese-white background, the letters in various colours. C.B.E. 1955.
D.Litt. University of Wales, 1960. F.R.S.L. Hon. Member R.W.S. 1961.
He was awarded the Hawthornden Prize for Poetry in 1938, and the
Russell Loines Memorial Award for Poetry 1956.

His publications include *In Parenthesis* (1937), *The Anathemata* (1952),
The Wall (1955), *Epoch and Artist* (1959).

ORR: We sit here in a room, the walls of which are covered with paintings and books. Which came first, the painting or writing?

JONES: Oh, the painting. The painting from the age of seven, and
writing not till I was thirty or so. When I was young I wouldn't
learn anything. My sister used to read to me because I couldn't read.

ORR: You used to pay her a penny an hour or something?

JONES: Yes, that's right. When we were children, when I was about
eight. It's very peculiar because so much would I *not* learn things that

97

I barely would go to school, so they let me go to an art school when I was just fourteen. It meant, of course, and this is increasingly annoying, that I didn't have any knowledge of languages or the apparatus of scholarship; I have had to do it all myself as I go along.

ORR: Do you find that there were any advantages, though, in not having been to a formal prep school?

JONES: Well, people who have been tell me that I *have* advantages. But, of course, I only see it the other way round.

ORR: Poetry and painting. In your mind have they got much to do with each other?

JONES: Absolutely! All the arts are one and the medium is—well, not *secondary*, but it's just another mode of making a thing.

ORR: If you have an idea, how do you decide whether this is going to make a piece of visual art or whether it is going to turn into a poem?

JONES: Oh, I have never had that experience, that choice hasn't really occurred. I don't think it would occur, but I'll tell you one thing that might be of interest. When I started to write that war book, *In Parenthesis*, in 1928, I thought I would do drawings and write pieces to go with the drawings; then I abandoned that idea and confined the thing, except for three illustrations, to writing.

ORR: Mr. Jones, your writing is sometimes extremely dense and enriched with historical and mythological allusions, and this does sometimes make it difficult for the reader, doesn't it? This is rather unusual in an age of what I suppose we must recognize as over-simplification. Do you feel you are very much against the current of the age in this?

JONES: Well, yes, appallingly so in one way. It is a thing that I can only question, I can't give any answer to. I only feel that all artists are against the current of the age in a way perhaps they've never been before. We know that in primitive societies, in tribal societies, the poets or bards had official status. It was absolutely necessary to that society. Well, that no longer exists, but even so throughout all literature there has been this business of a recalling of past images: all the past holds as far as your horizon, wherever you are in the world or whatever culture you belong to, you carry across to the next generation. And this is getting more and more difficult. I don't say it *can't* be overcome, I only question it, and it is to me a great difficulty.

ORR: You say you are gathering together the past. Does this mean that in some way you are transmuting the texture of the past, the shape of the past, even renewing the past?

JONES: Renewing is a *very* good word because, you see, that has always been so. The past takes on a new form because of the changed situation. I think one of the most interesting examples in modern times, in the English-speaking world anyhow, is Hopkins, because he was not consciously trying to do a new thing; one of his great influences was this mediaeval, incredibly intricate Welsh metric and yet, you see, it was almost like a time-fused bomb. It wasn't until 1918 that the thing exploded, and it wasn't until decades after 1918 that people in general have now accepted him as part of the corpus of English literature.

ORR: To come back to yourself, is not the sort of writing that you do going to become progressively more and more difficult in future generations, because the fund of knowledge which is available to man is growing vaster and vaster every day?

JONES: Yes, indeed, I do fear it. I think I said in the preface to *The Anathemata* that I may be trying to do something in a way that is no longer possible, but it is the only way *I* know how to do it.

ORR: Do you find that you can remember the sources of the allusions that you want to work into your writing?

JONES: No, not easily. I am conscious of the source and then if I'm going to employ it I have to find it out, because one can have a thing in one's head but can't immediately fetch it out from its particular sort of filing box. It sometimes takes me a very long time to trace the origin and very often one finds one has got the wrong one.

ORR: This presumably means that you write slowly?

JONES: Very, very laboriously and there is more cutting away than adding: I mean, stripping off and making as compact as possible, but it is a very, very painful process. I found in writing *The Anathemata* that I went out so far on limbs, as it were, that I couldn't get back again to the main trend with any sort of intelligibility, and that necessitated a good deal of pruning. You see an enormous number of facets of the thing, and one thing suggests another, but if you aren't very careful it takes you too far from the concept and you can't get back to it again except at very great length, and that might be artistically bad.

ORR: How do you know what to keep in and what to throw away?

JONES: Well, I try to just eliminate the things that go too far out on this by-path; I try to make that amount of judgement, and it really is where form and content come in, because form and content should be *one*; that is the thing one should aim at, and I think in the world's great art works that is precisely what happens. That is the thing that has always worried me about our time and our artists. Let us for a moment confine it to painting: you can't make a distinction between abstract painting and non-abstract painting; the truth is that *any* painting of greatness has an abstract quality and *all* painting is representative, not as we ordinarily say 'representative' but representative of *something*, of some idea. So that you can't divide the two, they both have form and they both have content. I mean, when you look at a Lascaux cave painting or at a Tintoretto, you don't ask which is form, what is content? You just see one thing. And that, I think, should be the first aim of a poet or of an artist of any sort. The form and content are as *one* as possible.

ORR: Do you find critics helpful at all? Are they in any way complementary to what you are doing?

JONES: No, not really. Of course, sometimes *constructive* criticism is, it depends upon the sensitivity of the critic. I don't know whether the critic's job is meant to help the artist; perhaps it is more to help the public, but whether he does or not, of course, depends upon his own integrity and his own sensitivity.

ORR: Is the idea of communication to a large audience important to you in your writing, or don't you think about it?

JONES: No, I don't see how you can possibly think about it. I never think about it at all when I am doing the stuff because you only say, either in words, or if it's a visual thing, drawing, what seems to you to be appropriate to that particular form and content.

ORR: When you're writing you don't think, 'Oh yes, this might not be understood, we must make it clearer'? Or do you simply do that by adding an apparatus of notes?

JONES: Yes, rather by the latter method, and although people have said that they think that notes are pedantic, *I* think they are the reverse, because it is useless to pretend that there's a common culture existing, as there might perhaps still be in different parts of the world where the poet would be understood because he was within a confined and received and inherited tradition. I would give anything to have Dante's annotations to 'Il Paradiso', for instance. After all, one might say even the word 'Aphrodite' might not be understood now by lots of chaps, and as civilization gets more complicated I think that the place for explanation may be in notes, it seems only mere politeness.

ORR: But you don't feel that there's a danger that ideally you would like to be writing for an academy of people whose interests and whose studies have been along the same lines as yours?

JONES: No, I don't feel that, but I *do* think that we are in a state of crisis. I think it is an integral part of the increasingly rapid change in our times. It is *extremely* difficult to find words which are valid as *signa* to people. I don't know how that is to be overcome, but I think we are in an exceptionally difficult situation with regard to that.

ORR: Do you feel that perhaps the nature of our civilization is changing and that therefore perhaps the nature of our arts should change with it?

JONES: Yes. Sometimes, when I am more than usually depressed, I don't see how things that I call the arts can go on at all, but that is only at certain moments. I know that at the turn of every civilization these difficulties must have arisen, but I feel that owing to the particular character and the enormous acceleration of what is happening today it does make it excruciatingly difficult, more difficult I should think than ever before to carry across.

ORR: And, of course, one has the knowledge too, hasn't one, that people are less and less willing to tackle difficult things, be they paintings which are difficult to look at or books which are difficult to read?

JONES: Yes! And I hate this thing that people talk about, the antagonism between the humanities, the arts and the sciences; but it *does* seem to me just from talking to people, and especially young people, that they find it difficult to think in terms of analogy; there is something about technological science in the modern sense which doesn't easily accommodate itself to forms that are purely signs. It is utile, it is utilitarian, one thing follows from the other and that is that.

ORR: Well, it's so specialized, in fact, that it doesn't accept associations which may not be strictly relevant?

JONES: Yes, and I am told by schoolmasters that they find that boys don't easily accept the language of allegory which, of course, is almost the the whole language of the arts, isn't it?

ORR: Do you find it more difficult to write today than you did, let us say thirty years ago, when you were writing *In Parenthesis*?

JONES: Well, yes, I do but then that's partly because as you get older whatever you do is more complex because you are aware of the complications that are going to arise. When I began to write *In Parenthesis* I didn't think about that at all. I had no idea it would ever be published: I simply wrote. I tried to make in words something that I wanted to say. It was as simple as that. I said in the preface to that book 'this is a shape in words', and people thought that was a rather affected thing to say, but I still stick to that. I think that is precisely what I was trying to do. Only my main trouble, you see, is over this business of *signs*; if I say sacraments then that will have overtones and undertones of a specific sort, but it's the same thing. I mean, you hold up this thing and you say this *means* so and so. Now that seems to me pretty alien from the trend of thought in techno-logical man. But man—unless he changes—couldn't do anything, he couldn't even raise his hat to a lady; everything we do is sacramental in that sense. But whereas once that was all taken for granted, I think that our modern age is dividing it out in a way that has perhaps never been divided out before. I'm sorry to keep on quoting myself, but I think we stroke cats and tie ribbons and give girls boxes of chocolates and so on, which is all part of the sacramental world from my point of view.

ORR: Well, do you like the world in which we live now?

JONES: No, I don't like it at all. I can't see what it can lead to from this stem. I'm not talking for the moment metaphysically, just that one finds a frightful dichotomy between the things that I have had to do with as an artist; it's difficult to swim against the stream, and I don't believe it is a good thing to do. I suppose that maybe something will emerge which one can't envisage, which will restore this balance. If not, then man will cease to be the kind of creature that I have believed him to be.

ORR: Do you believe that the arts, in fact, *do* anything? That they make people more sensitive, more receptive?

JONES: Yes, but I hate the thought of what is called 'cultural activity'. To me it must be interwoven through one's life and, of course, it is more and more difficult. The Hegelian, Dr. Caird, who was Master of Balliol in about 1900 said that it is the peculiar strength of the modern time that it has reached a clear perception of the finite world as finite. That in science it is positive, i.e. that it takes particular facts for no more than they are, and that in practice it is unembarrassed by superstition, by the tendency to treat particular things and persons as mysteriously sacred. Well, poor old Caird didn't understand the implications of what he was saying. I mean, he would be horrified by the thing in full application. But if you push it to its furthest conclusion you just don't have *man*, do you? You don't have what *we* call man. It's absolutely barren. I hate the notion of sounding like a person who is opposed to progress; I mean you can't hold up or write off technological advances. But this notion that a thing can't be the sign of something other destroys all the sacramental thing, in religion and outside religion; all the arts are part of that thing, and so are perfectly ordinary acts of courtesy to a degree that people don't realize. I don't really want to talk about religion, but the real snag is that the Christian religion, and as far as I can gather, most religions, is fixed to the sacramental idea.

ORR: It's fixed also, isn't it, to the idea of mystery, the sense of wonder which must be present in man if he is to survive as a growing spiritual being. I am reminded here of Marlowe: that speech at the end of *Edward II*, young Mortimer who scorns the world and 'goes to discover countries yet unknown'.

JONES: What a marvellous play. Terrific! It's interesting your mentioning the Elizabethan thing because all that New World finding was, I suppose, psychologically an escape from the awful wranglings and misery in Europe, and they really thought they were going to get away from it. And to some extent they did but, of course, it was only temporary.

ORR: As we think perhaps we are going to get away from it by going to . . .

JONES: Mars! Yes, carry the same stuff with us there! I am really worried about sign and sacrament. That is what the arts depend on, however abstract they are or however realistic they are.

ORR: So that words are not purely functional like screws and nails?

JONES: Exactly. And that's where Joyce seems to me to be so absolutely incomparable because he made one word, even a comma, have more facets of meaning, recall more things than any writer that I know. It's an amazing achievement but it *may*, as some think, be the end of that kind of achievement. And yet it is the essence of the central thing which all artists have to do in some way or other: making significant as much as possible in as compact a space as possible. All great things are like that. I mean, you just strip off layers and you find more underneath, and you strip off another and there is more underneath. The notion that Joyce was destructive is so ludicrous, because nobody could have been more concerned with informing every word and every jot and tittle with some sort of significance. It was rebellious, of course, rebellious against superficiality and preconceived notions. No one can draw upon more than is within their own inheritance. This is certainly true in my case. I can only work within the limits of what I feel or know or have inherited, and that's not much, but that's all I can do. I very much believe that history and mythology for the poet are like what is called nature for the ordinary visual artists. But if the world is going so far that things can only mean just what they *are*, it is a bit of a poser. And yet it is utterly impossible for people at the end of one cultural phase and civilization to have the foggiest notion of what is going to emerge, you know. I mean, even a man at the end of, say, the Roman Empire, could no more envisage the Gothic world than my grandfather could have envisaged the aeroplane.

24th November, 1964.

Thomas Kinsella

THOMAS KINSELLA was born in 1928 in Dublin. He works in the Irish Department of Finance. He is married and has three children.

He has published *Another September* (1958), *Poems and Translations* (1961), and *Downstream* (1962).

ORR: Mr. Kinsella, can you recall *what* started you writing poetry? Was there any one thing?

KINSELLA: No thing: one slight feeling of curiosity to see whether the thing could actually be done. The system of education under which I laboured for most of my adolescence never suggested to me that the writing of poetry was a human activity. Poetry was a literary product. We didn't understand that human beings in the ordinary course of their lives produced this. It existed in textbooks and it was there to be explored. It struck me as being an interesting experiment to see if I, personally, could produce anything which could pass for a poem. I tried a sonnet and I succeeded in making one with strict rhymes and iambic pentameter lines and so on. It was quite some time after that before the possibility of continuing to write verse entered my mind. I think it was meeting the particular woman whom I eventually married that got me seriously writing love poetry, which was the first poetry I now regard as valid.

ORR: What other themes have attracted you later in your poetic life?

KINSELLA: I think they can all be summed up in the 'passing of time' and its various effects; I think, in particular, death, the death of individual people. Some of the poems which I like most of mine are the cold-blooded lamentations for individuals whom I've known and liked and who have died. The 'artistic act' is another. My earliest poems were about the artistic act and I still do them, but they are becoming

THOMAS KINSELLA

slightly more elaborate and in a peculiar way the idea of artistic creation and the idea of the passing of time are becoming fused together. I have not yet written a poem in which this process is embodied. I have a distinct feeling, for instance, that one of the main impulses to poetry or, for that matter, to any art, is an attempt more or less to stem the passing of time; it's the process of arresting the erosion of feelings and relationships and objects which is being fought by the artist, not particularly because one relationship or one object has all his love at the moment, but simply that he is there to combat the erosion.

ORR: And have you written very much on larger themes, on themes which are supposed to appeal to what we now call 'committed poets'?

KINSELLA: Yes, I have detected recently a trace of moral feeling and judgement in what I am doing. Only quite recently the reaction was almost invariably cold-blooded, simply the blank stare, the noting down of the event and allowing the poem and the reader to take their own conclusions. But I have written one poem, 'Old Harry', in which I've allowed myself the luxury of a bitter and unforgiving judgement on a particular act. I must confess I enjoyed that immensely.

ORR: Yes, I've noticed in some of your poems that your own standpoint is, probably intentionally, ambiguous. You don't come down on one side of the fence or the other. You are, as you say, the spectator with the blank stare. Do you feel that the poet should adopt a moral standpoint which is evident to his reader?

KINSELLA: I don't think it is necessary to him as a poet. As a human being I presume it is essential. I think the function of the poet has something to do (and I feel, for the time being it has) with this business of stemming the flow of time, of halting the instant, and that the quality of the instant itself, while being important and having something to do with the actual stature of the verse, doesn't impose any actual, necessary, stateable conditions, it can be anything. I can imagine an imperfect sense of justice not flawing a poem. I feel, for instance, that the 'artistic act' is one almost of levitation above the event, even if the poet himself is involved. This is purely instinctive: I don't think I could justify it. If the poet is involved in an event which he is called upon to judge, he must levitate above the circumstances and judge it as if he himself is simply a factor. I don't think that he is necessarily called upon to judge it as an involved person.

ORR: This must be surely very difficult in the case of this poem you have written on the theme of the atomic bomb, which is something we are all involved in, and something it is very difficult to extricate oneself from.

KINSELLA: It is. But my attempt at levitation there has been to make the subject of the poem not so much the dropping of the bomb, which as a human being I regard as a morally ignorant act: the subject of the poem is not this, but is simply the possibility of the monstrous choice in the human brain, something which must be accepted because we have continuing evidence of it and always have had. It is possible to levitate above this condition because we are all implicated in it. It is not divorced from the possibility of perfectly orthodox religious faith. The religion in which I was bred and educated, the religion of Catholicism, has a great deal in it: perhaps it is the origin of these feelings. I don't feel this with any great immediacy, but I find in practice no actual clash between, say, the dogmatic and disciplinary requirements of Catholicism and this accepting and categorizing state of awareness of the poet.

ORR: I know we tend to stick labels on things and people all too easily these days, but do you think it is at all informative to a reader to speak about you, then, as an Irish Catholic poet?

KINSELLA: Well, I think it is completely misleading because Irish Catholic poets do exist. They may write Catholic poetry and I don't: they may write Irish poetry and I don't think I do. I am Irish and I accept it; I am Catholic and I find no obstacle to poetry in that. My poetry is a completely separate activity. It is my own full personality judging and collecting my experiences and I find myself, for instance, consciously eschewing Catholic subjects or Irish subjects as being limited in themselves. I cannot think at the moment of anything except two very short poems in *Moralities*, one of the 'Seventeenth Century Landscape near Ballyferriter' and the other of 'Sisters', where the references are completely and exclusively Irish and where the actual facts behind the references would certainly be unknown to a non-Irish person.

ORR: I have noticed, coming new to your poems as I have, that they make a considerable impact on a first hearing, a first reading. They read well, and they sound well. Is this intentioned? Is this something you think of when you are writing them?

KINSELLA: Yes, I am striving continually for greater clarity and directness and regular pace—fitting the pace to the poem and making it an immediately comprehensible whole as far as possible. But that absorbs about fifty per cent of my effort. The rest is absorbed in making my poems coherent. I try to make them defendable in depth. I think that is where the real value of them, if any, should lie.

ORR: What about literary influences on your writing? I notice, for example, in one of your poems you mention the drowning Ophelia, and there are occasional fairly obvious and simple literary references. Could you say who are the writers who have moved you most deeply as a poet and have influenced you?

KINSELLA: Of poets, those I respect most are the formal constructors of poems. I certainly enjoy the other kind of poetry, the inspired utterance, and—I suppose my favourite poet is in fact Anon.—all songs of all time, and also Robert Burns. But the poems which I really admire most are of another kind. They are the conscious, constructed real fabrications of the human intellect and spirit like Dante and Keats, and the later Yeats.

ORR: What about contemporary poets? I suppose Mr. Eliot is an inescapable influence?

KINSELLA: He has been an inescapable influence for some time. But I think finally I escaped quite easily, having watched what seems to me to be the slow and inevitable destruction of his own output by himself as he parodies it in his most recent verse plays. It has shown up all his weaknesses and removed thereby a great deal of his quality as an influence. I'm not saying, of course, that it has anything whatever to do with the great verse which he *has* written and which I still do enjoy: in particular the 'Four Quartets', which has, incidentally, that quality of magnificent intellectual form and of absolutely fresh diction, language created for the purpose.

ORR: Have you ever felt you wanted to write like this?

KINSELLA: Never, except in my very, very adolescent stage. I feel it is something which is totally beyond me. I construct from facts and objects and individual experiences and I formulate generalizations very, very laboriously. But the ability to move in an atmosphere of generalizations I do not possess.

ORR: Is the writing of poetry hard for you? Does the composition of a long poem like 'Downstream' occupy a considerable number of years, perhaps?

KINSELLA: Yes: The event in 'Downstream' took place (I think it was) in 1954. Almost immediately afterwards I realized there were a few seminal moments in the experience which could be worked into something. Over some years almost immediately after that I began to take a few notes, and other incidents occurred which have since been included and, indeed, excluded in their turn. But the process of writing commenced about four years ago and then dropped to make room for the writing of other work, or just for a rest, and then very intensely again, and it took at least six months to finish it.

ORR: And this, to a greater or lesser extent, is a fair description, is it, of how the poetic process works in your case?

KINSELLA: In my case, certainly. Yes.

ORR: The writing of poetry, of course, is not your main occupation, is it?

KINSELLA: No, it's really rather an intense hobby. I'm a civil servant and was actually a civil servant before I wrote any poetry. I never found any clash between the two. In fact, I've found that my mental state when composing a particularly difficult minute is not unlike the process of writing a poem.

ORR: Have you ever felt drawn to any of the other arts? Did you, perhaps, think at any time of being a musician or a painter or a sculptor?

KINSELLA: There was a time early on when I felt it would be nice to be all of these things, polycreator. But I certainly have written no music. I play a few tunes on the tin whistle and I am very fond of Irish traditional music. I do some sketching, but very, very rarely.

ORR: Do you find yourself much in the company of other poets and other writers? Are these your friends rather than civil servants?

KINSELLA: Yes, they really are. There aren't many of these in Ireland but I enjoy their company much more. More interesting!

ORR: At this stage of your poetic life (you've been writing poems for a number of years now) are you glad that it is something you started? Is it something that has brought you satisfaction? Is it something that you would rather have done in preference to anything else?

KINSELLA: Yes, no question about it. I am quite happy to have written what I have written. I have enough projects ahead of me of a kind which I think will be satisfactory for quite a long time. I couldn't ask for more.

24th September, 1962.

John Lehmann

JOHN LEHMANN was born in 1907, and educated at Eton and Trinity College, Cambridge. Partner and General Manager of the Hogarth Press 1938–46. Managing Director of John Lehmann Ltd. from its foundation to 1952. Advisory Editor *The Geographical Magazine* 1940–45. Editor of *London Magazine* from its foundation to 1961. Founder and Editor of *New Writing* and *Orpheus*. Editor B.B.C. *New Soundings* 1952. C.B.E. 1964. He was awarded the William Foyle Poetry Prize 1964.

His publications include *A Garden Revisited* (1931), *Prometheus and the Bolsheviks* (1937), *New Writing in Europe* (1940), *Forty Poems* (1942), *The Sphere of Glass* (1944), *Shelley in Italy* (1947), *The Age of the Dragon* (1951), *The Open Night* (1952), *The Whispering Gallery* (Autobiography I, 1955), *I am my Brother* (Autobiography II, 1960), *Ancestors and Friends* (1962), *Collected Poems* (1963).

ORR: Mr. Lehmann, why do you write poetry?

LEHMANN: It is very difficult to know why one *starts* writing poetry, and that may be a very different thing from why one *goes on* writing poetry. Perhaps one starts writing poetry because one's heard what a wonderful thing it is to be a poet, or because someone you know very well writes poetry: for emulation or for ambition. But I don't think you can go on being a poet unless you feel that there's some kind of music or substance in you that could only come out in that way, some kind of desire to assimilate, digest and shape experience in that particular way.

ORR: Can you say that your fundamental approach to poetry has changed radically since you began writing?

LEHMANN: I don't think my fundamental approach has really changed. I think I have changed in the things I wanted to write about, though there was a period in the thirties when I thought that one could write about politics, one could bring politics and ideas of social justice into it, much more than I do now, that one could use poetry in a kind of 'poster' way. I can't really say that much of the poetry I tried to write then touched the deeper levels of my mind—or perhaps only one or two poems—and I realized this after some years and became silent for a short while; and then during the war I began to feel my way again in poetry that was truer to myself.

ORR: Let's look at some of the themes you use in your poems. Can I take it from what you've been saying now that you are less influenced by what we might call themes of the moment?

LEHMANN: I think one's themes almost certainly, if one's a living person interested in the world around oneself, do come, originally at any rate, out of one's immediate experience, but I think it's fatal to try and be an entirely topical poet. I think one's topicality, one's up-to-dateness or modernity, or whatever you like to call it, will come out in ways that perhaps are not immediately apparent; perhaps by the tone of your voice, by your diction, rather than in using the latest political or topical or social theme of the moment.

ORR: Do you find you are more drawn to poems of action dealing with, let us say, war and death, suffering and pain, or more towards themes of reflection and meditation?

LEHMANN: I don't really begin to want to write poetry until a good deal of meditation has gone on about the subject that interests me. The subject might be war, the subject might be a riot somewhere in the world, but it has to be enclosed in a kind of envelope of reflection before it begins to turn into poetry in my mind.

ORR: Are you consciously influenced by the work of any other writer?

LEHMANN: Well, I should think I have been influenced by almost every conceivable writer. I think any poet who is sensitive at all is bound to be influenced by the most powerful voices of his time. The problem is to find your own voice after you have assimilated these influences, and it is very difficult for one to tell who are the chief influences. I think the modern poets out of whom I have got the most nourishment would be Eliot, Yeats, Edward Thomas, perhaps Cavafy the Greek poet, and Rilke the German poet.

ORR: You pay a great deal of attention in your writing to the stricter workings of verse forms. Can you say what value for you as a poet these have?

LEHMANN: I think that strict verse forms, working in them, does something to the mind. It quickens it in a way, it makes it more alert. To me, at any rate, it's like going into a lower gear in a car, and I think it's very valuable to have this verse shape, this stanza form to fight against. I think it gives the final product a greater intensity and vigour. Until this rather new and recent development of spoken poetry, I have thought that it was extremely important for poetry, in an age of prose (because I think we really live in an age of prose) to seek the utmost concentration and every device of music and internal tightening, to differentiate itself from prose. So much of the poetry that I have seen written during my thirty years as an editor, that has come pouring in, is too like prose to have the specific value of poetry, I think.

ORR: Does this mean that you write most or all of your poems with the conscious thought in your mind of having them read aloud?

LEHMANN: I don't think so at all. I have written one or two poems which were going to be read aloud anyway and I knew it, poems that were commissioned, shall we say, by the B.B.C., and there I have been very careful to make the grammatical structure, the sequence of thought, as clear as possible. But as in general my aim is to establish as great a surface clarity as possible, I do not think I really have ever been influenced by that.

ORR: Do you think that a poem, to have a real value for the reader or the listener, should make its major impact at first reading or at first hearing?

LEHMANN: I don't really think so. I think that a poem must engage you in some way, must engage your mind or your imagination at its first reading, otherwise it's going to be a flop. But I think a good poem very often reveals more and more the better you get to know it. It is like a fruit you chew and as you get towards the centre of it, perhaps the stone or the pip is the most succulent part of it. I feel a good poem is often like that. I have found how true that was very often when I tried to introduce new poems into my series of radio programmes called New Soundings. I found very often that in order that a listener should understand a good poem it had to be repeated. I did try and adopt the device of having the poem read once, then trying to explain it or talk about it, then having it read again.

ORR: Your poems are, as a general rule I think, immediately intelligible to a careful reader. What are your views about the more obscure poems, the poems which one has to read perhaps two or three times before you realize what they are at?

LEHMANN: Some of the poems I am most fond of are poems that you have to read several times and perhaps even consult notes about before you get the full value. There are plenty of pretentious poems that are extremely obscure and plenty of pretentious poems that have a large apparatus of notes and they are, of course, appalling. But good poems, I think, very often need some kind of exposition and I don't regret that myself.

ORR: You have done some work in prose, pieces containing perhaps a single thought or an atmosphere: pieces like *Morning* or *Springlight*. How did these come about? Are these pieces that wouldn't shape themselves into poems?

LEHMANN: No, they came about from a deliberate attempt to write prose poems, a kind of poetry which I think has been very much neglected in this country. It's surprising how very few poets have tried prose poetry in our tradition compared with continental tradition, the tradition of French, Italian and German poetry. *They* are constantly trying. It is very difficult, of course. 'Poetic prose' has a very bad name in our country and rightly, but prose poems are by no means necessarily in 'poetic prose'.

ORR: Does your environment play a large part in deciding the sort of imagery you use?

LEHMANN: Well, I think it's inevitable that the surroundings one knows best will influence one's imagery. For instance, in my poetry I am constantly coming back to imagery of gardens and water; rivers, seas, lakes. That goes very deep in me and the imagery of gardens and water and nature comes very naturally to my mind. I was brought up in the country in a very beautiful garden beside the River Thames, and I have never lived very far from water.

ORR: Do you find you have become more disciplined and more critical in your own writing as the years pass?

LEHMANN: I think I have become more critical about the language and diction. That may be something to do with having to read a great deal of bad poetry. As an editor for the last twenty-five or thirty years, an enormous amount of bad poetry has passed through my hands and one begins to get so sick of the clichés that are used in bad poetry and the imprecise use of language that I think one feels put on one's mettle to be as precise and pure in one's diction as one can. Not that one succeeds, but that is the impulse, anyway.

ORR: Do you undertake a great deal of revision of your own work?

LEHMANN: Yes, I do a great deal of revision. I am scribbling new versions of stanzas perhaps for weeks. But it is rather fun when it comes out right at the end, if you do think it has come out right. There are some poems you are never absolutely happy about.

ORR: Have you ever felt drawn to turn towards poetic drama as a means of expression?

LEHMANN: I would like immensely to be a successful poetic dramatist, but I have never felt I had the slightest gift for it.

ORR: Do you think there is a receptive public for poetic drama?

LEHMANN: Well, I felt during the war that there was growing up a tremendous interest in poetic drama, and for some years after the war there seemed to be a receptive mood on the part of the intelligent public for drama in some kind of poetry, whether a very loose kind of poetry like T. S. Eliot's or a much stricter kind of poetry like, shall we say, Stephen Spender's verse drama. I felt that there was that growing interest, and then it seemed to be nipped by a kind of frost. Perhaps the drama that started more or less with the great and justified success of John Osborne's *Look Back in Anger* at the Royal Court Theatre turned people's minds in an entirely new direction. I believe it may come back, but I don't see it there at the moment.

ORR: Now, what is the public for poetry pure and simple?

LEHMANN: Since the war there's a much bigger public that is keen to understand what one can call high-brow literature, perhaps. I think there's a much keener interest and wish to understand, but I think that poetry's still, for that new public, a little bit above their heads, with certain exceptions. And perhaps it proves how great that appetite is when something can be found to satisfy it. Perhaps the success of John Betjeman's poetry, for instance, proves that. But I think that most modern poetry is still rather too esoteric even for those who wish to learn a great deal more about poetry.

ORR: Do you think it is an advantage to the practising poet to have an interest in, or a feeling for, some of the other arts?

LEHMANN: Yes, I think it probably is. I know one or two of my contemporaries who derive a great deal of stimulation from their interest in music, for instance. I myself know very little indeed about music, but painting interests me enormously, always has, and it is possible that my desire for extremely sharp visual imagery comes from that.

ORR: Can you tell us how the creative process works towards a poem; how a subject presents itself to you and how it finds expression in the language you use?

LEHMANN: Well, of course, that's a very complicated question and a very difficult question to answer, because a lot of the time one is writing one isn't really quite clear what one's doing. But I should say, in three or four cases out of five, I am thinking about a particular experience or something someone has said to me, or perhaps something I have read in the papers, or a book I have read. Something particularly strikes me and I go on brooding about it and feel in the end that I want to write a poem about it. I then try and write down the ideas I want to get into that poem: I try and write them down on a piece of paper, and when I've got them into some sort of shape, then I have to wait until a line comes into my head. I don't think it's any use, for me at any rate, starting until a phrase or a line or a stanza form comes into the head. Once you've got that, then what you've written down helps you to distil everything into the shape you've chosen.

15th August, 1961.

James Liddy

JAMES LIDDY was born in 1934 in Kilkee, Co. Clare, Ireland, and educated at Glenstal Abbey School and University College, Dublin. He is a barrister by profession. He is an editor of *Arena*, and advisory editor of *Poetry Ireland*.

His publications include *Esau My Kingdom for a Drink* (1962), an address to James Joyce on his eightieth birthday, and a collection of poems *In a Blue Smoke* (1964).

ORR: James, have you ever stopped to consider why you write poetry?

LIDDY: Only very vaguely. I mean, it's not a question which interests me very much, because not *why* the poetry is written but *what the poetry is saying* is the immediate question.

ORR: Do you feel that a poet ought to write his work so as to do good to other people, to put it very crudely?

LIDDY: Yes, I would agree with that, but it would be done very indirectly, with subtlety and I think with charm, too, if possible.

ORR: You don't feel, then, that you perhaps might find a greater fulfilment in doing direct good to other people (this is a loaded question), doing something like Doctor Schweitzer has done, for example?

LIDDY: I would hate to be a liberal humanitarian, or a person who was obviously involved in a good cause. I would regard that as rather vulgar, actually. Poets do that sort of thing in a most refined, gentlemanly fashion.

ORR: So you object to the idea of causes?

LIDDY: Oh, I think causes are very bad except when they are indirectly, ideologically or imaginatively the cause of the expression or statement. Well, some causes are better than others, of course; but it's nothing to do with poetry.

ORR: But do you have strong political convictions yourself?

LIDDY: I used to have and I still have left-wing convictions. But I rather dislike having them. I mean, to have left-wing convictions is a sort of a parody. For a poet to have them, since the thirties, is a sort of parody of the poetic attitude, the poetic stance, and besides I think political opinions are in a pretty hopeless stage. I mean, you can't have any political opinions any more. But subconsciously I was a socialist when I was fifteen: a bit more when I was twenty, and that must have had some influence, but I have tried to get away from it.

ORR: What about your background and upbringing? Would you tell us a little about that?

LIDDY: Unfortunately my parents were rich, which is a great disadvantage, and the worst thing as a consequence of this is that I was well-educated. I went to university. I went to an Irish Catholic equivalent of an English public school, and this has arrested my development considerably. The result of which was I didn't write poetry until I was twenty-four, and I still feel isolated from ordinary people and from tradition in Ireland.

ORR: Well, just for the moment, I would like to take you up on that. Why do you say that an education and the bestowing of a number of material advantages have arrested your development? Do you really believe that one has to live in an attic and suffer and find things out for oneself in order to be a good and a real poet?

LIDDY: To suffer and to find things out for oneself, one has to be, or try to be, a simple person, a natural person and a person at ease with others and his environment. And the one thing that money or education does is to make one distinctly hedgy about ordinary people and ordinary things, and simplicity and naturalness.

ORR: Do you consider yourself, then, as an ordinary person?

LIDDY: I would like to be an ordinary person, but I am afraid I'm not.

ORR: In what way are you not an ordinary person? Does the fact of your being a poet make you extraordinary?

LIDDY: I was extraordinary before I ever became a poet. But I think that poetry is a terrible way of being extraordinary, it's a terrible way of being a bit outside, of being compelled to take an attitude which is not the attitude of other people. I think it's the kind of back door into normality or simplicity.

ORR: Can you define this quality of extraordinariness in yourself?

LIDDY: It's being an individual, consciously being an individual from an early stage of one's existence. To quote Cocteau's speech to the French Academy, when he was quoting Raymon Radiguet, it's like trying to be like other people and failing. He calls it originality, but I think that's a very high name for it. I would call it a sense of being different, of being extraordinary.

ORR: Has the reading which you have done and the absorption of other authors' ideas and styles made a great difference to you as a poet?

LIDDY: Yes I think it has. I have been rather influenced, principally by Patrick Kavanagh, an Irish poet of great power and depth: there's a Pasternak quality about him, about his poems. Poems of the caressing winds of nature, of love and of fulfilment, and the poetry of Dublin and the Anglo-Irish tradition, and a poet of waste if necessary; a poet of inspiration and of humour. He has influenced me more than everything else. And other Irish poets, like Yeats, of course. I was brought up on Yeats and Austin Clarke, and the whole Irish Renaissance is very deep in me.

ORR: Do you find that these are influences which in some sense are inhibiting, and you have to break free from them?

LIDDY: I think it depends on the influence. I think Yeats would imprison (and *did* imprison) a whole generation of Irish poets. But I think a poet like Kavanagh is not like other Irish poets, but is more direct and more simple, and more akin to the Gaelic Catholic Ireland, which I think is the better Ireland. I think he would liberate you, after the first state of influence was over, and not imprison you. A good poet really can never imprison you, except when you meet him for the first time.

ORR: Do you find yourself drawn to write about certain themes, certain topics?

LIDDY: Yes, I write about the idea of Christ, the idea of love for the world, and love as an explanation of man's sense of hopelessness and man's sense of suffering, and love as the only possible reply to the contemporary world and all its most horrible aspect. And besides that, I write about my friends, the people I love, the one person I love, and the places in Ireland, and occasionally about more international matters.

ORR: But is this readily identifiable, James, as mid-twentieth century poetry? Would somebody in a hundred years be able to put their finger on your poems, and say: 'Ah yes, we can see that this was written in 1960'?

LIDDY: I think that would be so, because it is identified in mood with, say, young poets in Russia, Yevtushenko and so on. It would be identified with the translations of the Catalan poets, the Catalan poets

I have read. It would be identified with James Baldwin in America and the search for authentic relations in a confused society; and it would be concerned with movements in many countries, excluding England and France which no longer seem young countries. But I would be identified because I would have the same mood as the young poets in Russia, or young poets in Spain or the young novelists, or even the 'beat' poets in America. I think I could be identified as a poet of the sixties, yes.

ORR: But you would resent being identified as a 'brand-name' poet, would you?

LIDDY: I don't think in a small country like Ireland one would be as easily identifiable as that. I wouldn't like it, actually. But I think that I would be related in some way to these other movements: a world movement of some kind, a movement where the members don't know each other, but just feel the tremors going across the continents.

ORR: Do you find yourself drawn, though, to seek the company of writers rather than, let us say, farmers or policemen or postmen?

LIDDY: I am drawn to the company of anyone I like, no matter what they are. But I do think that there's something in a poet, if I happen to like them, which makes my relation to them more intimate and more absolute.

ORR: Is this because they talk the same sort of language?

LIDDY: No, it's because they are poets. I think it's nothing to do with what they talk. It's something in them: it's the spark of fire, a bardic thing. Especially I am thinking of poets who are Irishmen; a quality of fire and defiance and of criticism of Irish society and of life.

ORR: You do think of yourself, do you, as distinctively an Irish poet and not just a contemporary poet writing in the English language?

LIDDY: Well, I don't know anything about being a contemporary poet in the English language at all. All I know is being a poet living in Ireland and feeling the outside world, but being a poet of particular place and of cultivation of a narrow acre, a small farm.

ORR: Let us turn to your poems themselves now. Do you write your poems to be spoken by your own voice?

LIDDY: No, in fact I sometimes don't like them being read at all by my own voice. But people who have read my poems, other poets, Michael Harnett in particular, and another young Irish poet called McDara Woods, have read my poems very well. I would hate a person who was an actor, or a person who wasn't a poet, to read them. Any poet can read my poems, but no non-poets.

ORR: Is it important to you what people think of your poems; whether they value them highly?

LIDDY: When I get depressed, I like my poetry to be admired but it doesn't matter to me when I am in good form whether they are good or not, if they satisfy me.

ORR: For you, is the writng of poetry a rewarding occupation?

LIDDY: For me it is as good as living, and it's rewarding in every sense except that you can't make a living by it.

ORR: Is it your sole occupation?

LIDDY: No, I am a barrister and I have the demands of a quite small practice. But still, these demands are quite heavy and I also have a messianic urge to found magazines, promote writers and reorientate the cultural values in Ireland, and that takes me away from writing poetry. So I have about three or four different professions, you might say. But the one which is really of any importance is the writing of poetry.

ORR: Are you a good judge of your own poems? Do you know which are the ones you should throw away, and which are the ones you should put out to the world?

LIDDY: I wouldn't know about that. I know the ones which I should definitely throw away. There's a halfway stage when a poem is half-good and half-bad, and if I like it for some personal reasons I might include it. But I have a general feeling for what my best poems are to date: I feel there are at least half-a-dozen which are better than the others.

ORR: Do you set much store by the formal disciplines of poetry?

LIDDY: I detest all regular forms of poetry. I hate regularity or any kind of metre. I don't think cadence or rhythm depend upon regularity. In fact, regularity is the death of cadence, so far as I am concerned. I don't know anything about verse forms, I hate them. That's why I find it very difficult to read poetry of any century but the twentieth century, with the exception of people like Shakespeare, who transcends the limits of formal disciplines.

ORR: Do you read much contemporary poetry, James?

LIDDY: I have read a great deal of contemporary poetry, in so far as I can get my hands on it. I would say I have read *too much* contemporary English poetry and too little contemporary American poetry and Continental poetry in translation: I am starved of that. By contemporary poetry, I mean poetry going back to nineteen-hundred or eighteen-ninety, to the symbolists.

ORR: Do you intend to go on writing poetry, or do you think that there must be some termination of this activity?

LIDDY: What I do lack is sufficient time to devote myself to writing poetry, and I know I could write much more poetry and therefore have a much higher percentage of successful poems if I spent more time at it. But I can't see any termination to writing poetry, except that I hope to be able to devote some time, in some mythical future, to writing *about* poetry.

ORR: But you feel there is a store there in your mind?

LIDDY: Well, a poet is the owner of a vineyard, and I feel there is a continual harvest inside for any good poet, and I feel that that harvest is in me if I can reach it.

17th October, 1963.

Edward Lucie-Smith

EDWARD LUCIE-SMITH was born in 1933 in Jamaica, and read history at
Merton College, Oxford. He is an art critic, book reviewer and broadcaster.
Until recently, he ran a discussion group for poets which was founded
by Philip Hobsbaum.

He has published two books of verse, *A Tropical Childhood* (1961) and
Confessions and Histories (1964). He is represented in *Penguin Modern Poets 6*
(1964). He was joint editor, with Philip Hobsbaum, of *A Group Anthology*
(1963), and editor of *The Penguin Book of Elizabethan Verse* (1965).

ORR: Mr. Lucie-Smith, did you begin writing poetry at an early age?

LUCIE-SMITH: I began when I was at school, when I first came to England,
when I was about fourteen.

ORR: You came to England from where?

LUCIE-SMITH: I came from Jamaica. I was born in Jamaica. My family
have lived there for many years.

ORR: Do you have distinct memories of this?

LUCIE-SMITH: Oh yes, I remember Jamaica very clearly, and indeed I
remember the sort of life one lived there. In a sense, I missed the war
completely and remained stuck in a nineteen-thirties childhood until
1945.

ORR: Does this make any difference to you now, and particularly in
your writing, the fact that you were brought up in Jamaica?

LUCIE-SMITH: I think a complete break in one's life always does make a
difference to one's writing. That one always has this kind of second
existence is, I think, a temptation and a danger, really. I think it is
something difficult for anybody who writes to cope with, this completely separate section of their life, because it is predigested material
for poems.

ORR: Do your poems arise largely from experience which you have had yourself, which you recollect, or do you draw your inspiration from other sources, from books, from paintings, from music?

LUCIE-SMITH: It used to arise entirely from personal experience, but I do not think that one can write poems on a large scale this way. I think Wordsworth is the only person who had a sufficiently powerful ego to write an enormously long poem on the subject of nothing but himself. Obviously a long poem always reflects, is always a kind of allegory of the person who is writing it. It reflects some personal preoccupation, otherwise it is simply pastiche.

ORR: Is the past important to you?

LUCIE-SMITH: I was trained as a historian. I think as a historian, as a result. I think of the past in rather an old-fashioned sense, as a series of exemplars demonstrating certain moral situations. I think this is a rather pretentious way of putting it, but it is the nearest I can get. I think that literature and morality are entirely intertwined (I know this isn't a particularly popular view), just as I assume that writers are dependent on society, that the writer who claims to be independent of social bonds is a liar. I think that all writers write for an audience, and the idea of the last man on earth writing poems is simply inconceivable. The poem is as much a product of the audience, of the society in which it is produced, as it is the product of the man who actually holds the pen or bangs the typewriter.

ORR: Does this mean that you are writing for a contemporary audience? And writing for them, does this mean that you are writing about contemporary events, problems, dilemmas?

LUCIE-SMITH: I am certainly not addressing myself to some imaginary posterity. I think that this has had a fatal effect on a great many poets. Poets are obsessed with the idea of not being appreciated, they feel that they have some right to be loved, and they feel that if they cannot make themselves loved, by hook or by crook, by their contemporaries, they will see to it that posterity values them. I do not see how one can predict what posterity will value: it is entirely up to them. I think one *must* write for a contemporary audience, that one falls into all sorts of falsities if one doesn't, and naturally the only problems one fully understands are contemporary problems. You can imagine what the problems in the past or in the future were like or will be like, but you cannot say for certain. You only feel the goad that pricks you now.

ORR: So you do feel drawn, do you, to write about contemporary problems?

LUCIE-SMITH: I am not really a writer of what has been rather viciously described as 'brand-name poetry', though I must say a great many of the contemporary poets I most admire fall into that category. Peter Porter, for example, is a very old friend of mine; I love his poetry, I think it is very good. But my approach is a bit more indirect, in that I try to find some situation which seems to sum up or typify something which is preoccupying me, something into which one can pour the feelings and the ideas which are contemporary, but this need not necessarily be a contemporary situation. The only way in which I go along with the 'brand-name poets' is that I think that poetry should be full of *facts*. When I write a poem about Rubens (or something like that), if you care to go to the books about Rubens and check up, you will find that it is reasonably accurate, that I am not indulging in fantasies of any kind.

ORR: Do you aim all the time at complete intelligibility and immediate intelligibility in your work?

LUCIE-SMITH: I aim at complete intelligibility, but I think immediate intelligibility is a slightly different question. I think that one has to be as clear as one knows how to be, but if one is discussing a difficult topic then people cannot expect the poem to be easy. Poetry, to my mind, all the techniques of poetry, all these elaborate ways with language, not only rhyme and rhythm, but all these other things which are so popular like counting devices, and syllabics and so on, these have two purposes. One is simply that they have a private purpose, which is that they provide a scaffolding on which one writes the poem: that after all, an elaborate stanza form, if you feel the need of a certain kind of architecture, this does supply the architecture. Also they keep that rather mischievous part of the mind occupied. You know that there is a certain department of the mind which is better kept amused at finding rhymes, while the rest of you gets on with writing the poem. But I also think that writing poetry is in a way making language more exact, that all these techniques are part of a machinery of exactness and I think that exactness and clarity are not necessarily the same thing. This is the difficulty. I work in an advertising agency and, believe me, one is always facing the question of over-simplification. The easiest thing to understand is the carefully calculated half-truth, and I do not think poetry has much to do with half-truths.

ORR: So you do not believe, then, in making allowances for the reader, either in the body of your work, or in a surrounding apparatus of notes which some poets feel it necessary to add on their works?

LUCIE-SMITH: If somebody wants to annotate my poems in the future, they are welcome, but I do not see why on earth I should do that job. It is not my concern at all. But I think that the compliment one has to pay the reader is that one must be as exact and astringent as one knows how to be. Whatever you are doing must be of good materials, so to speak. The language must be good language, it must not be slovenly, and if you depart from the normal conventions of prose—grammar, this must be for a purpose, you must know why you are doing it.

ORR: So, in fact, you are writing to communicate, are you, and not just writing, as we may think some poets write, for themselves and for other poets?

LUCIE-SMITH: 'In my craft or sullen art and exercised in the still night' . . . Yes, I think of it as a 'craft or sullen art' and even 'exercised in the still night'. But I think that if one sits down to write a poem, one presupposes that somebody is going to read it. I do not see how on earth one could do anything else, and therefore the idea of communication does come into it: that, in a sense, a poem is a shared experience, that the poem itself exists; but what also exist are the man who writes and the man who reads.

ORR: Is the sound of your poems, the sound that they make when they are spoken, read aloud, important to you?

LUCIE-SMITH: Yes, it is important and I write for my own voice as well. I think every poet tends to do this. I am very interested in sound and rhythm, though I must say I disagree with a lot of poets I know on this subject. I am much more keen on architectural rhythm than on the mimetic rhythm you find everybody propagating nowadays: the idea that the rhythm will be all right if each phrase mimes what you are saying. I think that the phrase ought to mime what you are saying, but within an overall rhythmic architecture, and that if it does not, the poem tears itself to pieces, it becomes choppy and bitty and breathless. I have always done a lot of reading of poetry aloud. I have acted for years as host to a group of poets, and the idea is that I send out duplicated sheets of about six poems, and these go out to everyone on a mailing list. Then on Fridays I keep open house and everybody comes, and the poet reads aloud these poems and after each poem everybody has the right to criticize: they praise, they can be very rude sometimes. I think this is very healthy, that it does establish first of all the idea of communication. But, of course, all this reading aloud has changed not only my poetry, but the poetry of people who come. For instance, the group has been very much the centre of a revival of rather longer poems in English poetry, and also it has been responsible very largely for the new interest which has been taken in monologues. There are more monologues being written now than at any time since Browning or the early Pound. The long gap between the Pound of 'Altaforte' and today has certainly been bridged again.

ORR: Do you think that this might in any way be a movement towards a kind of verse drama, this expansion of the length of poems that we are seeing now?

LUCIE-SMITH: I am not sure that a monologue and a verse drama are quite the same thing. A monologue aims to *construct* the supposed listener without giving him anything to say. There is always, so to speak, a silent protagonist in most monologues, but I am not sure about verse drama. I think this is a very tricky sort of question. I think the trouble with most verse dramas, quite frankly, is that they are very badly constructed, that they are extremely self-indulgent about language, that the authors of them have been much more fascinated by, and much more in love with, the words they were using than with the characters.

ORR: You are thinking here perhaps of somebody like Christopher Fry?

LUCIE-SMITH: I am thinking of Christopher Fry, yes. I used to be a great addict of his works, but I do think that they pall upon one terribly, that one loses one's taste for this particular kind of verbal showing-off.

ORR: What induces you to find the poem the perfect form rather than a novel or a short story or a play?

LUCIE-SMITH: I think it is partly my interest in rhythm and partly this obsession with the old Yeatsian idea of 'the fascination of what's difficult': that it is very difficult to write poetry, and that one cannot make any excuses, one cannot say 'After all, I am writing a novel' or 'It doesn't matter if I am slapdash, this is only journalism.' I think that poetry is obviously that department of literature where slovenliness is least forgivable. It is a sort of challenge. And therefore I think that that is the reason really that it's harder.

ORR: Do you consider yourself part of a movement in contemporary poetry or do you consider yourself as a poet in isolation?

LUCIE-SMITH: This is a slightly difficult question. I have often been considered part of a movement in contemporary poetry because of the group, and because of the fact that I am the man who does the actual running of it. I have even edited with the original founder of the group, the poet Philip Hobsbaum, an anthology recently. I think one of the main oddities of this situation is that I am one of the least characteristic of all group poets, in so far as group poets have characteristics. So I do not really know what to answer. Yes, I do see other poets. Yes, I am linked up with what people have been pleased to write about as a literary movement. But I rather challenge anybody to say how, in what way, my work reflects that literary movement. I have tried to learn from it what I consider to be the more basic things. I am very interested in how people react. There is nothing like a live audience for telling you what's tactful linguistically and what's not tactful. And the great difference between successful writers of poetry (by which I do not mean writers with worldly success, but people who write good poetry) and people who write poetry which somehow just does not work, is that the people who write poetry which doesn't work have no tact with words, they do not know which goes with what. One of the commonest forms of all blindness in poetry is the blindness to puns.

ORR: Do you think perhaps that in a hundred years someone reading your poetry will find in it a kinship with other poems which have been written by other poets at this time?

LUCIE-SMITH: I am sure they will, After all, the time itself will see to that.

ORR: There is something, then, which can be identified as mid-twentieth century poetry?

LUCIE-SMITH: But there has always been something which could be identified as mid-nineteenth or mid-eighteenth century in verse. You cannot escape from your own epoch, and you are foolish to try. Great poets are not monuments of that kind, or even good poets. They are in a way good poets or great poets to the degree in which they are representative of their age. Dryden seems to me the perfect example of his period, of the late seventeenth to early eighteenth century, and the difference between Dryden and Pope is, in a sense, the difference produced by the fact that civilization itself is moving forward and altering. I mention these two poets because, after all, these are two great poets who lived, who acknowledged themselves as living in society. I mean they complained and satirized and flyted, but they did not see themselves as people who lived outside a context. I think it is extremely hubristic for any writer to think of himself as so great or so talented that he can ignore the world around him.

ORR: Do you depend much upon your reading of earlier writers and of contemporary writers? Is this important to you?

LUCIE-SMITH: I am an immoral reader of literature. I am always ashamed of how badly read I am. Everybody I know seems to be much better read than I am. I do steal from other writers, and I don't mind doing it. I think unconscious theft is always the danger, that kind of unconscious plagiarism: it struck you so much and it sunk so deeply into your subconscious that it comes out and you think it is your own, which is always a rather terrifying experience. But I think that Fuseli's reaction to Blake's drawings, that they were 'damned good to steal from', is quite a healthy one in an artist, really. I also use, even pervert and parody, all sorts of sources: pictures, lives of artists, archaeological works. My poem about the Scythians is based on quite extensive archaeological reading. I have always been interested in the Greeks and interested in this particular kind of South Russian civilization. This poem is a conflation of all sorts of things, from anthropologists', archaeologists' reports, illustrations of objects in the Hermitage in Leningrad, though the particular object, the vase which is described, is in fact several different existing objects put together.

ORR: So that your interest in other art forms, and particularly visual art forms, does have a direct bearing on your composition of poetry, does it?

LUCIE-SMITH: Oh yes. This is a means of getting outside one's self. I think it is characteristic of poets, certainly in my experience as a kind of bear-leader of poets, that they are passionately interested in themselves, and I am sure that I take a passionate interest in myself, really, but I also find myself a bit claustrophobic. One likes to have a door which one can walk out of occasionally, however comfortable the padded cell may be.

ORR: Is the writing of poetry something which brings you satisfaction?

LUCIE-SMITH: I enjoy the craftsmanship of poetry very much, and I get guilty and restless if I have not written anything for a long time. I get very worried. I am never satisfied with the results. I never think they are nearly what they should have been. One cracks open the nut and there is nothing inside, so one resolves to try again and do it better next time.

13th July, 1963.

129

George MacBeth

GEORGE MACBETH was born in 1932 in Shotts, Lanarkshire, Scotland. He was educated at King Edward VII School, Sheffield, and New College, Oxford. He has been a Talks Producer for the B.B.C. since 1955, editing and introducing programmes about poetry and the arts, including *New Comment* and *The Poet's Voice*.

He has published two books of poems, *The Broken Places* (1963), and *A Doomsday Book* (1965). He is represented in *Penguin Modern Poets 6* (1964). He edited the *Penguin Book of Sick Verse* (1963) and the *Penguin Book of Animal Verse* (1965).

ORR: George, is there a purpose that you can define behind your writing of poetry?

MACBETH: I feel very strongly that one shouldn't write poetry just because one wants to write poetry. Every poet wants to write poetry for this reason: that's where you begin. But unless you have some other motive as well, it is not likely to be very good. One wants to put across a description of certain experiences from which conclusions might be drawn, helpful to all kinds of people in a given society in the course of their daily lives.

ORR: Then the principle of communication is important to you, communication with an audience?

MACBETH: Oh, vital, I think, yes, though of course, it's somehow hard to define just what this audience is going to be. I mean, you know in hard practice your book is not going to sell more than a few hundred copies. Nevertheless, I think even though you know that, you must want it to sell more and must try to write as if it would sell more. I admire enormously writers who *are* able to get a big audience, and still write well. I think Betjeman is very much undervalued as a serious writer and I admire, on a much higher level, someone like Hemingway, who was able, it seems to me, to write with extreme fastidiousness and precision and accuracy and at the same time in a way which was totally clear to very ordinary people, not only in the United States, but in Western Europe, Russia and all over the world. I think this was a wholly admirable thing to have succeeded in doing in the twentieth century at a time when the modern movement was widely rampant, as it were.

ORR: Do you have a particular sort of person or a particular group of people in mind when you are composing a poem?

MACBETH: I would like to think that I was writing poems sufficiently clear in structure and in sufficiently clear language to be understood and enjoyed by the man in the street. I want very much to get away from writing for the converted, for those who are already interested in art. I think this must be done to some extent through the subject matter.

ORR: There is also another point. Do you write your poems with the thought of their being read aloud, being communicated by the voice?

MACBETH: Yes, I do. Of course, working as one does for the B.B.C., inevitably, to some extent unconsciously, one is concerned with these problems. I have written a lot of dramatic monologues recently which are poems conceived in terms of characters other than my own. Whereas I perhaps enjoy doing these myself, they are intended to be poems which could be interpreted by other readers and by actors in various ways, in the sense that a play could; indeed quite often it could be that an actor could make more of it than I could myself, because there would be poems which I hoped would leave a certain amount open to the interpretation of an actor or another reader.

ORR: Does this mean that you would like to go on to write a full-length verse drama?

MACBETH: I would certainly like to, but I think it is an immensely difficult thing to do. You see, it seems to me that in the past poets have tried to write verse dramas without having very much experience of the theatre and hence they have failed. But it is a very difficult business to see what kind of verse would go on the stage; particularly the step from being able to write a poem entirely in one character to a dialogue between two characters is, I think, a very difficult step to take.

ORR: And also, the poet has to become more of a professional in so far as he has to know about the techniques of the theatre and the techniques of communication in the way that, for example, an advertising agent has to know what is eye-catching and what is ear-catching. Do you agree?

MACBETH: Yes, very much so. And also I think you have to be prepared to abnegate a certain amount of responsibility. It seems to me that all good plays depend not only on the writer, but also on the actors and the producers, and it's a great temptation for poets, particularly since the Romantic Movement, to feel that the poem is entirely themselves, that they must control it down to its last detail. If you are going to write a play, you have to leave a certain amount open, I think, for others to fill in for you and the kind of conceit and egotism which is endemic among poets to some extent is a bit resistant to this.

ORR: You, inevitably, working as you do in broadcasting, must find yourself thrown into the company of other poets, other writers. Is this a useful sort of climate in which a poet should operate?

MACBETH: I think it depends on the writer a good deal. In my case, I like to think that it doesn't do me much harm. That is to say, I enjoy the stimulus and excitement of being involved in practical concerns, organizing affairs, managing people, making telephone calls and so on, all this practical business life attracts me, and without it I wouldn't be entirely happy. And I think (one hopes, anyway) that it doesn't interfere with the actual business of writing. I think, however, that certainly in the past, there have been cases of poets being, as it were, spoiled by this. They have become submerged under affairs, they have been too much affected by other people's styles and so on. I think you have to be very careful not to be too responsive to fashion and too responsive to the pressures of other people's styles.

ORR: But you don't deliberately go and look for the 'inward bliss of solitude', then?

MACBETH: Not me, no! I mean, quite frankly, if someone gave me a thousand pounds to go off and live in the wilds of Ireland for a year, I don't expect I would write a line. I would be bored to tears. I would come back to London and meet all my old friends and eat, drink and go to the cinema and theatre, and talk, and in the middle of the night start writing poems as I do now. I think there are two kinds of writers: those who need solitude, isolation and time, on the one hand, and those on the other hand, who need stimulus, excitement, pressures, and I think I belong to the second class.

ORR: You said just now that the world of practical affairs is immensely important to you. Does this mean that the writing of poetry isn't the all-absorbing occupation for you; that this isn't the one thing that takes precedence over all else in your life?

MACBETH: I think that if you think that poetry is more important than anything else you are *bound* to be a bad poet. Unless you think that something is more important than poetry, either religion, an attitude to the world, or what-have-you, is more important, and that you use poetry to further that, then you won't write very good poetry. I think the characteristic vice of poets is to treat poetry as *sui generis*, a kind of supreme thing, a god in itself.

ORR: Is your reading important to you, your reading of other writers? Are you influenced by other writers?

MACBETH: Well, I'm interested in two ways. There are a small handful of writers who seem to have mattered to me over the years immensely to a degree that no other writers have: people like Hemingway, Wittgenstein and D'Annunzio have been enormously influential in the whole way I look at the world. Then, on the other hand, there are lots of writers who influenced me minimally: a particular poem they write, a particular form they adopt is useful to me at one point in time. I am very interested in form as such, the whole mechanics of style and different rhyme schemes and metres and so on and, indeed, I think that constant variation in these and preoccupation with them is a means of conveying one's view of the world in an unboring way. I think that the vice of writers who are didactically orientated (as I think in some ways I am) is that they often don't vary their forms enough.

ORR: What about themes? Are there sets of themes which particularly attract you as material for poems?

MACBETH: Two kinds, really. That's to say, autobiographical ones which to some extent are concerned with my father and mother, who both died when I was fairly young, and whose deaths had an important effect on me for this reason and, on the other hand, poems about politics and the psychology of politics, particularly extremism in politics seen from the inside. It seems to me that fascism on the one hand and, on the other hand, atomic warfare are two rather crucial major themes which one must grapple with if one has a serious interest in the modern world.

ORR: You don't think there is the danger here of poetry spilling over into a kind of high-grade contemporary journalism?

MACBETH: It depends quite how highly you value 'high-grade'. You see Auden, to some extent, does spill over into high-grade journalism in his pre-war work. I think it depends on the intensity of feeling which you manage to bring to bear, the amount of information you have and often the kind of seriousness. You see, journalism presupposes a certain sort of superficiality, I think, whereas poetry, to me, depends on a rather profound concern. Whether of course you can succeed in that I don't know, but I think you can try to about politics.

ORR: Let's get a little closer to your poems. What decides for you the shape and size, the dimensions of a poem, because you say somewhere, 'To leave great themes unfinished is perhaps the most satisfactory exercise of power.' How do you know when you have finished a poem and how do you know, when you begin it, how long it's going to be, what sort of shape it is going to have?

MACBETH: I don't certainly know when I begin precisely what shape it's going to have. The poem from which you are quoting, which was the one called 'The Spider's Nest', the one spoken by Eugene Lee Hamilton, began as a poem in a sort of colloquial stress accent form. It didn't seem to be working in that form, and I moved it into a syllabic form which I had never used before and it did seem to work. And I often find this, in working on a particular poem, that if the form is changed halfway through the drafting, sometimes it's almost like a magnet with iron filings, all the things seem to fall into place.

ORR: I would like to go a little more closely into the subconscious conception of a poem. How does this happen?

MACBETH: Well, it varies. I keep a lot of notes about this because I am terribly interested in it, really. Sometimes a phrase is the first thing that occurs to me. I have just finished, as a matter of fact, a very long poem about the Aztecs, and this arose originally from the phrase suddenly coming into my mind after reading a book about them, 'Mankind is a doomed élite.' These words. And these words probably won't appear in the finished poem, but they are a kind of kernel or springboard from which the whole thing has developed. That's one way. Another way is being interested in a particular form. I am very interested in adapting Greek metres to English and sometimes I have felt I would like to write a poem in English hexameters, and that has been a motive to do something. Sometimes a particular incident: I have come home late at night and the cat has had a bird which is half dead and it seems to me it couldn't survive and so I have had to kill it, and I have written a poem about this. Sometimes I have been reading a book or seen something in a film and suddenly it led to a poem. One can't generalize absolutely. The emotion from which the poem can come can be generated by any one of a wide variety of different incidents, I think.

ORR: One final question, George. Where does the satisfaction lie for you in this business of writing poetry? Is it in the actual labours of composition or is it in looking on the 'high-piled books, in charact'ry' after you have finished the whole exercise?

MACBETH: It's both of course. Everyone, I suppose, is ambitious and conceited, and I get a great deal of pleasure out of seeing poems in magazines, books published and so on. This is jolly exciting but the key thing, I think, is the sense of power and excitement you get from the actual composition of the thing: control over experience and words in such a way that you can make something absolutely new. I suppose this must be characteristic of all artists, that it is ultimately a power thing: it's the sense that you yourself are entirely integrated and able to move the world in accordance with your own needs.

2nd August, 1963.

Charles Madge

CHARLES MADGE was born in Johannesburg, South Africa, in 1912 and educated at Winchester and Cambridge. After a year in Fleet Street as a reporter, he helped to found Mass Observation. Later he did social and economic research under the guidance of Lord Keynes and for P.E.P. He was a director of the Pilot Press for three years and edited *Pilot Papers*. In 1947 he became Social Development Officer at the New Town of Stevenage. Since 1950 he has been Professor of Sociology at Birmingham University. He has also worked on technical assistance assignments for United Nations agencies in Thailand, India and Ghana.

His publications include two volumes of poems, *The Disappearing Castle* (1937) and *The Father Found* (1941), and a sociological study, *Society in the Mind* (1964).

MORRISH: Professor Madge, can you remember when you started to write poetry?

MADGE: It was very, very early on, probably when I was about seven.

MORRISH: And what form did your poetry take at that age?

MADGE: Well, it was a very extreme kind of experience. I used to go into some kind of trance. People were not allowed to disturb me, and the result was a fairly intense kind of poetry. I think some of the more interesting poems that I wrote date from those first years.

MORRISH: How did your people react to your going into a trance?

MADGE: They didn't really know quite what to make of it. Nobody in the family was interested in poetry, but they were very tolerant of it, as a strange sort of thing in their midst.

MORRISH: So you hadn't had poetry read to you before you started to write yourself?

MADGE: I don't think I had, really. I mean, I must have come across a bit of it, but it wasn't an everyday thing to read poetry or hear it read.

MORRISH: Now, you have been writing poetry pretty consistently up to the war and you've recently started writing again, I believe, but there's been a break of about ten to fifteen years.

MADGE: There's been a break of something like ten years, which began soon after I went to Birmingham to take up a university teaching post there; whether it was the effect of the university or Birmingham or my subject, which I do find difficult to combine with poetry, I am not absolutely sure, but perhaps a combination of all three did close me up quite a bit. I am happy to say that I now seem to have opened out again and there seems to be plenty of poetry still left for me to write.

MORRISH: Your subject is sociology?

MADGE: Yes.

MORRISH: Have you reconciled the difficulties between the world of work and the poetic world?

MADGE: Well, I think some sort of reconciliation has taken place. I don't think there is any question of a synthesis. The two things are quite different and separate and I do not like them getting mixed up with each other, but they are not fighting each other as hard as they were, and the problems within the sociology seem to have sorted themselves out to a point where I can really feel calm and confident about the poetry again.

MORRISH: Has any particular work that you have done in the past influenced a poem or set of poems especially?

MADGE: Without wanting to sound 'spooky' I think sometimes a poem has been a bit prophetic of some jobs which I was going to do later on, or some place I was going to visit later on. There is a way in which the poems seem to reflect later developments. To a certain extent the poems do reflect the environment that I am in at the time; certainly when I went to Birmingham this produced quite a few poems which were straight reactions to the Midlands town-scape.

MORRISH: What poets have influenced you?

MADGE: My real poetic affiliation, I think, is to some rather famous names like Chaucer, Spencer, Milton. This is the sort of thing that I like very, very much, and from that I go on liking people like Gray, and I'm also interested in less important poets like Thomson and Young, all of whom are developing out of this tradition.

MORRISH: Are you influenced by the arts in general, music, painting? Do these stimulate you, help you with imagery?

MADGE: I feel very deprived if I do not have music and I also very much like painting and sculpture and architecture. I like to have this as a part of my life.

MORRISH: Would you therefore say that you are an urban poet, in so far as many of these interests are nowadays pursued in towns rather than in a rural setting?

MADGE: I think that the urban-rural contradiction is just one of the many that the poet has to cope with at present. I was brought up in the country. I much prefer the country to the town. In the town I like to have a garden, I like to have trees and so forth, but obviously it would be, to me anyhow, quite useless to go and tuck myself away in a rural setting: this would be too far away from life altogether.

MORRISH: How does a poem come to you? How do you start to write?

MADGE: Well, I often feel somewhat uneasy for as long as two or three days, and I am not quite sure what I am feeling uneasy about. And sometimes a mood of extreme depression comes over me, and then in the middle of this there appear a few lines which, if I have something handy to write on, I probably jot down, and this means that I then realize that there is a poem on the way, and if I am lucky the poem is going to appear. Sometimes a poem just comes and manifests itself and then goes away again.

MORRISH: Do you write quickly or do your poems take a long time to come to fruition?

MADGE: This has varied enormously. I mean, several of them were probably written down in a matter of minutes and some have come very, very slowly over a period of weeks or even months.

MORRISH: When you have once written your poem down, do you polish and re-polish?

MADGE: Well, if it has all come out in one piece I probably don't find it necessary to make many alterations. But if it has come more gradually, then the polishing process may be quite lengthy.

MORRISH: Do you feel that a poem should be able to be understood on a first reading?

MADGE: Only if by understanding one is meaning something rather broad and general. I mean, one ought to get a very definite impact from it, but one is not likely to be able to get the whole of a poem at a first reading if it's at all an interesting poem.

MORRISH: Do you like your poems to be read out loud?

MADGE: I much prefer them to be read out loud, yes.

MORRISH: Have you done very much poetry reading yourself, in groups with other poets?

MADGE: Not as much as I would have liked to have done, no. I think it is a very good thing for poets to read poetry and to hear it read, and it is just one of these unfortunate things that in the way that life has gone on, I don't think I've had as much as I would have liked.

MORRISH: Why do you write poetry? I mean, what do you feel that you have to express in a poetic form that you can't express, say, in a novel?

MADGE: Well, perhaps compulsive would be too strong a word, but there is something which dictates itself in the poem, and I am not really free to choose whether I write poetry or not. This is something which is decided for me. And therefore what comes out of it is also to some extent decided for me. This is only to say that one part of myself doesn't altogether know what's going on in other parts of myself. And the art of managing the situation, as far as I understand it, is not to be too concerned with what's going on in the part that you don't know about, but to be ready to let it speak when it wants to, when it's ready.

MORRISH: Have you travelled at all?

MADGE: I have travelled a lot in the last fifteen years, largely on various United Nations missions in India, Thailand. Last year I went to Ghana. Those have been quite an important experience in widening one's horizons.

MORRISH: What effect does it have on your poetry, do you think?

MADGE: Difficult to say. The poems predicted that I would travel, and no doubt this is one of the reasons why I did, because, after all, one can always fulfil one's own prophecies. And I did write a bit about India and just a very little bit about Thailand, but on the whole the experience was too profuse, there was too much of it to get into the poems without appearing a little bit pseudo-oriental.

MORRISH: I was interested to hear that you have been to the East, because what you've been saying about the way you write and your childhood experiences of going into a kind of trance before you wrote anything is rather reminiscent of certain Eastern mystic practices. Did you feel a kind of *rapport* with Eastern thinking when you were meeting people, seeing people's way of life in the East?

MADGE: Well, I have a very definite reaction against Eastern mystic ways of thinking. I think it is probably quite true that my own early experiences were rather similar to those of mystics, but from about the age of twelve or thirteen onwards I rejected mysticism in that form and rejected it rather dogmatically.

MORRISH: Why when you were thirteen?

MADGE: Because I began to get very interested at that time in natural sciences and this rose above mysticism as a predominant thing which formed my ideas, and as the two were irreconcilable, mysticism went out except as something which I knew as a possible emotional experience.

MORRISH: Have you any religious faith?

MADGE: I think I very definitely have a kind of non-religious attitude. I accept the aesthetic side of religion and I am not at all anxious to prevent anybody from being religious who wants to be. Certain forms of religion appeal to me more than others; for example, in Thailand there was a very attractive form of Buddhism, not at all mystical, but aesthetically very, very sympathetic.

MORRISH: Are your feelings about religious faith at all the result of your studies of mass behaviour?

MADGE: No, I think that studies of mass behaviour show one very clearly how much religion has meant to a great many people, and make one more tolerant and understanding of it than one would otherwise be.

MORRISH: Do you see yourself as working in isolation?

MADGE: I think I am a little bit isolated. I had, perhaps, some *rapport* with some of the people who were in Cambridge just before I was, but I don't think it is a very clear link. I was a pupil of I. A. Richards at Cambridge, and this gives one a bit of a link with some of his other pupils who were fascinating people.

MORRISH: Which particular pupils?

MADGE: Well, people that remain very strongly in my mind are Bill Empson, Humphrey Jennings, Hugh Sykes Davies.

MORRISH: One last question, Professor Madge. What do you still want to do in your poetry? Have you got a particular ambition, a new form you want to try?

MADGE: Only that I would like to disprove the doubt and fear which sometimes assails me, if poetry really has got much of a future in our kind of world; and whereas if you'd asked me this a few years ago I would have been rather pessimistic, I feel now that there is some chance that some of the poems I write will prove to me, temporarily anyhow, that there is quite a lot of life in it.

18th September, 1964.

Christopher Middleton

CHRISTOPHER MIDDLETON was born in 1926. He was in the R.A.F. 1944–48, Oxford 1948–52, Zurich 1952–55. He has lived in London since 1955, apart from a year spent in Austin, Texas, 1961–62. He is married and has three children.

He has published *Torse 3, Poems 1949–61* (1962) and *Modern German Poetry 1910–60* (1962, with Michael Hamburger). He is represented in *Penguin Modern Poets 4* (1963). He wrote the libretto of a modern comic opera *The Metropolitans* (published in German as *Athenerkomödie* 1963), with music by Hans Vogt. *Nonsequences Selfpoems* appeared in 1965.

ORR: Mr. Middleton, do you write your poems with the idea that they're going to be read aloud?

MIDDLETON: Well, if they don't *sound* right, then I know they are wrong. But I don't think about this sort of thing before I actually start working on anything. The sound of the thing makes a very great difference to the way it is put together.

ORR: And do you read them aloud yourself while you are writing them, or after you have written them?

MIDDLETON: I can hear them while I am writing them, and then I do read them aloud to myself when I have eventually finished them. But it isn't just a question of phrases. The whole thing has to be an organized pattern of related sounds from A to Z. I wouldn't let, for instance, a single sonorous phrase through simply for the sake of the sonority. It would have to have a functional relationship to the rest of the poem as a whole.

ORR: So you don't think a poem should be primarily a nice or exciting noise?

MIDDLETON: It is a very, very ticklish problem this altogether, because sometimes I'm only too concerned to get rid of sonority in order to get at functional sound effects. This may be something to do with the state of the language or simply an occasional state of my mind, but there is a big difference between a normal rhetorical sonority and the sort of sound effect that I am trying to get at, the sound effect which enacts perception or an intelligence about things.

ORR: Do you ever wish you were a poet writing in another language – let's say Italian, French or German?

MIDDLETON: Oh, no. I never really wished to be a poet at all, if you want to put it like that. I certainly do not regard it as an activity to be particularly happy about. In fact, when I am actually working on the poem I am in a state where these things, pleasure or pain, simply don't matter any more: whether one is happy about it or not is quite immaterial. But I never really think of myself as a poet; much more as a writer simply, who's involved in making meanings of things and delighting in making them in this particular way.

ORR: Can you describe the way a poem comes to you? I mean, do you wake up one morning, feeling as some of us wake up knowing we have got influenza, knowing you have got a poem coming on?

MIDDLETON: I'm not sure if it is quite like that. It could be something like it. On the other hand it isn't necessarily the whole poem that comes at once. Sometimes it's like that, yes. You are walking down the street or waking up or just going to sleep and suddenly the whole thing is there: at least, the total perception, which you then proceed to evolve verbally. And sometimes it can be triggered off simply by a phrase. Now the phrase seems to contain the whole germ of the poem. But that has to be worked out detail by detail and centimetre by centimetre.

ORR: So it may take you quite a long time to complete even a very short poem?

MIDDLETON: It may take months. Yes, I write very slowly normally. Sometimes the things happen in about a day, or two days, but every one goes through about twelve versions before I have finished it: that is a general rule. Sometimes more, sometimes less than twelve, but that's about an average.

ORR: And does the twelfth version bear much identification with the first one?

MIDDLETON: Sometimes yes, sometimes no. It is hard to say.

ORR: Do you strive, when you are writing, for intelligibility in what you are trying to communicate? Is this an important factor in your thinking?

MIDDLETON: It has become more and more so in the last two years or so. Well, not a kind of rational, discursive or prose intelligibility. The poem as I want to write it should be absolutely itself, unchangeable, and its degree of intelligibility to me is very closely related to the structural factor. It has got to be an intrinsic structure which has its own laws, its own mode of consciousness, a very specific mode of consciousness, articulated in its own peculiar terms.

ORR: Is it, then, almost as though there were a poem there, somewhere existing, and you had to dig it out?

MIDDLETON: That's a sort of metaphysicalization of the procedure, I suppose, yes. Sometimes it feels like that, but that, I think, is a kind of useful fiction to work with.

ORR: To come back to this question of intelligibility, you don't adopt the attitude, do you, that if your reader hasn't read, let's say Dante and Petrarch or Plato and Homer, he can't be expected to understand your verses?

MIDDLETON: Well, I have done some things like that, yes. There is a poem I did in this book *Torse 3* called 'Male Torso', which is a structure of images, all of which are rooted in myth or in literary versions of myth. I wanted to make the human being speak out of a consciousness of his imperfection, and so I was thrown back on the sort of mythological structures of consciousness. The human beings, or mythological beings whom I immediately, quite spontaneously, began to look to were Adam and Dionysus (Dionysus before he was actually born), and Odysseus, too, because these are three figures in my imagination who stand for the avid, imperfect, but somehow illuminated side of man, because without imperfection illumination can't occur. The mythological elaboration in the poem is, I think, dictated by its subject matter. It's not a wilful, arbitrary thing at all.

ORR: But surely, isn't this going to diminish the circle of readers who can understand this poem when they pick it up, or the people who are going to take the trouble to ferret out the meaning, having picked it up and realizing they don't understand it?

MIDDLETON: Oh yes.

ORR: And does this disturb you at all?

MIDDLETON: No, I think there's a sound pattern there which will engage and involve anyone regardless of his education or his actual literary awareness, simply because everyone has an ear and they are excited by the way in which words impinge on their ears and the kind of balletic arrangement of sounds in that poem is just as central to it as the mythological pattern.

ORR: Do you think, then, that in some way a poem should make an impact on a reader or a listener at a first reading or hearing?

MIDDLETON: Yes. But I would only say that because the poems that I've liked reading most myself have been ones which I have been able to understand at a first go. On the other hand, I have been equally fascinated by some of Geoffrey Hill's poems, for instance, 'To the Supposed Patron', the last poem in his book *For the Unfallen*. I couldn't understand that at all the first time I read it and at the tenth reading I was still as much in the dark, but I was riveted to it by the visual appeal of its images, the acoustic appeal of its sounds, its very interesting and exciting use of certain words.

ORR: Do you like reading your own poems aloud to an audience?

MIDDLETON: Not particularly, no. But to some extent, it is necessary to have a physical audience. One learns to understand one's own work and one's own problems a lot better if you've got them there as a sounding-board.

ORR: Is it important to you that people should understand your poems? I mean, are you hurt or disturbed by reviews which may appear of your poems in which the reviewer has obviously misunderstood or failed to understand?

MIDDLETON: I think reviewers tend, much too often, to make their value-judgements before they have even made a single move towards really coming to grips with the intrinsic character of the work that they are faced with. They are always in a hurry to say either this is good or this is bad, or to fit it into some overall scheme of ideas which they have got in their heads without actually seeing things as they are.

ORR: Now you are a reviewer yourself. Do you find this is a temptation which you have to resist?

MIDDLETON: No, I don't, largely because I think I have the good fortune to have a pretty solid academic training, and I am very cautious about making value-judgements for myself. I think an academic training, as long as you handle it the right way, with a spirit of curiosity and exploration rather than imperatives and apodictic judgements and all this, as long as you handle it that way, you can get some way, not simply towards informing a public what this thing is about, but also to helping the poet, in the sense that you are collaborating with his consciousness, not telling him what to do, but just indicating to him what it seems like to another person.

ORR: You don't feel that, for the young practising poet who has had an academic training, there is weighing down on him the whole weight of the tradition of English Literature and he's in the bottom of the pile trying to get out?

MIDDLETON: This may happen, I suppose, with poets who write in English and teach English literature. I am lucky in that I teach a foreign language and I know extremely little about English literature, as a matter of fact. But what I've read is probably minimal compared with what, say, a poet like Charles Tomlinson, who is a professional English teacher, has read. I don't feel this weight of convention or tradition on me at all.

ORR: It's interesting to recall, speaking of Charles Tomlinson, that I was talking to him not so very long ago, and he said that the writers who had influenced him most were, in fact, prose writers and, in particular, he mentioned Ruskin. How does this apply to you? Are there writers who have influenced you particularly in the formation of a poetic style?

MIDDLETON: Very difficult to say. I have never really been able to break away from the compulsive image of Joyce as the supreme artist. On the other hand, a diametrically opposite kind of intelligence like Samuel Beckett, the caustic, stringent, almost mathematical style, has been just as much a stimulus to me as the richer, allusive style in Joyce. I am thinking of Joyce, too, more as the author of *Ulysses*, perhaps, than *Finnegans Wake*. Oh, there are loads of authors I have been interested in. Once I was very strongly influenced by Lawrence Durrell: in a bad way, I think, but Durrell then, too, had a kind of mineral quality in his words. He was using words very friskily and as if they were objects, moving them around. The language was electrified in his poems.

ORR: Let me take this a stage further. Do you find that the main stream of your inspiration, if I can take a phrase like this, comes from reality, or does a great deal of it come from books, not necessarily works of literature, but perhaps of history, of philosophy, of religion?

MIDDLETON: Well it's, I suppose, multiple in any case. One could theoretically separate the two strands; I mean the two main things, whether it's existence itself or whether it's what one reads. Certainly even optical illusions can help, anything can really, as long as one is in this state and can have the capacity, the instantaneous capacity for absorbing something that happens to you, an experience or whatever and seeing its point. I mean that box of matches, there, I would find it very difficult to deal with that because there are certain things against which one is conditioned, but maybe there are moments when that box of matches would suddenly be absorbed and I would be walking around with it inside me and then I could do something with it.

ORR: Have you ever wanted to write other things: plays, novels?

MIDDLETON: Not really, no. I have written stories, a long time ago, but they were all bad. It's the intensity and density of what I want to say for which, I think, a poem seems to be the commensurate form. Lots of poets, I think, do write poems when they should really be writing short stories, or the things that they are saying in the poems could just as well have been said in short stories. I have never really had the impulse to narrate, though, which I think must be the thing which grips a story-teller whether he is writing a short story or a novel. Maybe I would like to write a play some time. But at the moment I am only interested in writing poems and that's hard enough.

11th July, 1963.

Adrian Mitchell

ADRIAN MITCHELL was born in 1932 in London and educated at Dauntsey's School and Christ Church, Oxford. He has been a journalist on the *Oxford Mail* and the *Evening Standard*, and is now working freelance. He is television critic of the *Sun*. He spent a year teaching at the Writers' Workshop of the Iowa State University, 1963–64. He adapted Peter Weiss's *Marat/Sade* for the London production.

He has published a novel *If You See Me Comin'* (1962) and *Poems* (1964).

MORRISH: Mr. Mitchell, when did you first start writing poetry?

MITCHELL: I started dictating it to my mother at the age of two-and-a-half and she wrote it down.

MORRISH: When did you start writing yourself?

MITCHELL: When I was about nine. I was at a school where poetry was encouraged very much. Then I transferred to another school where, in fact, they gave house-points for poetry, so it was sort of ranked with athletics and football.

MORRISH: You do a lot of reading aloud now, I believe. Do you find this is, for you, the best way of creating poetry, to read it aloud?

MITCHELL: I think it is one of the best ways of fulfilling it, because then you get rid of any ambiguities there may be. You can get straight across to an audience; you can find out how they feel about your poems, which ones they want to hear. It is useful in that way. It is also satisfying, I suppose, partly from a sort of personal kick that any performer gets.

MORRISH: Do you find that you have to simplify at all, because presumably your poetry has to be understood on first hearing?

MITCHELL: They have to understand a certain amount of it at first hearing. They have to be able to follow the poem. Not all the poems

I write can be read at such readings. There are a lot of them I do not read because they do not have quite that initial impact. But I think a poem which has an initial impact can also have various levels underneath, so that you get more out of it each time you hear it, or if you read it afterwards.

MORRISH: How do you feel about the method of delivery, as far as a public reading is concerened; because some question of acting comes in, surely, of being able to communicate what you are reading to an audience?

MITCHELL: You have one advantage over an actor (he has the technical advantage to start with, that he has been trained), that you *believe* everything you are reading and an actor can't possibly do that. You have the disadvantage, of course: you are not trained, and the only kind of training most poets have is in poetry readings. But since there are more and more poetry readings these days in England, this is getting to be a bit less of a problem. I think there are more good poetry readers among poets nowadays than there ever have been.

MORRISH: Do you like to think that poetry should be read to and understood by as many people as possible?

MITCHELL: Yes, I do. The thing that has worried me in the past (it doesn't worry me so much now because things are improving) is that the public for poetry has been very small, and the poems in the past have very often been confined just to literary magazines; and the people who read literary magazines have been the poets, and they have all known exactly what to expect of poetry and what they want from poetry. So they are never surprised, and if you are never surprised poetry does not do much for you. The same thing applies to poetry readings which used to be held in literary societies. Nowadays all sorts of odd people come who have never had anything to do with poetry before: partly because you have got a jazz band along, which helps, but they don't go to sleep while the poetry is on.

MORRISH: You would not find, I suppose, that you had much in common with the more academic writers of poetry at the present day: the university lecturers, for example?

MITCHELL: No, I don't think I have got much in common with them. Without knocking individual writers, I feel that a lot of modern poetry has nothing much to do with me and nothing much to do with most people, partly because it takes as its protagonists people whom most people don't know anything about. A very great body of modern poetry is concerned with using heroes of Greek myths, particularly more obscure heroes of Greek myths. Well, I wouldn't call Hector exactly obscure, I know a bit about Hector, but I know a lot more about such modern myths as Superman from the comic, or Harold Macmillan or Stephen Ward, for that matter.

MORRISH: Politically, you are very interested and committed, would you say?

MITCHELL: I would say that every writer is committed one way or the other. I would call myself a socialist writer, not a committed writer. Evelyn Waugh is a committed writer, but he is not quite committed to the same thing that I am committed to!

MORRISH: What aspects of your own surroundings influence you and inspire you to write particularly?

MITCHELL: Partly what I know about world affairs, in so far as they affect individuals. Sometimes it may be as simple as this: I had read about Dick Gregory going to Jackson; then I was sitting in a pub one day trying to work, because there was an electric drill outside my window and I couldn't work at home, and I read a cutting which said that when he got back to San Francisco after these demonstrations in Jackson and Greenwood, Mississippi, his son was dead. And I was very shaken up by this and I wrote a poem very quickly. Normally it takes a lot longer. Sometimes it is a newspaper cutting, sometimes a newspaper photograph, sometimes it's just talking to people, sometimes it is dreams. I write about war, partly, I suppose, because I was brought up in the war and partly because most of the nightmares I have had have been about war. And I think it is a thing that concerns me a lot.

MORRISH: Have your family been involved with war, both the First World War and the Second World War, very deeply that you should have had childhood nightmares about war?

MITCHELL: My father was in the First World War, but he could not bring himself to talk about it. He only talked to me about it about twice. As a family, we were less involved in the war than most people. We were in some air raids; we were in Bath when they blitzed Bath, but we didn't see much of it. But still, being brought up as a child in that atmosphere where, even if you're not being bombed you are likely to be, has, I think, affected my whole generation. I think this is partly why it is my generation and the generation just younger than mine which has been most concerned about nuclear weapons.

MORRISH: I gathered from some of your poems that you feel very strongly about the Bomb. Do you, in fact, feel pessimistic about the future of mankind or are you optimistic in spite of it?

MITCHELL: I am certainly more optimistic than I was when I wrote most of those poems. I still think the chances of nuclear war are about fifty-fifty. Still, in the long run, I am pretty optimistic about society.

MORRISH: Do you think this is because you yourself are happier than you were when you wrote the poetry? In other words, do you think it is a slightly subjective judgement that you have come to or that, in fact, things themselves are more optimistic.

MITCHELL: I think partly things are more optimistic; I think partly I am much happier than I was when I wrote most of those poems. I am sure also that I know a lot more about politics, and this has made me rather more hopeful in the long run. I am still pretty pessimistic in the short run, but in the long run I think things will go the right way.

MORRISH: Would you call yourself a satiric poet?

MITCHELL: Some of the time, and sometimes a destructive poet. It is very hard to be a constructive socialist poet, in fact. It has been done by Neruda and a few others, but this is a great problem and one that I am trying to tackle at the moment.

MORRISH: Have you been greatly influenced by satirical poets of the past, say Pope, for example?

MITCHELL: Not particularly Pope. I am much more influenced, I think, by poets whose general social attitudes I am sympathetic with, like William Blake, Wilfred Owen, some of W. H. Auden, Christopher Logue, Peter Porter.

MORRISH: Have any prose writers influenced you strongly, would you say?

MITCHELL: Oh, yes! Edward Lear, as a poet and a prose writer, too; James Thurber, Saul Bellow, the Bible, Nathaniel West.

MORRISH: Do you find making jokes in poetry presents certain problems when you are reading out loud to an audience?

MITCHELL: No, it doesn't. It's a help, if anything, when you are reading aloud because you can, just on a very simple technical level, gauge something about the audience from the kind of laughter, the amount of laughter. I like using jokes in poetry just as I like using jokes in ordinary life. The only difficulty this presents is with the critics, because there is a critical attitude, which is not common to all critics, that comedy is somehow inferior to tragedy. The worst critics even think it should be kept way apart. I think they should be mixed together. I believe in some of the greatest writers like Chekhov (who I am not comparing myself to in any way) you get a great many lines which are both very tragic and very comic.

MORRISH: Why do you write poetry, rather than a newspaper article about a social theme or, say, about the Bomb?

MITCHELL: Partly because my particular kind of views on politics are not very popular (there are very few places where my kind of views can be expressed in British newspapers) and partly because the few in which I could perhaps express my views have already got much better purely political writers than I could ever hope to be. Also because I see politics in terms of pictures, in a way. You see, when I think of the Bomb, I don't think of it as a deterrent or anything like this: I see in my mind all the pictures I have ever seen of the Bomb being tested, all the pictures I have ever dreamt of the Bomb and its effect on people.

MORRISH: Are you very concerned with problems of form when you are writing? Or are they secondary?

MITCHELL: They are pretty secondary. I let the subject dictate the form, which makes it sound much more simple than it is. In fact, sometimes there is a difficulty: I like using extreme forms sometimes. In that 'marrowbone jelly' poem, I use a sort of basic rock and roll rhythm, and I sometimes do that one with jazz. It is just for fun. And sometimes, as in 'The Dust': that is a very jolly rhythm, if you analyse it, for a very sombre poem. The 'Veteran with a Head Wound' has a very complicated form, but on the other hand, some of the others are completely free-form. I use rhythm in them but in an eccentric sort of way.

MORRISH: Do you feel that poetry is, and should be, different from prose, or that you could, in fact, write your poetry out as prose, paragraph after paragraph? Are you very strongly committed to the one form, or type of form?

MITCHELL: No, not at all. I am not committed to any form, and I think that between poetry and prose there's an enormous sort of no-man's-land and it is very hard to tell which is which on a lot of occasions. I don't think it matters. At poetry readings sometimes I read a bit of my novel, which uses rhythm and rhyme as well, but in the novel it is written out as prose. I read it out as poetry. Which you call it, doesn't really matter. I think it has to be judged on its value, not on its category.

MORRISH: Are you very critical of your own work?

MITCHELL: Yes, I think I am. Some people think I am not. I reject an awful lot of it, and I rewrite it a lot usually. Most poems get rewritten at least fifteen times, or more than that.

MORRISH: Do you find the process of writing hard, or in some sense a joy?

MITCHELL: It is very hard and it is very happy at the same time. I enjoy it, but it is painful. After I have written something, after I have finished something, I am usually fairly shaken up. This is partly because if it is a long piece I just have to go on writing it until it is finished, whether this takes three days or whatever. This is hard to do because I am a working journalist. But I enjoy the actual process of writing, although it is physically very tiring, apart from anything else. But I enjoy it most when I have finished it.

MORRISH: Would you say you are a religious man?

MITCHELL: No, I don't think I am. I certainly was religious in quite a conventional sense, but not any more, no! I am idealistic, but not religious.

MORRISH: Is there any reason why you are no longer religious in the traditional sense of the word?

MITCHELL: Oh, yes! Partly because I found the sort of Presbyterian beliefs in which I was brought up were gradually, one by one, making nonsense, and partly because I had to watch my mother die of cancer over three operations and about ten years. This is the sort of experience which in the *Reader's Digest* makes you believe, but in real life it usually doesn't.

8th August, 1963.

Norman Nicholson

NORMAN NICHOLSON was born in 1914 in Millom, Cumberland, and still lives in the house where he was born. He was educated in local schools, but a breakdown in health at the age of sixteen put an end to thoughts of a university career. During the war he lectured to WEA students in Cumberland, and these lectures formed the basis of his book of literary criticism, *Man and Literature*. His verse play, *The Old Man of the Mountains* was performed at the Mercury Theatre, London, in the 1945 season of 'Plays by Poets', and *A Match for the Devil* was performed during the 1953 Edinburgh Festival. He won the Heinemann Award for Literature 1944. He married in 1956.

His publications include three collections of poems, *Five Rivers* (1944), *Rock Face* (1948) and *The Pot Geranium* (1954). He edited the *Penguin Anthology of Modern Religious Verse* (1942).

ORR: Mr. Nicholson, obviously your upbringing and your life in this particular part of England, in or close to the Lake District, has had a great influence on you. Has it made you the sort of poet you are?

NICHOLSON: It's the reaction between that and the sort of *person* I am that has made me the sort of *poet* I am. I certainly could not have been the sort of poet I am anywhere else, even apart from using this particular sort of imagery.

ORR: You live almost between two worlds, don't you? Because not very far away from where we are at this moment there is industry, smoke, dirt and all the sort of things that we associate with the Industrial Revolution, and in another direction we've got fells, lakes and rivers. How do these two elements join together in your life?

NICHOLSON: Well, I don't really see them as two. In fact, one of the main features of my poetry is that of saying that they are *one*, because I do see the industry as coming out of the rock. This is a rather small town and though it may be rather dirty and smoky and drab and old-fashioned, in that it belongs to the last century, it's still to my mind as much a product of the environment as an oak wood.

ORR: Have your views on why you write poetry changed during the course of your occupation as a poet?

NICHOLSON: The first impulse towards poetry is not to express something or to say something, but it's like a musician who wants to play a piano: it's the desire to join in this exuberance which poetry is, I think, and it's only later that you may find that you have something to say. When I first wanted to write verse, it was because I had read Eliot and the rest, but principally Eliot. In those days, in the thirties, it was Eliot who set us off like a rocket and one wanted to write his sort of poetry. But it didn't occur to me for some years after I had been writing that I would ever want to write about this district. In fact, I can clearly remember the poem which seems to me to be the first of my poems, the first Nicholson poem. I can remember writing it. I was out one day after the war began, down in the mines, and I scribbled this and I was almost imitating Herbert. I wasn't writing the sort of poem which I wanted to write, and it wasn't till some months after that, that I found that I had begun to write without knowing it. I had begun to write in the way I was going to write. That's the poem, 'The Blackberry'.

ORR: Do you write your poems with the idea firmly fixed in your mind that they are going to be read aloud, that they are going to be spoken? In other words, do you think of your poems as songs?

NICHOLSON: Well, I am speaking them aloud all the time to an imaginary audience who, I think, is another part of myself. Also I tend to speak them rather more roughly, as I am talking to you now. I tend to drop, not exactly into broad dialect, but into something a little more like the way I spoke when I was a lad.

ORR: Are you very concerned with the formal disciplines of the poet's craft, things like regular metre, rhyme-schemes?

NICHOLSON: Not enough, I think, because I belong to the generation of the forties who have been accused so much of looseness. I think the accusations are far too wide, and there were a good many poets, anyway, who were not particularly loose in their construction and certainly not particularly meaningless. But there was a tendency to think that you just had to throw a few metaphors together and trust the reader to make a poem out of it. Some did that, but I think it is ridiculous to suggest that that was the whole trend of the forties. Criticism was overdone for a perfectly good reason: because the poets of the fifties wanted to write a *different* kind of poetry, and therefore they exaggerated the defects in their minds, the limitations of the poetry they *didn't* want to write. Formal? Well, I wrote quite a number of early poems in octosyllabic couplets and I did them in that because I liked the bounce of it. I was rather influenced by Scott, as a matter of fact, a poet whom nobody does read, so they never suspect me of reading him.

ORR: Do you feel your poetry should serve a purpose in the same way as, presumably, a man of the Church hopes that his sermon is going to serve a purpose? Do you see poetry in this way at all?

NICHOLSON: You know, you may see poetry in that way, but you don't see a particular poem in that way when you write it. No, you write a poem because you want to write a poem; if you don't want to write it, it will be no good. Its main purpose, of course, is to be poetry, and unless it fulfils that purpose it has no right to exist at all. I think it *can* fulfil a social purpose, and I see a place for didactic poetry, but I don't like poetry as the mouthpiece, or as the tool, you might say, of a particular movement or point of view at all.

ORR: Are you closely interested in contemporary social and political events?

NICHOLSON: Well, I am, yes; but as a poet. There are two different things here. As a poet I have written a poem about Windscale. But I am unlikely to write a poem about the possibility of renationalization of the steel industry. Now twenty years ago, when we were coming out of the Slump, those social questions hit one personally much harder, and I was far more likely to write a poem with social references then than I am now. At that particular time there was a poignancy and a personal element. When I talked about social problems, I was thinking about the problems of individual people I had been to school with, and I was seeing in the streets, out of work. And when it was like that it involved me as a poet. When I am considering the prosperity of England, or the unemployment figures, or even the possibility of world survival, it tends to become so abstract that, although I am very, very concerned as a person, I am not particularly concerned as a poet.

ORR: Let me ask you something different now. Can you describe how a poem takes shape, how it begins?

NICHOLSON: Different sorts of ways, but very frequently I am given a line, which is sometimes the first line, but quite frequently the last. And, given the line, I then either see what the poem is going to be fairly quickly or, on the whole, I give up. If it's a first line, I may start writing the poem and let the imagery make the poem. If it is not the first line, if it is more likely to be the last, then I actually work the ideas out and write a poem in which I know what I am going to say. But I think probably, more often than not, the poem has to discover itself as it is being written. I think the most profitable stimulus for poems, since I have not been writing them very frequently, has been the 'remark': mind you, that remark may be one which I have remembered from twenty years ago; I usually manage to give it to somebody else who didn't say it, put it in a different situation and, in fact, use one phrase to collect a number of memories from various experiences and turn them into one.

ORR: This is a sort of Wordsworthian concept, is it? 'Emotion recollected in tranquillity'?

NICHOLSON: Yes, it is exactly what he did, putting together different people and different times and places as in 'The Leech Gatherer'.

ORR: You feel, obviously, a great affinity with Wordsworth, not only geographical?

NICHOLSON: I don't, of course, accept his philosophy, but I feel a great affinity with the man, with the sense of his being here, and with a certain seriousness, which I am afraid irritates many people and irritates me at times. I don't think you'd find very much influence of Wordsworth in my first poems at all. In my first poems I was writing much more often about the country and when I was writing about the country I kept off Wordsworth. The Wordsworthian element usually comes into my poetry when I am writing about the mines and the streets and the blast furnaces and things like that, because I can let it come in then.

ORR: What about contemporary poetry? Do you read much contemporary poetry?

NICHOLSON: By 'contemporary', what do you mean? Since 1950? Well, it happens that some of the most important poets, I think, since 1950 are earlier poets: people like Andrew Young, for whom I have a great affection, and R. S. Thomas, who is an older poet who really has found himself, or who has been found, in these times. I enjoyed the poets of the fifties. I think, in a way, they were rather overpraised. Obviously they were doing something people wanted them to do. A poet like Philip Larkin, who is a very, very enjoyable poet indeed, seems to me a poet working on rather a lower level than many of the critics actually think. He is still a very good poet. But when he isn't a good poet, he is writing something which is next door to piffle. I mean that sort of poetry has to come absolutely off, or else it just becomes a list of objects taken out of the bargain page of a newspaper, you know. With Larkin, and still more with Betjeman, when they attempt a pseudo-simplicity, I think they become very sentimental, particularly Betjeman. I liked the rhetorical tricks of people like Amis and Wain: the poem which is made up of the game 'O'Grady says' – that one, and things like that. But I think they probably would have done the right thing if they had decided to concentrate on their novels. Of the next generation, of course, it's so hard to tell. I am not very fond of the poets whose chief theme seems to be stepping on snails. I mean, there are some effective poems among them, but I feel the cult of (using a loose word, but just to save time), the cult of nastiness can become just as sentimental as anything else. I wondered what Ted Hughes would do, but he's so individual a poet that I think you can only produce bad Ted Hughes if you try to imitate him. He's not, I think, going to help anybody else to write.

ORR: You don't feel that there is a danger, though, in the sixties that poetry is becoming a game which is played by perhaps an ever-increasing number of people, each writing poems for each other?

NICHOLSON: Yes, that is really the frightening thing. I think the trouble is that poetry is becoming a specialized subject written for university students. That's the thing I am afraid of. I am afraid, not just because it means a small public. You can have the world's great poems written for a very tiny audience. After all, I don't imagine Milton expected many, neither, I think, did Virgil expect many readers. But the trouble is, that there is a certain type of criticism which has been evolved now, which is obviously very useful in taking a poem to bits, but no poet ought ever to know anything about that criticism, because you are getting to the stage when a poet is terrified to write a poem, because he can analyse all the meanings that he doesn't want to be there, but which he sees other people will see. Shall we put it this way? How on earth could Herbert have written the poem about the Crucifixion if he could have foreseen Empson's criticism? I am not saying such criticism isn't relevant, but it would seem to me to destroy the poem almost before it is written, because the poet is going to be aware of interpretations, dissections going on that he doesn't want. Well now, unfortunately most poets, because they are honours students in English at universities, most poets have that kind of technical equipment, and I think it is going to destroy their powers of writing poetry or limit them very much.

ORR: Is the writing of poetry something which has brought you satisfaction, satisfaction greater than that you would have had from anything else?

NICHOLSON: I enjoy being alive, you know. I enjoy life very much, and writing poetry is part of it. It's a very complicated question, because you like writing the poem, it's a great satisfaction doing it, and then – let's be perfectly honest about this, it sounds very horrible, but you like being a poet. I mean, you like people knowing that you are a poet. You get pleasure, in fact, out of having written poems long after they are written. I think, too, to have written poems, even if they are rather bad, is to have gone through a certain experience which, by sympathy, by intuition, opens to you an enormous new realm of human experience. I don't mean that the person who hasn't written a poem, even a bad poem, can't understand other people's poems, but I am sure he can understand them better if he has written poetry because he can understand what the poet went through.

3rd April, 1964.

Ruth Pitter

RUTH PITTER was born in 1897. She wrote poetry from the age of five and received great encouragement from A. R. Orage, editor of *New Age*, and Hilaire Belloc, who had two of her early collections published at his own expense. She writes book reviews and articles, and lectures on a wide range of subjects. Has also appeared on radio and television. Awarded the Hawthornden Prize 1936, the Heinemann Award for Literature 1953 and the Queen's Gold Medal for Poetry 1955.

Her published works include *First Poems* (1920), *First and Second Poems* (1927), *Persephone in Hades* (1931), *A Mad Lady's Garland* (1934), *A Trophy of Arms* (1936), *The Spirit Watches* (1939), *The Rude Potato* (1941), *The Bridge* (1945), *Pitter on Cats* (1946), *Urania* (1951), *The Ermine* (1953).

MORRISH: Miss Pitter, has writing poetry always been your main occupation?

PITTER: Oh, by no means, because I had a living to earn.

MORRISH: What did you do?

PITTER: Apart from war jobs, I've always earned my living by doing hand-painted fancy goods. At first, I worked for some people on the East Coast, and then they came to London and I worked for them for a good many years there, and then we had an opportunity of setting up in business for ourselves. I went into partnership with a woman I worked with. We had a very good little business in Chelsea between the wars. The second war put an end to it.

MORRISH: So what did you do in the second war?

PITTER: Oh, I went into a factory.

MORRISH: Was this experience one that, on the whole, you enjoyed or did you find it very distressing?

PITTER: I didn't enjoy it at all. It was very distressing to lose the business one had sweated blood to build up and it was a very successful little business too. But I wouldn't have missed that factory for the world, because it was a new world to me.

MORRISH: You didn't experience a sense of isolation and loneliness?

PITTER: Oh yes, but it was very fertile, you know. I remember going home one night over the bridge to Chelsea, a wild March night with the water slapping against the piers of the bridge; and a man had fallen all the way down the lift shaft and sustained multiple injuries. I'd just groped my way out of a blacked-out dirty shop where there was a dispute going on, and I stood in the middle of the bridge and I thought: 'I can't go on like this. I must find some means of going on'. But I think that was the beginning of becoming a Christian.

MORRISH: What about your childhood and upbringing? Has this been a rich source for your writing in later years?

PITTER: Oh yes. My parents were teachers. They were devoted to the kind of poetry that means something to children, and I think with this experience I was imprinted with poetry at a childish level. Immediately comprehensible poetry and standard authors have always had a value to me which nothing subsequent can quite have.

MORRISH: Your own poetry seems to me to be written to be understood fairly easily. Do you find obscurity, as in such a lot of modern poetry, desirable?

PITTER: It depends on the motive for obscurity. I do bury an occasional bone myself, but if anyone can find the clue, they will be able to dig it up. This is always the case in, for instance, Hopkins, the great model for the moderns. But they do not follow their model always, because Hopkins can always be elucidated if you have enough general knowledge. I think the sort of modern poetry, where you have to be at a particular week-end, or in a particular group to understand it, is no good. That sort of obscurity is illegitimate. There's no good poetry without obscurity, really, but the obscurity must be of a justifiable kind. I always say, take your meaning as far as you can take it, and then if you are forced into obscurity your obscurity will be valid; there will be some sort of blessing on it. It seems to be subsidized from on high. But you must take your plain meaning as far as you can.

MORRISH: You've mentioned Hopkins. Has he greatly influenced you?

PITTER: I don't think I knew him early enough to be imprinted at the really plastic level. But I do value Hopkins intensely for his natural mysticism. He's a very good example, too, of natural mysticism issuing in Christian mysticism all in one piece, and for that I revere him very much. But I think his use of words, the meaning he can get into words is so poetical, it's almost Pauline. There are passages in Hopkins that could have been said in no other way and which express meanings which you would not think mere language was capable of. They embody that truth, that pure meaning, that haunts language and is not explicit in it. I think that's what poets are always after, the pure meaning, as in Owen Barfield's *Poetic Diction*.

MORRISH: What other poets have influenced you?

PITTER: Well, one doesn't really know. I think collections of poems have influenced me, because one got them all at once. *The Golden Treasury* influenced me very much, but I have lived to realize that you can have a bad case of *Golden Treasury* ear in later life and one gets sophisticated and guards against it. *The Golden Treasury* is really rather unbalanced, but for many years people didn't like to say so, it was so revered. Then Ernest Rhys brought out a *New Golden Treasury*, which was in effect supplementary to the old one, and this included many more early poems, and those I fell in love with at once, because I think at the source a young person will always find something pure and powerful to nourish and simplify. I mean such poems as 'The Bailey Beareth the Bell Away' and 'Alison' and 'Lenten is Come with Love to Town' and poems like that, they took possession of me. And 'The Maid of the Moor'. You remember 'The Maid of the Moor': found quite by accident on a bit of paper?

MORRISH: Do you feel really that what you have read, either in poetry or prose, when you were a child is what influences you afterwards more than anything else that you read?

PITTER: Oh, undoubtedly! I know the sutures of the skull close in infancy, but I think we have some kind of sutures of the skull that don't close until we are adult. My generation was childish for a long time. When I was eighteen I was still in pigtails and sailor collars and liking it, and we had a long, long childhood. It was like a long dream, and we were rich in the harvest that we could reap from our childhood, because it simply was so long. We were bringing a child's sensibilities to bear on things, for all that time.

MORRISH: Do you think that perhaps this was a very splendid thing, because you had time to know that time was passing, time to rest off and examine what was happening, instead of being rushed, as one perhaps is nowadays.

PITTER: I remember being nine years old, though, and regretting that I should have to be ten. Nine years old, I thought, was the ideal age to be. If I could have put it that way, I would have said that I was a very old, experienced child, but not yet any kind of woman. But after that you start having to be a woman and this is an onus and a distraction.

MORRISH: Can we turn to themes now? Are you conscious of having any particular themes which recur again and again in your poetry? I was thinking, for example, of man versus nature. I always think in your poems that you almost feel man is of *secondary* importance before the perfection and beauty of nature. I don't find any hint of the savagery and cruelty of natural things, of natural existence.

PITTER: You're right there, because when I find the savagery and the cruelty, which I am well aware of, I try to burn that up, you know, like burning smoke up. I want to have as an end-product something that will please and soothe, that may have some bitterness, because you can't be a human being without some bitterness and some violence creeping into your work. But, on the whole, I wish it to be for delight and for solace because that is the way I see all art. People nowadays call that hedonism. But I won't have it, because I think the purpose of our creation is for delight.

MORRISH: You mentioned earlier on that you had become a Christian during the second world war. Are you conscious that you have been progressing towards your conversion to Christianity through all your life, or was this quite a sudden occurrence?

PITTER: It was fairly sudden, everything happened together as it does, you know. I went through all the fancy religions at second hand, because my mother went in for them. Then I became rather Julian-Huxley-scientific-humanistic, a very typical young thing to be, and I thought, 'All this religion, how could it be true?' Then, after having been in some tribulation and some danger and some unfamiliar surroundings, I began to be very much cut-up about all these things and finding life dreadfully stressful. And then I heard a series of broadcasts by C. S. Lewis that *started* me on the road, anyway. I think he undermined one in a good many directions, but my humanistic citadel didn't fall until I was incautious enough to go to some lectures on fundamental philosophical principles. I there met Newman's Doctrine of Assent, I think it's called, where Newman said, in effect, that if you believe in a thing, you must act upon it. There I was, up against the decision, so I decided and went off into the Church of England, where I had been baptized long years before. But it was a great disappointment to me, in a way. I had wrong ideas. I had been such a stranger to churches for such a long time that I thought I had only to turn to any church to meet George Herbert or somebody on that level, and I thought 'I shall be parting with part of my freedom, but I shall be under direction.' When I found the parson was a stuffed shirt and the people were there only in the sense that the old stones in the wall were there, I realized that it was on one's own contribution that the whole thing depended. This was very unpalatable. I am still wondering what one can do about it.

MORRISH: Apart from your religious conversion, what other great experiences, or perhaps sad experiences in your life, have coloured your poetry?

PITTER: Well, nothing much because I have kept it more or less watertight. If it was for delight, you had to keep the miserable things out of it. I don't like to propound anything without offering some sort of solution, and one's troubles are, in effect, unsolved experiences. You can outlive them. You often transcend a question without finding the answer to it. It goes by. But this is not the sort of thing I feel I can put into poetry. If one had a miserable love affair (and, of course, one led a Bohemian life and one had many) then this was not the stuff for what I wanted to write. I think instinctively I was anticipating Monsieur de Rougemont's *L'Amour et L'Occident* and C. S. Lewis's *Allegory of Love*, because I always had an instinct about mixing love up with things, it never seemed right when you had done it. It wasn't that I minded showing my feelings, but the result seemed impure; one hadn't enough control to present the solution one wished.

MORRISH: You've mentioned both the word and the idea of *control* several times. Do you find that discipline is something you personally need and appreciate very much?

PITTER: Oh yes! It leaves one so free. If you are always showing what you are up to by exhibiting reactions or doing a splurge of any kind, it takes an awful lot of nervous energy, for one thing, and for another, you've done something irrevocable. But with control, you have at least a chance to work things out in private and, as I say, outlive them, without having done too much damage.

MORRISH: Do you find writing poetry very hard, because you're conscious of the disciplines of technique, formal problems and so on?

PITTER: Oh terribly, especially lately, because I am well aware that my technique has more or less stuck. I find now I tend to be either formless or pompous and either way it doesn't seem to belong where we happen to be now. I know this is a bad reason for not writing, for one should never write with a mental squint and one eye on the audience, never, but you can't be unaware of the ambience of your own time. It would be wrong if you were. Everything that happens modifies everything that has gone before as well as everything that is happening now, so I can't be unaware of it. I am rather suspended, like Mahomet's coffin. It is very hard work, but I don't think it matters terribly because I always say that there will be plenty writing without me, and lyric poetry particularly tends to die out as we get older.

MORRISH: Do you write and rewrite, correct and re-correct?

PITTER: I have done of late years. When I was young I used to brood upon it, so I was sure that once I began I could end. I would write it down like a shopping list, after I had incubated it long enough: very much, surely, as A. E. Housman's process in *The Name and Nature of Poetry*, very like that. The theme strikes you like a blow in the face. It comes up from the unconscious mind somewhere. You feel about until you can get a phrase or something that you can put down and then, if you can do that, you can return to the mood at any time and, with any luck, the rest of the poem will crystallize out of it. And, from the fragment, you can deduce the shape it wants: deducing the prehistoric skeleton from one bone. Also there are interior rhythms in us: whether it's our own physiological rhythms I don't know. You can almost hear a silent music, you can almost beat time to it: and, if you have something to say, it's well to wait until it seems to fit in with the silent music inside, which has its own way of doing things.

MORRISH: One last question, and rather a tough one: why do you write poetry?

PITTER: Oh, because I am *made* that way. I don't know why I did it when I was five years old. I don't know why I still try now I am sixty-six.

24th March, 1964.

Sylvia Plath

SYLVIA PLATH was born in 1932 in Boston, Massachusetts, of Austrian and German parentage. She graduated from Smith College, Massachusetts, in 1955, and from Cambridge, England, where she had been studying as a Fulbright scholar, in 1957. She then became lecturer in English at Smith College. She returned to live in England in 1960, and died in 1963. She had two children.

Her first collection of poems, *The Colossus*, was published in 1961. Her novel, *The Bell Jar*, was published under a pseudonym in January, 1963. A later collection of poems, *Ariel*, was published in 1965.

ORR: Sylvia, what started you writing poetry?

PLATH: I don't know what *started* me, I just wrote it from the time I was quite small. I guess I liked nursery rhymes and I guess I thought I could do the same thing. I wrote my first poem, my first published poem, when I was eight-and-a-half years old. It came out in *The Boston Traveller* and from then on, I suppose, I've been a bit of a professional.

ORR: What sort of thing did you write about when you began?

PLATH: Nature, I think: birds, bees, spring, fall, all those subjects which are absolute gifts to the person who doesn't have any interior experience to write about. I think the coming of spring, the stars overhead, the first snowfall and so on are gifts for a child, a young poet.

ORR: Now, jumping the years, can you say, are there any themes which particularly attract you as a poet, things that you feel you would like to write about?

PLATH: Perhaps this is an American thing: I've been very excited by what I feel is the new breakthrough that came with, say, Robert Lowell's *Life Studies*, this intense breakthrough into very serious, very personal, emotional experience which I feel has been partly taboo. Robert Lowell's poems about his experience in a mental hospital, for example, interested me very much. These peculiar, private and taboo subjects, I feel, have been explored in recent American poetry. I think particularly the poetess Ann Saxton, who writes about her experiences as a mother, as a mother who has had a nervous breakdown, is an extremely emotional and feeling young woman and her poems are wonderfully craftsman-like poems and yet they have a kind of emotional and psychological depth which I think is something perhaps quite new, quite exciting.

ORR: Now you, as a poet, and as a person who straddles the Atlantic, if I can put it that way, being an American yourself . . .

PLATH: That's a rather awkward position, but I'll accept it!

ORR: . . . on which side does your weight fall, if I can pursue the metaphor?

PLATH: Well, I think that as far as language goes I'm an American, I'm afraid, my accent is American, my way of talk is an American way of talk, I'm an old-fashioned American. That's probably one of the reasons why I'm in England now and why I'll always stay in England. I'm about fifty years behind as far as my preferences go and I must say that the poets who excite me most are the Americans. There are very few contemporary English poets that I admire.

ORR: Does this mean that you think contemporary English poetry is behind the times compared with American?

PLATH: No, I think it is in a bit of a strait-jacket, if I may say so. There was an essay by Alvarez, the British critic: his arguments about the dangers of gentility in England are very pertinent, very true. I must say that I am not very genteel and I feel that gentility has a strangle-hold: the neatness, the wonderful tidiness, which is so evident everywhere in England is perhaps more dangerous than it would appear on the surface.

ORR: But don't you think, too, that there is this business of English poets who are labouring under the whole weight of something which in block capitals is called 'English Literature'?

PLATH: Yes, I couldn't agree more. I know when I was at Cambridge this appeared to me. Young women would come up to me and say 'How do you dare to write, how do you dare to publish a poem, because of the criticism, the terrible criticism, that falls upon one if one does publish?' And the criticism is not of the poem *as poem*. I remember being appalled when someone criticized me for beginning just like John Donne, but not quite managing to finish like John Donne, and I first felt the full weight of English Literature on me at that point. I think the whole emphasis in England, in universities, on practical criticism (but not that so much as on historical criticism, knowing what period a line comes from) this is almost paralysing. In America, in University, we read – what? – T. S. Eliot, Dylan Thomas, Yeats, that is where we began. Shakespeare flaunted in the background. I'm not sure I agree with this, but I think that for the young poet, the writing poet, it is not quite so frightening to go to university in America as it is in England, for these reasons.

ORR: You say, Sylvia, that you consider yourself an American, but when we listen to a poem like 'Daddy', which talks about Dachau and Auschwitz and *Mein Kampf*, I have the impression that this is the sort of poem that a real American could not have written, because it doesn't mean so much, these names do not mean so much, on the other side of the Atlantic, do they?

PLATH: Well now, you are talking to me as a general American. In particular, my background is, may I say, German and Austrian. On one side I am a first generation American, on one side I'm second generation American, and so my concern with concentration camps and so on is uniquely intense. And then, again, I'm rather a political person as well, so I suppose that's what part of it comes from.

ORR: And as a poet, do you have a great and keen sense of the historic?

PLATH: I am not a historian, but I find myself being more and more fascinated by history and now I find myself reading more and more about history. I am very interested in Napoleon, at the present: I'm very interested in battles, in wars, in Gallipoli, the First World War and so on, and I think that as I age I am becoming more and more historical. I certainly wasn't at all in my early twenties.

ORR: Do your poems tend now to come out of books rather than out of your own life?

PLATH: No, no: I would not say that at all. I think my poems immediately come out of the sensuous and emotional experiences I have, but I must say I cannot sympathize with these cries from the heart that are informed by nothing except a needle or a knife, or whatever it is. I believe that one should be able to control and manipulate experiences, even the most terrifying, like madness, being tortured, this sort of experience, and one should be able to manipulate these experiences with an informed and an intelligent mind. I think that personal experience is very important, but certainly it shouldn't be a kind of shut-box and mirror-looking, narcissistic experience. I believe it should be *relevant*, and relevant to the larger things, the bigger things such as Hiroshima and Dachau and so on.

ORR: And so, behind the primitive, emotional reaction there must be an intellectual discipline.

PLATH: I feel that very strongly: having been an academic, having been tempted by the invitation to stay on to become a Ph.D., a professor, and all that, one side of me certainly does respect all disciplines, as long as they don't ossify.

ORR: What about writers who have influenced you, who have meant a lot to you?

PLATH: There were very few. I find it hard to trace them really. When I was at College I was stunned and astounded by the moderns, by Dylan Thomas, by Yeats, by Auden even: at one point I was absolutely wild for Auden and everything I wrote was desperately Audenesque. Now I again begin to go backwards, I begin to look to Blake, for example. And then, of course, it is presumptuous to say that one is influenced by someone like Shakespeare: one reads Shakespeare, and that is that.

ORR: Sylvia, one notices in reading your poems and listening to your poems that there are two qualities which emerge very quickly and clearly; one is their lucidity (and I think these two qualities have something to do one with the other), their lucidity and the impact they make on reading. Now, do you consciously design your poems to be both lucid and to be effective when they are read aloud?

PLATH: This is something I didn't do in my earlier poems. For example, my first book, *The Colossus*, I can't read any of the poems aloud now. I didn't write them to be read aloud. They, in fact, quite privately, bore me. These ones that I have just read, the ones that are very recent, I've got to say them, I speak them to myself, and I think that this in my own writing development is quite a new thing with me, and whatever lucidity they may have comes from the fact that I say them to myself, I say them aloud.

ORR: Do you think this is an essential ingredient of a good poem, that it should be able to be read aloud effectively?

PLATH: Well, I do feel that now and I feel that this development of recording poems, of speaking poems at readings, of having records of poets, I think this is a wonderful thing. I'm very excited by it. In a sense, there's a return, isn't there, to the old role of the poet, which was to speak to a group of people, to come across.

ORR: Or to sing to a group?

PLATH: To sing to a group of people, exactly.

ORR: Setting aside poetry for a moment, are there other things you would like to write, or that you have written?

PLATH: Well, I always was interested in prose. As a teenager, I published short stories. And I always wanted to write the long short story, I wanted to write a novel. Now that I have attained, shall I say, a respectable age, and have had experiences, I feel much more interested in prose, in the novel. I feel that in a novel, for example, you can get in toothbrushes and all the paraphernalia that one finds in daily life, and I find this more difficult in poetry. Poetry, I feel, is a tyrannical discipline, you've got to go so far, so fast, in such a small space that you've just got to turn away all the peripherals. And I miss them! I'm a woman, I like my little *Lares* and *Penates*, I like trivia, and I find that in a novel I can get more of life, perhaps not such intense life, but certainly more of life, and so I've become very interested in novel writing as a result.

ORR: This is almost a Dr. Johnson sort of view, isn't it? What was it he said, 'There are some things that are fit for inclusion in poetry and others which are not'?

PLATH: Well, of course, as a poet I would say pouf! I would say everything should be able to come into a poem, but I *can't* put toothbrushes into a poem, I really can't!

ORR: Do you find yourself much in the company of other writers, of poets?

PLATH: I much prefer doctors, midwives, lawyers, anything but writers. I think writers and artists are the most narcissistic people. I mustn't say this, I like many of them, in fact a great many of my friends happen to be writers and artists. But I must say what I admire most is the person who masters an area of practical experience, and can teach me something. I mean, my local midwife has taught me how to keep bees. Well, she can't understand anything I write. And I find myself liking her, may I say, more than most poets. And among my friends I find people who know all about boats or know all about certain sports, or how to cut somebody open and remove an organ. I'm fascinated by this mastery of the practical. As a poet, one lives a bit on air. I always like someone who can teach me something practical.

ORR: Is there anything else you would rather have done than writing poetry? Because this is something, obviously, which takes up a great deal of one's private life, if one's going to succeed at it. Do you ever have any lingering regrets that you didn't do something else?

PLATH: I think if I had done anything else I would like to have been a doctor. This is the sort of polar opposition to being a writer, I suppose. My best friends when I was young were always doctors. I used to dress up in a white gauze helmet and go round and see babies born and cadavers cut open. This fascinated me, but I could never bring myself to disciplining myself to the point where I could learn all the details that one has to learn to be a good doctor. This is the sort of opposition: somebody who deals directly with human experiences, is able to cure, to mend, to help, this sort of thing. I suppose if I have any nostalgias it's this, but I console myself because I know so many doctors. And I may say, perhaps, I'm happier writing about doctors than I would have been being one.

ORR: But basically this thing, the writing of poetry, is something which has been a great satisfaction to you in your life, is it?

PLATH: Oh, satisfaction! I don't think I could live without it. It's like water or bread, or something absolutely essential to me. I find myself absolutely fulfilled when I have written a poem, when I'm writing one. Having written one, then you fall away very rapidly from having been a poet to becoming a sort of poet in rest, which isn't the same thing at all. But I think the actual experience of writing a poem is a magnificent one.

30th October, 1962.

William Plomer

WILLIAM PLOMER was born in 1903, and his early life was divided between England, South Africa and Japan. From 1940 to 1945 he served with the Naval Intelligence Division. He is an Hon. D.Litt. and was awarded the Queen's Gold Medal for Poetry in 1963.

He has published five novels, amongst them *Turbott Wolfe* (1926, reissued in 1965), and *Museum Pieces* (1952). He has published four volumes of short stories, two autobiographies, *Double Lives* (1943) and *At Home* (1958), and lives of Cecil Rhodes and Ali Pasha. He has edited three diaries, *Kilvert's Diary* (3 vols: 1938–40), *Japanese Lady in Europe*, by Haruko Ichikawa, and *A Message in Code: the Diary of Richard Rumbold, 1932–61*. He wrote the libretti of Britten's *Gloriana* (1953) and *Curlew River* (1964), and an introduction to Britten's *War Requiem*.

ORR: Mr. Plomer, could we begin by asking you about your upbringing and how much this has to do with the sort of poetry you write?

PLOMER: That's a very large question, but I'll try and answer it. My upbringing was a very irregular one and it occurred in different countries – two different countries mainly – so that I never knew quite where I belonged. I think that might well have something to do with inclining one towards poetry, because it seems to me from observation over a good many years that poets are generally rather misfits in the world, and I think I was a misfit from a very early age, and that might have started me writing poetry.

ORR: This was a sort of early angry young man then, was it?

PLOMER: I was an angry young man, yes. My anger reached its first climax in South Africa about forty years ago, when I certainly flew into a rage over the state of things there, and looking back it seems to me now that I was, perhaps without knowing it, a pioneer in that

173

particular sphere of anger. The first book I wrote is now being re-printed after all this time, and it's got a long introduction by Laurens van der Post, who is an old friend of mine. I read his introduction with great interest and found that unconsciously I had apparently put forward opinions which have now become more generally held, and it's thought that this book has had an influence.

ORR: When we were talking to Stephen Spender recently in one of these interviews, he said, talking about his writing in the nineteen-thirties, that he felt it a duty to write about public suffering. Now, did you in the thirties have this sort of feeling?

PLOMER: I had no sense of duty, but, you see, I began a little earlier than people like Spender and Auden and so on. I began writing in the twenties. My first book came out in 1926 and it did really touch on important public issues in Africa. When I lived in England in the thirties and knew well, at that time, Stephen Spender, among other people, I was a little puzzled by their concern with European and English politics because I had been interested, not only in African politics already, but in Japanese politics. I had lived for two or three years in Japan, and felt rather a veteran compared with those poets of the thirties who were concerned, very properly, with the Civil War in Spain and with unemployment in England. These things, I agree, were very important but they didn't move me in the same way, because my earliest and strongest emotions as a writer were in Africa and in Japan. I took rather a wider view than they did, I think.

ORR: Would you consider yourself a political animal?

PLOMER: No, not at all.

ORR: But do you have a strong social conscience which emerges in your writing, or can you analyse it this way?

PLOMER: I am very interested in people and in relations between differ-ent sorts of people of different races, ages, classes and characters. In that sense I am socially conscious. I remember once, after giving a public reading of my poems, I asked the audience if they would like to ask questions and somebody said, Are *all* your poems about people? Nobody had ever put it to me quite like that before, but when I stopped to think I found that practically all my poems are about people, not about abstractions or states of mind or other things. I think I can say that I have a social sense to that extent, but it isn't political.

ORR: You've written in your memoirs, which I've been reading recently, about the literary circle and the friendships you enjoyed there with people like Virginia Woolf, Stephen Spender, Hugh Walpole, E. M. Forster, the Sitwells. Do you find the world we live in today, the literary world of today, is very different?

PLOMER: Several of the writers I knew well, the older writers, were revolutionary in their ways. E. M. Forster was certainly revolutionary and still is, I am glad to say. The Sitwells in their way, though it isn't realized now, were revolutionaries. The Bloomsbury writers were revolutionary; they rebelled against everything they had been taught. But all those people were born in Victorian times. They had grown up with a background of security and money and social status and were highly educated, and they took for granted a great many things which the young today can't take for granted. The young today generally have to face the problem of earning their livings, and they haven't the same sense of leisure or of this long, solid tradition of leisure and culture behind them. I think that's the difference I notice most.

ORR: You have written that you don't find it a difficulty, as a poet, to be connected, when you're earning your daily bread, with the business of literature.

PLOMER: I can, I think, speak with a certain amount of experience about this matter because when I was young I was busy with things which were extremely unlike literature. When I lived in Africa I lived for some time as a farmer and spent my time with sheep. I then lived in Zululand when I was a young man, trading with the Zulus. That was pretty far from literature but when I lived in Japan I suppose I got rather nearer to literature as I was teaching English to earn a living. I've certainly earned my living by doing non-literary things. But I still feel that it is no disadvantage to me as a writer to be concerned with literary matters, and for the last thirty years or so I have been involved in literary friendships and literary interests. I've been a constant reviewer of books. I've worked as a publisher's reader for a great many years, I've done all sorts of different things in the way of writing, and I've found that the more one practises the more one learns about the craft of writing. In recent years I've done some work with Benjamin Britten, writing libretti, which is something quite different to poetry.

ORR: Do you draw upon the other arts for inspiration and for help?

PLOMER: When young, I looked a great deal at paintings and I think painting helped me a great deal. I have naturally a keen visual sense and I think I learnt a great deal in forming such taste as I have, and in composition, by studying painting and enjoying it very much. To music I came rather later and now I am learning more from music than from painting.

ORR: Do you find your poems arise, though, from things that you've read or pictures that you've seen or from music that you've heard, or do they arise more often from direct personal experience?

PLOMER: Now, I think, always from the unconscious or from direct personal experience. Never from works of art, at least not now. They may have when I was young. I think there is a tendency, as I am interested in people, to dramatize emotions, to give them the form of specific characters in specific situations which are not necessarily my own, if you see what I mean. The emotion or the impulse to write the poem may arise in me, but the form that it takes is nearer now to a dramatic form. It may not arise like that. It may arise simply in some haunting phrase or word or rhythm or some visual thing or something of that kind which starts it off. The process is always very peculiar.

ORR: And when you are writing your poems, do you think of them as things to be read aloud, to be voiced, or as things to be looked at on the printed page?

PLOMER: I think, chiefly as things to be read aloud. Auden once said that if a poet felt in sympathy with his audience, the language tended to be direct and simple; if he felt lonely and separated from his audience the language then became more obscure. I read a great deal in public to various kinds of audiences and I feel that I am in touch with them very easily and that they understand what I am reading, and I like them to understand what I read. I am not writing down to them. I just feel that the writing, the production of a poem, is not a solitary thing entirely. It's a co-operative act between me and the people who are going to listen to it, or read it on the printed page. I do have strongly the idea of reading poetry aloud.

ORR: And do you place a great deal of reliance on the traditional poetic devices, rhyme, assonance, alliteration, regular rhyme schemes, regular metres?

PLOMER: I think I do, rather more than I should wish. I think that's partly because of my generation and upbringing and also because I have an inclination to order and moderation and clarity and what is now, I think, rather badly regarded, a certain formalism. I rather regret that. I hope if I live and if I'm capable of developing, that I shall be a little freer in my way of writing, in the way that a painter sometimes becomes looser in his handling of paint as he gets older.

ORR: Are there particular themes which attract you now as a writer?

PLOMER: I do notice that I'm a little less inclined than I was to write sardonic and satirical ballads and that I am a little more, perhaps melancholy, or shall we say a little more sober in my poetry, and I think that's fitting because I am getting older. I think an old man given over to sharp satire might be rather tiresome. I hope I shall become a little more, what shall we say, meditative, as I get older as a poet.

ORR: Do you find it becoming more difficult to write poetry as you grow older or no?

PLOMER: I think it *is* more difficult, because when young, one has a lot of false confidence as well as real confidence. As one gets older, one is more and more critical of the words one puts on a page. One thinks there are so many books in the world and so many people writing and so many poets writing and so many young poets writing, how dare one put a poem on paper unless one feels that it really is of some weight or value? I think a sort of modesty sets in, or ought to set in perhaps, as one gets older, and that is a brake on one's fluency, if any.

ORR: Does it disturb you that there is such a small public for contemporary poetry today?

PLOMER: It doesn't disturb me. I have never been worried about small publics, whether writing prose or poetry. I think a poet who is any good is bringing something new into existence, and he can't expect people to take to something new, because people don't. They like what flatters their prejudices and their interests. They like what they're used to, and you've only to glance at the history of poetry, particularly in the last century, and you can make a long list of poets, beginning with Blake, who wrote almost in isolation, because they were ahead of their time.

ORR: Do you feel drawn towards poetic drama as a form of expression?

PLOMER: I don't really, no. My poems do occasionally take a slightly dramatic form, the form of a dramatic monologue or dialogue, but I haven't really felt drawn to writing plays, either in prose or in verse. That rather surprises me because, as I'm interested in character and situation, I should have thought that I should have written plays, but there must be some lack in me, I think, a kind of pessimism which sets me against building up a large machine of character.

ORR: What form does the satisfaction you derive from writing poetry take?

PLOMER: In the first place, it's the satisfaction of giving exact expression to a puzzling mixture of feelings and ideas which haven't sorted themselves out. One has to get the form exactly right. I suppose at the back of one's mind all the time, half consciously, is the idea that it will be read or heard by other people and may mean something to them, but the primary thing is to get it right for oneself. It's like a man making a machine or an invention. He's got to make the thing *work* before it can be of any use to anybody else, and his chief satisfaction is in inventing a new thing which works.

22nd September, 1964.

Peter Porter

PETER PORTER was born in 1929 in Brisbane, Australia; his parents were of English and Scottish origin. He came to England in 1951. He is married and has one daughter.

He has published *Once Bitten, Twice Bitten* (1961) and *Poems Ancient and Modern* (1964). He is also represented in *Penguin Modern Poets 2* (1962).

ORR: Peter, you are an Australian by birth. Does this make a great deal of difference to you in your writing of poetry? If you had been born, let us say, in Budleigh Salterton, would this have produced a different sort of poetry?

PORTER: I suppose it would, inevitably. I feel, though, that I am not conscious, when I write, of being an Australian, but merely of being a person. As a matter of fact, coming to England, although I have been here a long time, has been a continual day-to-day experience of being confronted with myself as an Australian which I would never have had if I had been in Australia, because here there are things about me which Englishmen recognize as not being English, in fact, as being Australian, which I completely ignore. I very rarely write about Australia as a place. I do sometimes, but not as often as I write about things which have interested me in England. But being an Australian *does* make a difference. It makes a difference to the cadence of verse. It makes a difference to the way in which you hear the dying fall. Everybody has a kind of half-close in poetry which he works towards and my half-close has a rather more dreary, sort of Methodist, note than other people's half-closes, because this is the Australian temperament, the Australian dying away, the Australian accent, the whole dried-up feeling which you get in Australia.

ORR: Does it make any difference to the sort of imagery you use, the fact that you are an Australian?

PORTER: No, I am an urban poet, almost entirely, although I was brought up in Australia. Well, I say 'although I was brought up in Australia': in fact, it is perhaps 'because'. Australia is not at all like people's image of it. It is a great big suburb. It is the biggest suburb in the world. I find it a very easy transition to the urban landscape of London and of England. In fact, the only difference is that the urban landscape of England is rather more heavily asphalted.

ORR: Do you find it helpful being in England, being in London, and being a poet in a sort of greenhouse, where lots and lots of poetry is being grown?

PORTER: I find it much more interesting. I would rather be here where all the poets are. If your question means, do I think that it is good to have a kind of hot-house literary atmosphere, I would say 'yes and no' because you have, after all, Elizabethan-Jacobean England where all the poets seemed to know each other, mostly with cordial distaste, and this produced a lot of work, some good, some bad, and I think we do get something of this sort in any large metropolitan place, especially in London. I believe it is different in America because of the topographical difficulties; but certainly in London there is such a thing called literary life, though it is not quite what some people in the provinces think it is. Literally, if you set out in a rather pushing way to get yourself invited to a lot of places, you probably could meet a great number of literary people in, say, one month in London, but you would have got nothing from them really. You would have got no closer to their works or even to their personalities.

ORR: You do not find there is a danger, do you, of poets writing for other poets, or even writing each other's poems by mistake?

PORTER: No, I don't think so. People are too egotistical to write each other's poems. I think, though, that sometimes you come across in the works of somewhat weaker figures reflections of the personalities of stronger ones, but these are written in hopeful admiration. They are certainly not in emulation. They are not written to succeed. They are written because the weaker poet cannot get the other poet out of his system.

ORR: Do you find this happening to you?

PORTER: I don't think so. There is only one poet I ever self-consciously set out to imitate, and that is George MacBeth; only because I thought that MacBeth had produced something new in poetry. He was not necessarily the best poet living, of his age even, but he had done something that I had not seen anybody else doing. I think I did once or twice bear him consciously in mind when I was writing.

ORR: Peter, are there any dominant themes which press in upon you when you are writing poems, themes that you feel drawn to, constantly and continuously?

PORTER: Difficult to say. There are dominant moods rather than dominant themes. I regard it as a great pity that due to some psychological pressure I find it easier, to use a metaphor, to lower a bucket into a well full of depression than a well full of elation. I think, on the other hand, that the way the bucket comes up tends to alter the prevailing mood. That is to say, that a poem written out of depression is not necessarily a depressed poem. I think it is a great pity that we have all, to some extent, lost the ability to write what I can only call poems from the pleasure principle. The only thing I can say is that some of the poems which are written out of apparent moods of misery may still possess the energy which is proper to the pleasure principle.

ORR: Do you have deep religious convictions?

PORTER: No, I have deep religious non-convictions. The idea of the numinous 'What is God? What is good?' seems to me the only interesting idea in the world, other than certain ideas about sex. But I am fascinated by all the orthodoxies that I have ever come across, extremely interested in dogmas, but I do not support any of them. And I take a strong polemical view against them. I do not like them. I would like to see them overthrown, but they still fascinate me.

ORR: Something I would like to ask you now: what about the influence of alcohol on poets? We read a great deal about poets sitting down with a bottle of some sort or other beside them and this helping them to produce or clarify some theme or idea which they are trying to put down on paper. Is this, do you think, helpful or completely misleading?

PORTER: Well, one has to be honest about this. The connection between poets and booze is a very close one, and one very much written about. The public knows that too many poets drink too much. I think nevertheless that the main purpose of alcohol in most poets' lives, in those that I know, is to make up to them a loss that they cannot be poets all the time, and some of them have a great aspiration to be poets all the time. And they find that lots of drink is some sort of substitute for the poetic experience. I do not mean so much the poetical trance of Graves. I mean the only time that *amour propre* seems to be absolutely a good thing to the poet is when he is writing a poem. This is not the time to get self-doubt. Whatever you think about the poem later, you want to be damn certain that what you are doing with it is utterly the thing you want to do. You want to have a kind of divine arrogance about it. No matter how good it turns out, it has to be written full-bloodedly. This feeling, once experienced, is so exciting that a lot of poets, not being able to call the feeling down from the sky (because you can't, it waits upon you) resort to stimuli like booze.

ORR: Now let's turn more closely to your own poems. Do you write them with the idea of having them read aloud, of having them performed?

PORTER: No, but I write them in what I would call a public voice. I write them more in a speaking voice than a reading voice. I think that this business of the difference between the poem on the page and the poem in a public performance is rather unreal, because there is a third state which is not talked about, which is the poem as a form of conversational communication as distinct from rhetorical communication. I think that most of my poems are written in a voice which approximates to the argumentative voice rather than to the speech-making voice.

ORR: Is the sound of your poems important to you, though?

PORTER: Yes. It is the sound they make in my own ear, to me, which is important.

ORR: Rather than the physical sound?

PORTER: Yes, I am afraid so. Far from wanting to capitalize upon the exotic quality of being an Australian with an Australian accent, I find this acts as an inhibition in me. And I find myself wincing a little at the tone of my poems as I read them: they seem to be more crass in performance than I meant them to be when I wrote them. Therefore, I prefer to think that they may make a smoother or more mellifluous sound in the inner ear, as I say them to myself without speaking them, than they do when I am speaking them publicly.

ORR: Do you find you assume a personality in your poems, a personality which is alien from your own real personality?

PORTER: I think not. I would rather not do so, as a matter of fact. I think it is a great pity. I would agree with Auden that poets' autobiographies are the dreariest and silliest things. One doesn't want the poet to be in his poems the sort of chap he actually is in life. But, by and large, I think in my poems I probably am; but I don't write more than a percentage of poems in which the 'I' person is me. I mean, I write quite a number of dramatic monologues and quite a number of rather vague pieces where it isn't quite certain who the first person pronoun is.

ORR: Do you aim all the time in your poems for intelligibility?

PORTER: Largely, but not to the detriment of leaps of the imagination.

ORR: In other words, not immediate intelligibility, but intelligibility after a time of study?

PORTER: I think I would always aim for intelligibility after a time of study, though I would admit that there are many cases of ambiguity in my poems where any amount of study would produce a number of conflicting possibilities. These poems are perhaps the least successful, but they are not necessarily the ones least dear to me. They are often the ones I like best.

ORR: Are you a good judge of your own poems?

PORTER: Fair, I would say, fair. I can see what my major faults are: that I am far too journalistic in style in many ways and also I can see that I am rhythmically deficient in many ways. These I would claim to be my major faults and I can see what I think are my best poems. People don't always agree with me, of course.

ORR: That epithet 'journalistic' is used in a pejorative sense about many of our contemporary poets. Do you think it is really right to use the word in that sense? After all, there are many, I think, great English poets, Pope for example, of whom one can say the same thing.

PORTER: Indeed. On the whole, I think it isn't a pejorative epithet, but I turn it masochistically on myself often because I look at some poems which I can only regard as failures and say: 'The idea which was in your mind was complex, you have allowed it to be rather stupidly simplified in the interests of a package deal. You have settled for rather less than you meant.' I feel this. I use the word 'journalistic' in that sense, not as concerned with certain material things. I don't give a damn about critics who object to too many brand names, too much contemporary imagery, which they always find a pejorative label for, like 'coffee-bar' or 'kitchen sink', or something of that sort. This doesn't worry me, because if you look back at any of the admired periods, the Jacobean, the Augustan, even Chaucer, it is absolutely reeking with brand names and with proper names and with the real names given to the things which occupied people at that time. And if you look back into classical Roman poetry, the poetry of the Silver Age, especially the later ones, I mean Martial and Juvenal, it is even more so. Their poems are almost incomprehensible to modern readers because they are so stuffed with names and places and people who were their concern.

ORR: Do you think at all of your poems being read in, let's say, a hundred years. In other words, do you think of posterity?

PORTER: I never think of it at all.

ORR: Do you think there is anything to be gained from thinking in this way?

PORTER: For the right temperament, I think there is, but even for the right temperament it is a very dangerous thought. I fully agree with Graves, it is like weeping on your own tombstone. I don't think you should do it. I mean, Donald Davie does it and other people do it and it does act as a stimulus to them to classicize, but it is seldom very useful. I think you should read and you should write, almost, as it might be put, while you are running. You shouldn't stop and look at the scoreboard.

25th August, 1963.

John Press

JOHN PRESS was born in 1920 and educated at King Edward VI School, Norwich, and at Corpus Christi College, Cambridge. He has worked for the British Council since 1946, and has served in Greece, India and Ceylon as well as in England.

His main publications are three critical works, *The Fire and the Fountain* (1955), *The Chequer'd Shade* (1958) and *Rule and Energy* (1963); and two volumes of poetry, *Uncertainties* (1956) and *Guy Fawkes Night* (1959).

MORRISH: John, I would like to start off with a quotation from your book *Rule and Energy*. You say a poet's job at any given moment is to solve certain problems, technical, intellectual, imaginative and spiritual, knowing that their solution will pose a further set of difficulties and challenges. I was wondering if you could perhaps expand this with reference to your own work.

PRESS: Obviously the particular problems which I have faced have changed over the years. When I began writing seriously, which was just before the outbreak of the Second World War, and then when I was in the army in East Africa, I felt that the various problems posed by the war, by killing, by the slaughter and so forth, were very urgent problems. I wanted to take advantage of all the ways that had been opened by Eliot and also by Yeats, but at that time I really wasn't technically competent to do so. And I am very conscious that in my early work I was very much too verbose, and I fell much too readily into very strong, rather obvious and regular rhythms, and this was sheer technical incompetence. In recent years I think that the most successful of my poems have been both more economical and at the same time more elaborate, if that isn't a paradox.

MORRISH: You mean they're more elaborate in the range of theme, or technically, or both?

PRESS: I think that the actual use of words has become more economical and also that the rhythms have become subtler and richer. This is what I hope.

MORRISH: Do you write your poems expecting them to be understood at a first reading?

PRESS: I don't expect that they will be understood completely at a first reading, but I don't expect that any lines or phrases or general ideas will be completely incomprehensible. It's very much easier to be incomprehensible, to leave in a phrase which has a meaning for you, and so you don't worry whether other people know or not, but I think that this is bad, I think this is lazy, and I think that it leads to the wrong sort of complexity.

MORRISH: You've mentioned Eliot and Yeats. What other poets have influenced you, do you think?

PRESS: I remember writing, when I had just started to write poetry, a very bad poem, which I have never published, which acknowledged a debt to Blake, Hopkins, Yeats and Donne. And these four were the great formative influences twenty-five years ago. I was also very much influenced by Housman. Since then, though I have continued enormously to admire these four poets and other poets such as Pope, Keats, Clare, I am not conscious of having been influenced directly by any other poets.

MORRISH: So you haven't found, in your later work at any rate, influences from which you've been trying to free yourself, influences of which you disapprove?

PRESS: No. I was rather amused when Raymond Mortimer reviewed my last volume, *Guy Fawkes Night*, and said that he detected in it traces of John Davidson. Well, in fact, I may have read a few poems of Davidson but as far as I am aware there is absolutely no influence whatsoever and it's very odd to see how critics, and good, intelligent critics, can imagine all kinds of influences which as far as the poet is aware simply are not present.

MORRISH: Have you found your reviewers and your reviews at all helpful or do you tend to read them, if you read them at all, for the entertainment that they offer?

PRESS: I tend to read them really for entertainment, amusement, interest.

MORRISH: Do you think this is because the critics themselves are poorly qualified critics at the moment?

PRESS: No. I think that critics can help on very minor matters; for example, if a critic were to say, 'So-and-so is too fond of the adjective "pearly"', then I think this might be valuable. But if a critic says, 'The lines of Mr. So-and-So are rhythmically dead', this isn't any help because you can't by willing make your lines become rhythmically alive and it is only, I think, on very small specific points that criticism is of any value to the man who is being criticized. Like everybody else I am delighted if somebody says, 'This is magnificent.' I'm not depressed unless it's criticism from somebody whom I respect. For example, when Professor Kermode reviewed a prose book I had done and said that this showed a lack of historical sense and so forth, I was sorry, because if Kermode thinks this, then I think probably it's true, but if it had been said by somebody else I would have just thought, 'Well, this confirms my opinion of so-and-so.'

MORRISH: Do you write your poems quickly and then revise and revise until you are satisfied with them, or is it a very slow laborious process to get even the first draft on to paper?

PRESS: It varies. I have written two or three poems almost straight down and had to alter maybe a couple of words in fifteen or twenty lines. Other poems have taken me maybe a week or ten days, a number of workings and many, many corrections. There is no general rule.

MORRISH: The question which always fascinates the layman is how a poem actually arrives. Can you describe the nature of your own poetic inspiration?

PRESS: Very often with me it begins as an actual phrase, a few words. Sometimes, and this is very, very difficult to explain, it begins as an actual cadence, a rhythm, not composed of words but almost made up of a musical rise and fall, and very often I know that a particular poem needs to be written, sometimes in a certain metre, sometimes in a certain form. For example, I wrote a poem recently about the death of a poet and from the very beginning I knew that this particular poem must be a sonnet because the whole idea, although it was still a wordless idea, seemed to me to demand the shape of a sonnet; and I am very much influenced by the way that the poem sounds and by the shape that I feel it ought to assume.

MORRISH: How interested are you in technical innovation nowadays? Are you continually experimenting?

PRESS: I don't feel a passionate need to innovate metrically. I wrote a poem recently and showed it to a friend and he wrote back and said, 'Is this written in syllabics?' When I looked at the poem again I found, in fact, it was written in syllabics, though it rhymed and wasn't purely syllabic, but I hadn't sat down and said, 'Now I am going to write a poem in syllabics.' It simply turned out to be a poem in syllabics. And I'm content on the whole to use the metres and the stanzaic patterns and other set forms that have been used, after all, as Donald Davie, I think, once said, by ninety per cent of English poets from Chaucer onwards.

MORRISH: What do you see as the role of the poet, particularly in modern society? Do you feel yourself out on a limb, a rather isolated individual?

PRESS: I think primarily a poet has to solve not problems of society but problems that matter to him, and I don't think myself that the problems of a poet in modern society are very different from what they were, let us say, five or six hundred years ago; they may be different from those of a poet in ancient Greece. Obviously there is this interaction between the individual and society, but my own belief is that, fundamentally, we are first and foremost individuals, living in society with social obligations. But the really vital things, the deepest things, remain now, as in the past, personal things.

MORRISH: You don't feel that this personal profound integrity has perhaps been shattered by two world wars? In your poems, for example, I have found many allusions, direct and indirect, to the cruelty and horror of the concentration camps.

PRESS: Yes, this is the terrifying thing: that we now, for the first time, I think, in history, have not merely the means of crushing the individual as an individual, but know that we have this power and are doing it scientifically. I don't think that the tortures that we inflict on one another are necessarily worse now than, say, in the Peloponnesian War, or at any time in the past; there've always been massacres and so forth, but what I think is new is the deliberate use of torture, not simply to inflict pain or to make people do what you want them to do but with the deliberate purpose of obliterating their individual identity.

MORRISH: I wasn't quite meaning that. I was thinking rather of a state of society which has perhaps become so destructive that the creative subconscious of a poet can be damaged so that his creativity is impaired. Do you feel that the arts, let us say, are now threatened by the happenings of this particular century?

PRESS: I think that they're endangered, but I think that on the other hand the way that we live now has liberated all kinds of forces which have been either dormant or suppressed in the past. I think that for the great mass of human beings all over the world, scientific and technological inventions mean that millions, for the first time, are having the chance to realize themselves as individuals and that the world can free itself from primal hunger, poverty, early death, and that this is pure gain.

MORRISH: Do you feel that a poet should be open to as many influences from other arts as possible?

PRESS: Yes. There is a great deal of talk about the necessity for reforming education so that the artist becomes acquainted with scientific theory and so forth. I think it is very much more important that an artist should become acquainted with other *arts*. For example, I don't feel that I have been imperfectly educated because I don't understand the second law of thermodynamics. I *do* feel that I'm imperfectly educated because I can't play a musical instrument. And I believe that a poet who really understood at least one other of the major arts would be very much better equipped to be a poet than one who had a smattering of scientific theory, unless he was passionately interested in science, in which case obviously let him study science as deeply as he can.

MORRISH: What about work going on in his own field, poetry, in other countries? Some English poets have been accused of insularity because they seem to be unaware, and moreover quite uninterested, in what is going on outside this country.

PRESS: This, I think, is very much a matter of temperament. I feel that poetry is, in a sense, the least international of the arts, and that it needs extraordinary linguistic gifts really to understand the poetry of another country, particularly of one's contemporaries, because contemporary art, for a variety of reasons, is more difficult to digest than the art of the past. I am very glad that I know a certain amount of French poetry, though not very much contemporary French poetry, but I don't share the view of Donald Davie that the imaginary museum is the natural place for poets to wander in.

MORRISH: You, as a poet, have written books about poetry, the nature of inspiration, and so on. Do you feel that this is in a way an explanation and justification of your own poetry as well as being an explanation of other people's work?

PRESS: I try not to make it so. I think that poets when they're writing criticism tend all the while to be making an indirect defence of themselves. And I try to adopt the principle of Darwin that when you come across a fact that is inconvenient for your theory, you should note it down immediately, otherwise your subconscious will ensure that you forget it. And I've tried, whenever I've made a statement which I realized to be a justification of my own work, to see whether this is a just statement, or whether it is a disguised form of apologia.

6th November, 1964.

Carl Frederik Prytz

CARL FREDERIK PRYTZ was born in 1922 in Oslo. He studied philology at Oslo University from 1941 to 1943, when the University was closed by the Germans. He was a refugee soldier in the Norwegian military camps in Sweden in 1944 and 1945 and came home as a welfare officer. He has since worked in publishing, in radio and television, in documentary films and as a literary critic and translator. He has travelled widely in Europe and the Far East.

He has published *Da senker jeg mine våpen* (poems, 1945), *13 norske lyrikere. Essays om poesi og livsholdning* (essays on poetry and the poets' attitude to life, 1956), *Noen vil alltid våke* (poems, 1957), *Til deg min kjaerlighet. En bukett gjendiktninger etter Jacques Prévert* (poetry translations, 1959), *Klokken i havet og andre dikt* (poems, 1960), *Konkylier. Gjendiktninger etter Kathleen Raine* (poetry translations, 1961), *Innenfor* (poems, to be published 1966).

ORR: Carl, do you read a great deal of English poetry?

PRYTZ: No, I do not. I don't read very much now. I was a literary critic for ten years and I think it was too long. It was not good for me as a poet. I read more or less for my own inspiration. I do not read many novels; I read a bit of poetry, philosophy, religion, books that people don't talk about.

ORR: You have a dual function; you are a poet, a Norwegian poet, who has been translated into English and you are also someone who has translated English poets into Norwegian. How do you think the translator ought to work? Should he attempt first of all to present a literal equivalent in the tongue into which he is translating or should he attempt to be a part-poet himself? Should he try and re-create another poem in his own language?

PRYTZ: I think you have to do that, you have to be a poet to translate poetry. I could not say what is the more important thing to do; but, of course, you have to try and transfer all the qualities of a poem. Then there are, of course, a lot of cases when you can only transfer one of, let's say, three or four different qualities. You have to make a choice; but you should try and transfer *all* the qualities.

ORR: You have translated Ezra Pound and also Kathleen Raine into Norwegian. Why particularly these poets?

PRYTZ: Well, I don't know why Ezra Pound. I hadn't translated anything from other languages into Norwegian and, well, just for fun, I translated some of his years ago. A few of them have been published in literary magazines. But then some years ago I happened to find an article in a Norwegian newspaper about Kathleen Raine and that struck me very deeply and I thought she was a sort of kindred spirit. In fact, I was then writing a long poem of my own, a sequence of poems, but I didn't dare to buy her collected poems until I had finished that, because I feared I might be too much influenced by her poems. When I finally bought the book and opened it, I came across some poems I would very much have liked to have written myself and, in fact, one of them I nearly have written. I do not know if I will continue to translate poems; but, you know, you cannot write your own poems all the time. It is a good exercise to translate, so that when a poem comes to you, you are able to express it.

ORR: Are you critical about your own writings?

PRYTZ: My first volume of poems was published in 1945 and, looking back on it now, I think most of the poems are very bad. If I ever publish my collected poems, I think there are very few that will be republished in that book. It always takes some years from when a poem has been written until it is published in book form, so you have a lot of time to consider, probably to rewrite it dozens of times.

ORR: Are your poems, the ones on smaller subjects (I am not talking about the poems which you write, or feel you ought to write, about great world problems), are they the sort of things which you see from within, through yourself, through your own personality, or are they observation? Do you see a man in the street or a flower in the fields and say: 'Well, that will make a poem'?

PRYTZ: This is a difficult question, because poems come in so many different ways. I do not know what makes one out of thousands and thousands of observations, everyday observations, into a motive of a poem. It has something to do with human relationships; I mean it is an observation which you can interpret and put into a larger pattern.

Life comes to us, streaming towards us, thousands of unselected details, and the problem is to interpret them into a pattern, isn't it?

ORR: Carl, what is the point to you of writing poetry? Have you ever tried being anything else?

PRYTZ: Yes, I was in the publishing business. I was a literary critic. For me, it is not very good to live by something very close to poetry, such as criticism. I live by other things, so as to get time and freedom to write my poetry. But I have also found that I have been inspired by most of the things I have ever done.

ORR: Is poetry the thing that brings you most satisfaction; is this to you the ultimate goal?

PRYTZ: No, I would like to write a lot of other things too. You shouldn't talk about things you haven't written, but I hope I will write plays; not novels, I think, but plays.

ORR: Why not novels?

PRYTZ: Well, I like concentrated form, you know; a very good poem could say as much as a novel of two or three hundred pages.

ORR: When you write a poem, do you see the whole poem before you even start? Maybe in only a vague outline, but when you start to write the first line, don't you, in your mind's eye, see the end of the poem too?

PRYTZ: I think it is not fully adequate to ask if I see the end; maybe I don't see the beginning or the end. I don't know where I start; but I do. When I write the poem, many of my poems, I think it's a sort of description of a mental experience and it's just to find the right words to give an absolute, true description of that experience. It is not making up anything, you know.

ORR: And does this poem usually come a long time after the actual experience?

PRYTZ: Very often, yes. I know that I have written down a few lines, something struck me as a motive, and up to, I think, thirteen years is the most.

ORR: What about the sort of imagery you use in your poems? Does this come from personal environment, and is this something you are conscious of?

PRYTZ: Nature plays a great part in my poetry, as in all Norwegian literature, much more than here. I always forget figures, but I think it is only one-tenth of Norway that is cultivated and for week-ends, for summer holidays, winter holidays, we all go skiing or rowing, walking in the woods and the mountains. Nature means very, very much to us and that's a great source of inspiration for every Norwegian, whether he writes or not.

ORR: But nature is a thing which comes into almost every poet's image and vocabulary, doesn't it? I mean, we don't have, do we, a great number of poets (I don't know if you have any in Norway) who write about the towns, whose imagery comes from man-made objects, trains and aeroplanes and things like that?

PRYTZ: Not so many, but we have them in Norway. But they would not just write about the towns. Compared with English poets, I mean, we haven't that sort of academic poetry that you have here.

ORR: Why is this, I wonder?

PRYTZ: Well, the whole structure of Norway is much more democratic, you know, we haven't these class divisions as you have. We haven't an academic atmosphere, milieu, like you have in Oxford, in Cambridge.

ORR: Do you mean there is not a place where poets and scholars, writers and artists meet and live in their own little world?

PRYTZ: No, no.

ORR: Writers and artists in Norway are very much of the people, are they?

PRYTZ: Yes, they are. Very few of them have university degrees, you know.

ORR: Do you ever find you get completely stuck with a poem, you can't finish it?

PRYTZ: Oh yes, that has happened. One of my longest poems, I had to just leave for more than a year before I completed it. But, of course, I have draft sketches of poems years and years back that I have never completed.

ORR: But do you ever sit down at a table, take out your pen and start to write a poem and find that it just won't work, it just won't come?

PRYTZ: Yes, I have done that too. But I think then I have not been prepared. The whole question, or one of the problems, is to know at which time to sit down and try to write: not too early and not too late. The ideal thing is to sit down and write when the poem is completed in your unconscious. But if you start too early, you'll maybe squeeze the life out of it.

ORR: It will come up like forced vegetables with no taste or flavour?

PRYTZ: Yes, yes. Then if you do it too late, it may have been suppressed by other things and it's not there any more.

26th March, 1962.

194

Herbert Read

HERBERT READ was born in 1893 at Kirbymoorside, Yorkshire, educated at Crossley's School, Halifax, and Leeds University. He served in the Green Howards 1915–18 and was awarded the D.S.O. and M.C. Assistant Principal H.M. Treasury 1919–22, Assistant Keeper Victoria and Albert Museum 1922–31. Professor of Fine Art, University of Edinburgh 1931–33, Lecturer in Art, University of Liverpool 1935–36. Editor of the *Burlington Magazine* 1933–39. Leon Fellow University of London 1940–42, Professor of Poetry, Harvard University 1953–54, Lecturer in Fine Arts, Washington 1954. Knighted 1953. He is married and has five children.

He has published a number of works of literary criticism, including *Reason and Romanticism* (1926), *Form in Modern Poetry* (1932) and *The True Voice of Feeling* (1953). His books on art include *The Grass Roots of Art* (1947), *Icon and Idea* (1955), and *A Letter to a Young Painter* (1962). He has published several volumes of poetry, including *A World Within a War* (1944), *Collected Poems* (1946) and *Moon's Farm* (1955). His autobiography, *The Contrary Experience*, appeared in 1963.

ORR: Sir Herbert, how does the creative impulse for a particular poem come to you?

READ: I think that's quite a mystery. I'm not a deliberate writer of poetry, I wait for the occasion. I won't call it the inspiration, but the mood and some unconscious factor which just sets off the creative process.

ORR: Has this always been so in your writing of poetry?

READ: There are one or two of the longer poems which are more deliberate: for example, *A World Within a War*, where I did feel that I wanted to express once and for all my attitude to my experiences in the first world war. There, I think, there is a deliberate structure and a deliberate composition.

ORR: Does your own environment and upbringing play a significant part in forming the imagery of your poems?

READ: Yes, very much so. I think all the imagery would be heard to come from my north Yorkshire landscape and my life there in my childhood, the historical associations of that district, and, of course, to some extent the sound of the poetry must be imagined in the dialect of that district. I do actually pronounce some words, too, with a north country accent. I don't say I do that deliberately, I do it because that's my natural mode of expression and I don't want to depart from it, because it is intimately linked both with my background and with my poetic feeling.

ORR: Do you write your poems with the conscious thought in your mind when you are writing them of having them read aloud?

READ: Not necessarily; though I have written quite a number of poems which one would call Imagist poems, which arose out of the Imagist movement which I participated in as a young man, and I don't think the Imagist poem is suitable for reading aloud. It can be read, of course, it can be read with feeling, but the whole idea is to present a visual image from the medium of words. The actual musical sense of the poem is not so important.

ORR: What value do you place on some of the stricter poetic forms, forms like the sonnet, or devices like rhyme or regular metre? Do you place much value on these in your own writing?

READ: Well, this is a very interesting and subtle question. I have always called myself a writer of free verse, *vers libre*, but the writer of free verse is always aware, or should always be aware, of the stricter forms. I write, for example, sometimes a free verse sonnet. It doesn't conform to any of the rules of any of the sonnet forms. At the same time, it bears a relationship to those forms and has to be seen in contrast to those forms.

ORR: Do you think it's a good thing for a poet to have acquaintance with some of the other arts?

READ: I don't think it's necessary. I think some of the best poets have been completely lacking in any musical sense, for example, any love of music or any interest in music. But that doesn't imply that their poetry is not musical in the poetic sense: on the contrary, perhaps the inhibition of the aural sense of music has developed their verbal sense of music.

ORR: Have you ever felt drawn to writing work for the theatre?

READ: Yes, from the beginning I hoped I would write poetic drama. I am not so interested in the possibility of writing prose drama, and I did right at the beginning of my career write two or three poetic dramas which were so Yeatsian that I destroyed them before I became rash enough to publish them. I have written a full-length poetic drama which has recently been put into print by a private press.

ORR: Are you consciously, or have you been consciously influenced by the work of any other writer?

READ: Well, yes, in my early days I was very much influenced by the whole of the Imagist school, more particularly by Hulme, who only wrote a handful of poems himself, but I think very important poems in the sense that they were prototypes for Pound and Eliot and the whole of the Imagist movement, Aldington, Flint, and so on. In those days, roughly from 1912 to 1920 or so, there was a very active fertilization going on in English poetry, partly from these cross-currents which came from America, that is to say Pound and Eliot, but also purely English development too, represented by Hulme, a reaction against what we called Georgian poetry in those days, a violent reaction against this traditional poetry, and as one who took part in that reaction I was naturally influenced by my friends and fellow-poets of the period, but not since then significantly, I think.

ORR: Now, you have spent some time in America. Are there any streams which you can detect in the poetry there which are very different from the current of poetry as it runs in England today?

READ: Well, I think contemporary American poetry is, in a way, much more philosophical or metaphysical than English poetry. It deals much more with ideas generally rather than feelings. It has become in a way much more difficult, not so simple. What we value so much in English poetry, this lyrical simplicity and almost naïvety, as represented for example by William Blake or Christina Rossetti, it doesn't appeal at all to the modern American poet.

ORR: You used the word 'metaphysical'. Is it possible that what is happening in contemporary American poetry may be akin to something which happened in English poetry three centuries ago, at the time of John Donne?

READ: Yes, I think there has been, of course, a direct influence of Donne and the metaphysical poets of the seventeenth century. It appeals to the rather academic mind of the American poets. I think you should remember that most American poets seem to be attached to educational institutions of one kind or another; usually they are university lecturers or something like that. Anyhow, they are much more academic in their approach to poetry, I think, than poets in Europe, and that means often that they are very conscious of the past, of the seventeenth century and later periods, and do more consciously imitate those schools of poetry. At the same time, of course, there is also in American poetry an indigenous and American element which comes out in the vocabulary and the imagery.

ORR: Do you think that the public for poetry, and I am talking here particularly of contemporary poetry, is growing in this country?

READ: Well, there are certain signs, such as the extraordinary sales of John Betjeman's *Collected Poems*, which point to a potential audience for poetry of perhaps seventy or eighty thousand, but of course the normal circulation of a poet is much less than that. Even poets like Eliot don't reach such figures immediately. As a publisher, I know quite a bit about the chances which even good poetry stands, and they are extremely poor. There is no guarantee that poetry of good quality will sell at all. It will get reviewed, something like two or three hundred copies of a volume might percolate to libraries and public institutions, very few to private buyers. The sale of poetry at the moment depends on, well, extraneous factors like the readability of the poetry: that is to say, when you get a poet like Dylan Thomas who is a very good reader and broadcaster, almost an actor, then he will get an audience through these means of publicity. Then people will buy his poems because they have heard him read them, and that is an exceptional gift and really not relevant to the quality of the poetry. Indeed, I could put it the other way; there is much good poetry which the poet himself can't read with any ability, and therefore doesn't gain this kind of audience through the voice. That may be a misfortune, but I think the audience for poetry is very limited unless there are extraneous factors, something that gives the poet publicity as a person. If there is a public image, then people will buy his poems, but if there is no image they will not buy poetry as such.

ORR: What value do you think can be placed on contemporary poetry for the common reader, the man in the street, particularly since you have mentioned that in America poetry is becoming more and more an academic pursuit. Do you think that poetry can have, in this age, for the man in the street, a real and lasting value?

READ: No, I don't really believe in this image of the man in the street in relation to any form of art. Art is always a minority occupation: it's the product of exceptional sensibility, as we know it. We talk about genius: genius is something exceptional. A great poet or a great painter is a genius, and just as the creator of art is exceptional, so I think, to a lesser degree, the appreciator, the consumer of art is rather a special kind of person with refined sensibility. Now, the only question is whether this sensibility can be educated, and I am optimistic enough to think that it can. It isn't being educated by our present methods of education, but I think that one could teach people to appreciate poetry, as one can teach them to appreciate music, but it has to be done deliberately, and it would interfere with a great deal of what goes on in the name of education now.

ORR: But this is something that you would like to see and you think is worth while doing?

READ: Oh, not only like to see, I mean that's putting it mildly! I think it's essential if our civilization is to survive, because I think a civilization only survives on the highest level of its sensibility. If the general level of sensibility falls, then there's a dulling of intelligence throughout the community, and that goes not only for the arts, but for the sciences too. The arts are, if you like, a kind of (what shall I say?) one can call it the leaven, that's an old biblical image; one doesn't really need a symbol because it's really a physiological thing. It's something which happens in the mind, in the brain, in the nerves, in the senses. Unless the whole mental organization is kept on the *qui vive* by the arts a civilization doesn't develop, doesn't progress in its highest intellectual attainments.

29th March, 1961.

James Reeves

JAMES REEVES was born in 1909 and educated at Stowe School and Jesus College, Cambridge. Schoolmaster and lecturer in teachers' training colleges 1933–52. Since 1952 he has been a freelance author, editor and broadcaster. He is married and has three children.

His publications include *The Wandering Moon* (1950), *The Blackbird in the Lilac* (1952), *The Critical Sense* (1956), *Prefabulous Animiles* (1957), *Mulbridge Manor* (1958), *The Idiom of the People* (1958), *The Everlasting Circle* (1960), *Collected Poems* (1960), *Ragged Robin* (1961), *Sailor Rumbelow and Britannia* (1962), *The Strange Light* (1964), *The Questioning Tiger* (1964).

ORR: Mr. Reeves, in the introduction to your *Collected Poems* you say at one point: 'To me the deliberate choice of a theme has always been impossible.' Can I ask you to elaborate a little on this? How does a theme come to you?

REEVES: It is very difficult to say; what I meant was this, that if I say: 'Now everybody's thinking about atomic bombs; I am very depressed by them; I will write a poem.' If I were to do that the poem would, I think, be a failure. It wouldn't satisfy me; it wouldn't seem to come from me, but just from my brain, and I think a poem should come from one's emotions more than one's intellect. I wrote a poem once called 'Green Hallows' when I was in a state of rather heightened emotion about a particular situation, and I didn't really know what the poem was about until afterwards. Then I realized that it was about frustrated ambition, and so on. But, I think, had I been fully aware of the emotional situation and all there was behind it, I shouldn't have been able to write the poem as I did then.

ORR: Is it difficult for a poet like yourself to write to order?

REEVES: Not only difficult, but impossible. I was recently commissioned to write a poem: admittedly it was only a children's poem, but much to my disappointment I simply couldn't write it. I have to write when I feel some sort of compulsion from inside, but no compulsion from outside is any use at all.

ORR: Do you believe that poetry should set out to be topical, that it should deal with H-bombs or racial problems, or any of the events of particular topical significance in the world today?

REEVES: Well, I can only speak for myself. I think that if one were personally moved and involved in one's private life with something which happened to be a problem of the sort you mention, a world problem, one might write a successful poem on that subject. But I don't hold with people who think that poets must be what they call 'committed'; that is, writing poems about what everybody regards as important things of the day. A poet is 'committed' to living his life, with as much integrity as possible, in the world as it is, and in that sense he will write poems which are relevant to the world situation, but only indirectly. So far as I am concerned, I would like to think that I am a man of my time, in the sense that I am affected by everything that goes on. But that one should expect to find all those preoccupations in my poems seems to me more than anyone has a right to ask.

ORR: You say also in your introduction to your *Collected Poems*: 'To me poetry is rooted in the particular and the immediate', and you go on to explain that you yourself don't feel that *as a poet* you can be deeply moved by things you read in the newspapers, but you are moved more by things you yourself experience at first hand. Now, does this exclude, for you, tackling historical or mythological fantasies, for which you would have to depend for your material on things that you had read and things that you hadn't experienced directly?

REEVES: Well, I'm glad you said 'as a poet', because I do think that one has to distinguish, whether one likes it or not, between what one thinks and feels *as a poet* and what one thinks and feels *as a man*. I doubt if any poet can get into his poems everything that he feels as a man. Certain situations are poetic, by which I don't mean poetical, but poetically fruitful, and certain others, perhaps, move him too much. You may read in a newspaper about some frightful disaster and boil with indignation, but to write a poem immediately might mean that one merely wrote a piece of journalese. I think it has to enter into one's subconscious before it can be made conscious. Now, you ask about a mythological or historical situation. Well, I think one can

202

see in any situation of the past, whether historical or mythological, a reflection or an image of one's own situation, not necessarily always, but at a particular moment. You may feel that, say, the myth of Artemis and Actaeon is relevant to a particular situation which is occupying you emotionally, and you may want to express what you have to say about it through that myth. I don't think one actually ever writes a poem about a historical situation objectively, and it's not the kind of poetry I would write, or be particularly interested in writing, if one could.

ORR: If I may make one last reference to something that you yourself have written about poetry: you said that it may be that this is an unpoetic time, and I wanted to ask you whether you were thinking here more of the poet or of the reader. Surely poetry is something which is in the poet and will come out willy-nilly, regardless of his circumstances or his environment. For example, Wordsworth today could surely write the same sort of poetry in the Lake District, about the Lake District, as he wrote a hundred and fifty years ago.

REEVES: When I say it's unpoetic I mean that it's very difficult for anybody to get any local roots. In what circumstances, for example, could Wordsworth have become rooted in the Lake District now? Then again, poetry is anti-specialization. A poet is a man who knows everything, potentially, and nowadays there's no use for people who know everything; people only want somebody who knows everything about one small thing, and it gets smaller and smaller, and therefore poets have no authority. A poet is regarded as an odd, eccentric, and I mean literally eccentric, person who is not by his nature at the centre of things. Look at the examples of people today who try deliberately to write poems about current newspaper preoccupations. To me they don't really succeed. In an age of increasing specialization, a poet seems to be an increasing anachronism. I don't mean that poetry is dead, I don't think it will ever be dead, but how much it will be taken notice of I don't know. And, of course, it is no good pretending that poets go cheerfully on without any notice being taken of them. Most sensible poets, most poets I know, are acutely conscious of the lack of concern with poetry, the lack of authority that poets have. If you go back sixty or seventy years, Tennyson was credited with a sort of authority that now a great publicist or thinker or 'brainstruster' has, and he managed at the same time to maintain his status as a poet. I don't see how that could happen nowadays. That's what I mean by saying it is an unpoetic age. But I don't mean that there isn't poetry there for people to read, and poets to write poetry.

ORR: Isn't poetry primarily a selfish occupation as far as the poet is concerned? Isn't it something that the poet needs to do himself whether anyone reads his works or not?

REEVES: I think a poet must imagine an audience of some sort. He writes certainly for himself; but, after all, speech is communication and that means communication with somebody. Now, if you take a poet of a hundred years ago, Emily Dickinson, she undoubtedly imagined to start with that she was a possible communicator with other people, but as she got older she realized more and more her isolation, and that nobody was listening. She made one attempt to get a man to understand her poems and he proved so hopelessly bad at it that she gave it up and simply went on writing. Why, one doesn't know. She says, to preserve her own sanity and to keep herself company, and a poet may well be talking to himself to banish fears, as I think she was largely. But poetry which has no audience must lack something.

ORR: Do I take it, then, that you write some or many of your poems with the idea of having them read aloud?

REEVES: No, I think essentially I would write for silent reading. I like to think that a few people read them to themselves. No, I don't think, to my mind, apart from children's poems, the speaking aloud is important. But I think what is important is the kind of noise a poem makes in the inner ear. I am not indifferent to sound. It is not just an intellectual statement to me. It's a whole, it's a musical statement, but the music may be a silent one.

ORR: And in your case it more often is?

REEVES: I think so, yes.

ORR: Do you go along with Dr. Johnson who once said words to this effect, that 'there are words and images which are suitable for use in poetry and there are words and images which are definitely not suitable for use in poetry'?

REEVES: No, I wouldn't say that at all. I think one must choose the just word for the particular situation it is wanted for. I said 'choose', but again I think there is a great deal of unconscious choice in writing a poem. One chooses not, as it were, from all the words available, not from a dictionary, but from all the words that come into one's mind, and if one is lucky, what one accepts as the right word comes into one's mind straight away. If one's not lucky one has to search for it. Now, I think that it's very wrong to go out of one's way to search for an obscure, or bizarre, or new word; but, on the other hand, of course, a word or a phrase may come into one's mind which one sees at once is stale, and in that case it has got to be rejected consciously and something else found. But I certainly don't think there is any such thing as poetic diction. I should think there's almost no word which might not come into some poem or another, though not necessarily by me.

ORR: Do you believe the stricter poetic forms have much value for the contemporary poet?

REEVES: I think that the unit of speech in English poetry is either an iambic eight-syllable line or an iambic ten-syllable line, and we cannot very well get very far from either, although, of course, the variations are infinite.

ORR: Can we turn now to the imagery you use in your poems? Is this imagery drawn from a specific source that you can identify?

REEVES: My mind would tend to go back to my childhood. I was very much rooted in the past, my own past, until after the age of forty. Since then I think I have been less attached to it, but where it comes from now I don't know. I think perhaps later poems of mine have been rather more intellectual in imagery and less local and less immediate, which I think may be a loss, but certainly the imagery of my own childhood has less attraction to me now than it had until ten years ago.

ORR: Have you at any time felt drawn towards poetic drama as a means of expression?

REEVES: Yes, I have. I have written two. I wrote one when I was very young. It was very romantic; it didn't come off. I've always liked poetic drama, but then I really don't think I have very much gift for drama. I think one has to know what it's about, and I didn't know what it was about. It is not just a poem divided into different speakers. A dramatic or, as I prefer to think, a theatrical situation, with words, is what it should aim at being, and I think very few people have been able to do it. I tried a short one for the radio in dramatic form some years ago, but it wasn't liked and I have never done very much in that way. I would like to write for the stage, but I don't feel that I really have the power. For instance, it is bound to be a rather sustained effort and most of my poems are short. That's an immediate disadvantage. To write in the bits of non-poetry between the poems, so to speak, which make sense has always seemed to me to be frightfully difficult.

ORR: Can you say that you have been influenced consciously by the work of any other writers, poets or prose writers?

REEVES: Yes, dozens. I think that a poet ought to be influenced by *all* poetry, and if you find that a young poet now is noticeably influenced by, say, Dylan Thomas, then what you mean is that he is not sufficiently influenced by everybody else. And I don't think that the chasing of influences among reviewers is very fruitful, though it's very widely practised. Now, in my case, I have been very much influenced by what I see as the whole of English poetry, and more of it at different times than others. When I was much younger I was very impressed by Milton, and influenced probably by 'Lycidas', but not, I think, very identifiably, and since then I don't think I would say I have been influenced by Milton. I have been influenced by Arthur Waley, who is a poet I very much admire, by Vaughan, by the seventeenth century generally. Reviewers sometimes call me a quiet poet, which is only partly true. I have always rather liked the poetry of understatement, which is why I prefer, say, Hardy to Yeats, or the seventeenth century to the Victorian romantic poets. I don't think that I am recognizably influenced by any one poet, living or dead, to the exclusion of all others. Among American poets I have been influenced by E. E. Cummings (though possibly not recognizably), by John Crowe Ransom, possibly by Emily Dickinson. In England I have been influenced by Arthur Waley, Housman, whose compression and under-statement have always appealed to me, by Robert Graves. I have certainly been influenced by Eliot: I don't think you can escape it, I mean he is so very much in the air. I would almost say that any poet since 1925 or 1930 who has escaped the influence of Eliot is probably very marginal. His work is probably very much on the edge, or else he may be rather old so that his formative period was before the publication of 'The Waste Land'. But certainly I would say that any poet of fifty now living whose work seems to have any significance must have been influenced by Eliot. And, of course, one can be influenced by a poet without being in any way like him. One might say that I'm influenced by Cummings, because I admire him, but I doubt, I very much doubt, if you could find any lines in Cummings, or any lines in me which sound like an echo. To be influenced by does *not* mean necessarily to echo. I have been influenced by composers. I am very much influenced by Mozart, but it is impossible to say in what way.

27th November, 1961.

W. R. Rodgers

W. R. RODGERS was born in 1909 in Belfast. He graduated from Queen's
University, Belfast, studied for the ministry and was minister of Loughgall
Presbyterian Church, Co. Armagh, 1934–46. In 1946 he became a
scriptwriter and producer for the B.B.C. Features Department in London,
and initiated a series of 'biographical' broadcasts, including portraits of
W. B. Yeats and James Joyce. In 1951 he was elected to the Irish Academy
of Letters. He has been a freelance writer since 1952.

His publications include *Awake, and other poems* (1941), *Europa and the
Bull, and other poems* (1952).

PRESS: Your poems first began to appear, I think, early in the war when
you were in your late twenties. Had you been writing for many years
before this?

RODGERS: No, I came fairly late to the writing of poetry. I had always
been interested in it, but nothing ever added up to a poem, but then
in the nineteen-thirties, for one or two reasons, I found that there was
something I wanted to say. What was quite a discovery to me in the
nineteen-thirties was the thirties poets: Auden, MacNeice, Spender.
That was really exciting and I was particularly taken by Auden's
work. I thought, well, if Auden can write in this very irregular way
and rhythm, I'll have a go at it myself, so then I started. I think I was
about twenty-eight when I wrote my first poem.

PRESS: Have you consciously been influenced very much by your Irish
background and education?

RODGERS: I think so. I think one has certain advantages in being born in
Ireland, because poetry is taken much more for granted than it is in
other places and it still has a great deal of public esteem. There is a
censorship of books, and a rather absurd one, in the Republic of

Ireland, but you will never find them censoring a poet, no matter what he says. As I say, one had certain advantages even. Everybody wrote poetry, even the shopkeepers would write verses which they would put up in their windows. When I was a very small boy going to school in Belfast, I passed a tailor's shop and I still remember one of his verses which ran:

> When winter issues his decree,
> And biting winds blow from the sea,
> Then come with me and don with glee,
> A Garmoyle coat at three pounds three.

Well, of course, that shows you how long ago it was. Now it would be £13. 19. 11½d, and it would neither rhyme nor go in poetry.

PRESS: Your poems have a very strongly marked musical pattern. Have you been very much moved by music or is this musical pattern a verbal pattern?

RODGERS: I am fond of music, but I think what a French critic once said is quite true, that the music of poetry is absolutely different from a musical composition. In fact, I find when I am writing any verse, the one thing which I absolutely can't stand is the sound of music anywhere near me. It just interferes.

PRESS: And does a poem begin with you normally as a musical phrase, as an image, or as the memory of a particular experience?

RODGERS: It can begin in many ways. It can begin with a phrase. There is one poem I wrote called 'Lent'. It's seldom that one can fully remember how a poem came about, but that one I remember particularly well: it started off with an image of a bay by the sea and rocks. I spent a summer beside the Mountains of Mourne (you know, the ones that roll down to the sea), and I spent it in the company of a geologist and I used to roam the shore and he had a little pack and a little hammer and he knocked a bit off a bit of rock and he said, 'This is greenstone'; another bit he said, 'This is felspar porphyry'; another bit he said, 'This is basalt'; another bit granite. I had no more on my mind, on my conscious mind, than this image of the shore and rock. But then the rocks turned into basalt, because it was a very impressive rock, I remembered, it was a very severe, reserved kind of rock. It had none of the spark or the wit of granite. Then, very much, in fact, it reminded me of Lent and the starkness of Lent and the reticence of Lent. The word 'Lent' introduced me to a cousin of it called 'relent', and 'relent' then, by association, reminded me of Mary Magdalen relenting, so it ended up that I wrote a poem about Mary Magdalen relenting. But initially I had thought just of starting to write about a place and a seashore.

PRESS: When you write your poems, do you normally write very quickly or do you build up these elaborate poems almost like a mosaic, phrase by phrase?

RODGERS: It's a kind of brick on brick, it's a kind of architecture, slowly. Well, I mean, four lines might run to half a dozen pages, absolutely crammed with words, every possible alternative variation until I chip the line that I want out of the stones.

PRESS: Have you written less as the years have gone by?

RODGERS: I never was very prolific in writing: I always take my time about it. It's almost as if I thought I had forever. But quite clearly, there comes a time when one sees that one *hasn't* got forever, and there is so much that one hasn't put down that I think I'll have to start and work faster now.

PRESS: Do you write a poem to be read aloud or do you think of it primarily as a visual pattern?

RODGERS: Well, I feel strongly that poetry should be read aloud. So often nowadays words are treated like children that should be seen and not heard. But I think poetry should be heard. As Yeats once said to a friend, he said, 'If you are writing poetry, write it as if you're shouting to a man on the other side of the street and he has to hear you.' Of course, a great deal of poetry now is written for the eye, the medium is rather changing. But in the old days, I mean before books, in antiquity, all words were read aloud. My father was an old country-man and he belonged to a kind of older world: I remember as a small boy, I was quite impressed, he always read aloud if he were reading the newspaper, and then one day I realized that he couldn't take in the meaning of the words unless he spoke them out and that that was what had obtained for centuries before books and writing.

PRESS: Do you think that poetry can have a wide audience even if it is read aloud?

RODGERS: I am always surprised by the interest that there is in it when it is read aloud. I never expect many people to be interested in poetry. Very few people buy poetry, and I strongly suspect that of the people who buy, a great many people never read it. But we have three things in this country, I think, which have a place of their own in England still: racehorses and bishops and poets get a special place and a special licence.

PRESS: Have you any particular themes which continually haunt you, themes either from mythology, from contemporary life or from your own experiences?

RODGERS: Well, I think all poetry is written out of conflict, out of a clash between two opposites, that that is where articulation comes from. As Yeats said, 'Out of the quarrel with ourselves we make poetry.' I remember once having a drink in a pub in London; Louis MacNeice was there and Dylan Thomas and a few other poets and Louis said to one of the poets, he says, 'Are you writing anything at the moment?' A kind of flush came over the other man's face and he says, 'Oh, Louis, I'm far too happy to write poetry.'

PRESS: Then poetry, first and foremost, is a means of resolving your own conflicts?

RODGERS: Yes, but it becomes more than that. It should, in the end, be impersonal.

PRESS: It is both the result of a conflict and an impersonal work of art?

RODGERS: Yes. In the course of writing, of course, it clears. I suppose you could call it a kind of therapy, but that is only incidental; and when one has written a poem, I'm never interested in it again. It's as if it had done something, solved something and let's get on to the next thing.

PRESS: You have no conscious, didactic purpose in writing?

RODGERS: Not really. I have opinions which come into my work and, of course, one always starts by having very strong opinions, you know; they may be political, they may be social opinions, and when one first starts to write, and when one's first published, it is rather a grievance and a great disappointment to find that all critics write about the technique and the craft of your writing, but they never mention the ideas which you are trying. It's like, 'Don't look now, children, at what the monkeys are doing, but notice how beautifully they're doing it.'

PRESS: Do you believe in such things as classes in creative writing?

RODGERS: Well, I've had no experience of that. I often think it might be a help. But, of course, it's like the schools of the prophets: *they're* not the ones who prophesy. I mean, the prophet comes out of the wilderness: a very ignorant man, usually.

PRESS: Poetry is something that happens, that can't be planned or mapped out?

RODGERS: It can't be planned. If I were asked to define poetry, I think the best definition that occurs to me is – I will put it in the form of a story. One day the writer, Frank O'Connor, met the poet, W. B. Yeats, in a street in Dublin and he said to the old poet, O'Connor said, 'How are you today, Yeats?' Yeats said, 'Not very well, O'Connor, not very well. I can only write *prose* today.'

PRESS: Do you read much contemporary verse, particularly of poets younger than yourself?

RODGERS: Oh yes, I think there is nothing so pleasant as finding, coming across a new poet who is good.

PRESS: Have you come across any like that?

RODGERS: Oh well, one does occasionally. I mean, I like the poetry of people like Larkin and Thom Gunn and so on. I should like to know more about American poets, but they're strongly ignored, I think, in this country in the normal teaching in schools.

PRESS: Do you feel that they are very different from contemporary English poets?

RODGERS: No, but I think they are much more experimental. They have a wonderful energy and excitement about them which I don't think we have at the moment in England.

PRESS: Do you feel strongly drawn towards technical experiments?

RODGERS: Well, nothing matters in poetry except, you know, the fascination; as Yeats said, 'The fascination of what's difficult'. And it is always the new thing, in being different, that matters to people who write poetry. I remember one day Louis MacNeice and I thought we should go and spend a couple of days with Dylan Thomas in Oxford. So we did that, and the first night the talk was so good that we never went to bed. Very convivial talk, of course. So about dawn, MacNeice and I thought we could like to take a walk to see Oxford in the dawn; he had never seen it then, although it was his own university town, so we sallied out; and we were carrying briefcases and somewhere in the High Street a police sergeant stopped us and insisted on seeing what we had in our briefcases and they had to be shown. And we came back and we told this to Dylan, and Dylan said, 'Why didn't you tell them that you always carried a change of verse and a clean pair of rhymes?'

PRESS: You felt great sympathy for Dylan Thomas?

RODGERS: I was very fond of Dylan, yes.

PRESS: Your method of composition that you described earlier on, this elaboration of a few lines and then the reduction to a few lines, was this characteristic of his way of writing also?

RODGERS: Well, I think most poets write and rewrite, and rewrite and rewrite, and even Dylan Thomas, for instance, even that well-known anthology piece of his, 'Fern Hill', he wrote that two hundred times before he got it right, and even then there was one phrase in it which he felt he'd never got right.

4th September, 1964.

C. H. O. Scaife

C. H. O. SCAIFE was born in 1900 in London. He was a boy actor in London before enrolling for eight months in the 18th Battalion, Royal Fusiliers, when he was fourteen. In 1916 he resumed his studies, at King's College, London, and in 1920 he went to St. John's College, Oxford, where he read history. He was Newdigate Prizeman 1923, editor of *Oxford Outlook* and President of the Union 1924. He has acted in various plays, including his *Death's Triumph*, produced by Tyrone Guthrie in 1924, and *Hamlet* in the Anmer Hall Company's production at the Westminster Theatre in 1937. Assistant Editor of *The Egyptian Gazette*, Alexandria, 1927. Senior Lecturer in English Literature, University of Egypt, Cairo, 1928. In 1941 he joined the Libyan Arab Force and was wounded in the siege of Tobruk. He then worked for the Ministry of Information in Egypt, Palestine, and Iraq until 1945. Educational Adviser to the Government of Iraq 1945–46. He became Visiting Professor of English Literature at the American University of Beirut in 1947, and joined the permanent staff of the University in 1957. Until last year he was Chairman of the Department of English.

His publications include *Towards Corinth* (1935), *A Latter Day Athenian* (1937), *In Middle Age* (1953), *Morning, Noon and Night* (1955), *In the Levant* (1958). He has also contributed to an anthology, *Traffic with Time*, published by Khayat's, Beirut, 1963.

SCOTT-KILVERT: At what time of life, roughly, did you begin writing poetry?

SCAIFE: When I was about seventeen, during the first war.

SCOTT-KILVERT: Have you written fairly continuously since then, or has it come at lengthy intervals?

SCAIFE: Lengthy intervals, yes. When I am busy I find that unless I prime the pump by writing nonsense verse or something like that, I tend not to write at all.

SCOTT-KILVERT: How does the process of composition come to you, so to speak? I mean, do you wake up early in the morning feeling there is a poem on its way, or do you find you have to make some sort of mental effort in the first place and then it begins coming?

SCAIFE: Well, when I was much younger, of course I wrote with much greater facility than now. One begins to realize how much of that is one's own egoism, and not really a poem wanting to be written. I think that is part of the experience. In recent years I have found that very often I have had to *start* the process: for instance, if one simply sets oneself down a rhyme scheme and fills in the lines with absolute nonsense, if there *is* a poem that will perhaps start it off. It won't, of course, if one hasn't got anything to write about.

SCOTT-KILVERT: When you've written a poem is it there all finished or do you then maybe come back to it six months or a year later?

SCAIFE: I have found that very rarely. I think the better poems that I have written have been ones when I have made a note that there is a poem clustering round that experience or that thought or whatever it is, and then sometimes very soon after, or sometimes a long time after, I've made the poem, but all the working on it goes in the period when it is being written. I have very rarely found that I come back to it after a long time unless one's really botched it badly and put it aside, and come back to it as a really new poem.

SCOTT-KILVERT: Is there any particular theme or range of themes which has consistently attracted you?

SCAIFE: Yes, ever since I have lived in the Near East, the excitement of being there, the sense of the past, is one of the things that I have always wanted to write most about.

SCOTT-KILVERT: I was going to come on to that. I noticed in your poems that there was evidently a source of inspiration in the Mediterranean landscape or the sea. Is there something which resides in how it looks or is it a particular quality of silence? This is something which has always struck me, that in Greece or in Egypt, if the place is quiet it is somehow much more quiet than it is in England. Is this something which has impressed itself on you?

SCAIFE: Yes, very much so, and the visual registering and experiencing of the landscape has always at the same time made me very conscious of the continuity with the past.

SCOTT-KILVERT: Is this something which you feel is largely visual or is it mental as much as anything else: something one imagines rather than something one sees?

SCAIFE: Well, it is, I would say, a total experience really. It's not merely visual. That is why, I think, it tends to turn me to writing poems about it, because it's got so many levels of significance and experience.

SCOTT-KILVERT: Has your poetry been influenced at all by the writers of any of those countries, either by the Greek ones or the Arabs?

SCAIFE: I was influenced very much, but I can't quite say how, by a highly selected amount of Cavafy's poetry; I knew Cavafy in my first year in Alexandria in 1927, and I liked him very much and was immensely influenced by him talking about his poetry and reading a certain amount of it. We did some translations together, although I didn't know Greek. And it isn't that I particularly wanted to imitate him, but his attitude towards that part of the world certainly opened windows to me.

SCOTT-KILVERT: What are your own feelings about the use of traditional forms in poetry, of a regular metre and of rhyme, which I notice you use quite a lot, and of closely organized forms, such as sonnets, for instance?

SCAIFE: I began writing very much as a student of English literature, you know, in 1917 or so; when one began to get a little experience one realized how very, very derivative everything was and that that was something one had to get rid of. So that I found that for a long time I wrote most easily and, I thought, effectively, in a sort of free verse, sometimes using rhyme, sometimes not. Walt Whitman had a tremendous effect on me when I was about sixteen or seventeen. And then gradually, as one became more experienced and a more mature person, I found that one could turn to the classical and established metres and so on without using the clichés. And then, of course, I think they're *immensely* helpful. I found that I could write very stimulatingly with triple rhyme. It helped me a lot: turning the pattern back so that it would end after a certain number of stanzas in triple rhyme, repeating the first rhymes. I found that was very, very useful.

SCOTT-KILVERT: You mentioned Whitman just now. Do you think of any other poets as having been a strong influence?

SCAIFE: Well, I don't want this to sound priggish and pompous, but I have always felt that I wanted the cadence of Spenser and of Milton and the great ones; I have always felt that I want to hear that kind of cadence, not imitating them, but one would want to produce lines which would stand the same sort of test.

SCOTT-KILVERT: Is there any modern poet in whom you have found that kind of influence which affected you?

SCAIFE: Well, I have found that most of those colloquial cadences of Eliot were tremendously attractive and revealing when one first came across him in 'Prufrock' and 'The Waste Land' and, of course, inevitably in Yeats. But I have read all the books that have been put out by the Poetry Book Society in duty bound, and only a few of them really move me. I find I have to make an effort to get through. Only a few of them seem to me to have these accents, but there are some and it is delightful when it comes.

SCOTT-KILVERT: Do you regard your own poetry as belonging to any particular school or group, or do you regard it as rather isolated?

SCAIFE: I think it is very isolated. At least, it never gets published in papers and journals and so on. I don't often send it, but the few times I have it came back regularly.

SCOTT-KILVERT: Do you think of your own poems in terms of their being read aloud? Is this something which influences your composition?

SCAIFE: Very much indeed. I apply that as a very important test. I nearly always get the thing in my mind before I write it down. I don't write the whole thing, but the phrase or the image or whatever it is, and the cadence is awfully important. The result is, of course, that frequently one writes a line which sounds beautiful when one says it, but is, in fact, purely prosaic. And then one has to be careful to take it out afterwards.

SCOTT-KILVERT: Do you think of there being any close connection between poetry and music, or do you regard the kind of music which is in poetry as rather different or subtler?

SCAIFE: I think of them as very closely connected. And I'm always rather frightened when I find the number of important authorities on verse who seem to be tone-deaf with regard to music.

SCOTT-KILVERT: This has been true of many poets, of course.

SCAIFE: It has been. One has to accept it as one of those miraculous facts, but I can't understand it.

SCOTT-KILVERT: Well now, you have done a good deal of teaching of literature overseas. Do you find that in poetry and the English classics, there is something which is indefinably national and insular and rather difficult to convey to a foreign audience, or is there a quality in poetry which you can come across even if it isn't your own mother tongue.

SCAIFE: Both. I have found that grandeur of conception and execution on a large scale, and intensity of experience and expression, are not difficult to convey to non-English-speakers. But the quality that gives a particular poetry its flavour—in English poetry, for instance, the lyric cadence which is so very characteristic and which is so large a part of its Englishness—that is very difficult to get over to people who aren't familiar with the language.

SCOTT-KILVERT: What is it that you feel you *can* get over? The idea, the concept, or the image of a line or of a particular poem or what?

SCAIFE: One can get over quite easily to foreign students the grandeur of conception behind a thing like Wordworth's 'Prelude'. I mean that it is on a very big scale and a great deal of it is charged with intense experience. That's common. What is much more difficult to get over is what is contributed to the significance of a poem, say 'Lycidas', by the *music* of the phrases; that is much more difficult to get over. You can get over the formality of 'Lycidas', you can get over the political references and all that sort of thing, but its innate beauty which is so *very* important, that is much more difficult. The cadence to one's ear, the music of the poem, that is *very* difficult to get over to a foreign listener, even to a European listener, in terms of its contribution to the significance of the poem.

SCOTT-KILVERT: Moving on to a different topic, do you find poetry more difficult to write as one advances in years, or has the process of having acquired a technique for what one is writing made it easier as time goes on?

SCAIFE: Much easier—when one's got something to write about. But on the other hand I find that I can't rely on that. I had an interesting experience when I was in hospital recently for about four months. There are four or five dreams which I have had over years, going back a long time. I thought perhaps one might write them up in prose, and then it occurred to me that they'd make rather a good series of sonnets. And once having realized this, I found that I could go at them bald-headed. I worked pretty intensely, although I had to work without pencil and paper because I was not able to see. Each one would be completed in, say, three days, working it over in my mind. But when I had used those (I think there were about five of them) I hadn't any more dreams to write about and I didn't go on writing sonnets. I wrote just one more on another theme which was suggested to me by a talk I heard on the wireless.

SCOTT-KILVERT: Did you find that the process of having to compose by ear, not having a pencil and paper, or by memory, did this make it much more difficult?

SCAIFE: More difficult in one way but much more intense in another, because while one was doing it, you see, there were no other distractions. The horrible thing was, of course, having to keep on turning it over in one's mind for fear of losing the *mot juste* which one had been working for half an hour to get, until one could find somebody to write it down. I found *that* was very irritating, and also how the lines would keep on muddling themselves up.

SCOTT-KILVERT: Well, finally, one very general and perhaps rather difficult question. What do you think is the particular satisfaction which one gets from writing poetry which makes one go on writing it?

SCAIFE: Of course, I ought to be fashionable and say 'communication'. It isn't really. Needless to say, I love it if somebody else enjoys the poem; nothing could be more gratifying. I think it is the feeling of its having floated off from one and existing independently. It is extremely satisfying. The process is, as well, very satisfying, when it begins to come right, you know. And I am a great believer that the poem builds itself. Very often one begins at the end, I find, and then it begins to develop, as it were. It's an irritating process, not by any means essentially pleasurable, but it is very satisfactory when it is there. It's a fulfilment, something done, and there it is and you can turn to it and it's got its own independent existence. You begin to lose interest in it almost at once, it's quite true. I find it very difficult to remember my own poems. I have to learn them up again.

SCOTT-KILVERT: And if the audience comes along later and finds it equally pleasurable, that's fine, but primarily this is a matter of satisfying one's own standards?

SCAIFE: I think so. I think that's much nearer the truth than saying that one's longing to be heard, much though one enjoys it when one is heard.

16th November, 1964.

Vernon Scannell

VERNON SCANNELL was born in 1922, and educated at elementary schools; he spent a year at Leeds University. He has written two experimental verse features for the B.B.C., and the libretto of an opera, *The Cancelling Dark*, with music by Christopher Whelen. He won the Heinemann Award for Literature 1960.

His publications include four collections of poetry, *A Mortal Pitch* (1957), *The Masks of Love* (1960), *A Sense of Danger* (1962), and *Walking Wounded* (1965); and four novels, *The Fight* (1953), *The Face of the Enemy* (1961), *The Dividing Night* (1962) and *The Big Time* (1965).

MORRISH: Mr. Scannell, are there any particular questions and problems which preoccupy you and form, as it were, a constant theme throughout your poems?

SCANNELL: I think the two main themes of romantic poetry (and I think that I probably am a romantic) are simply love and death. These, of course, cover many kinds of love, anyway, and probably many kinds of death too, but certainly profane love and sacred love and love in all its strange forms. Certainly a preoccupation with death.

MORRISH: Can you remember what it was that gave you your dread of death? Was there any particular experience when you were a child that frightened you?

SCANNELL: Not as a child, no. I think that perhaps the war brought the reality of death home to me very sharply. I think most young people are protected by this peculiar sense of personal invulnerability. Death is something that happens to other people and not one's self, but when you're suddenly and traumatically brought up to it and you see friends and people you were talking to moments before smashed to pieces and so on . . .

MORRISH: I was going to ask you about the war, because the Second

World War produced really no war poets as such. Why do you think this is?

SCANNELL: That's not quite true. There was, for instance, Keith Douglas, who was a very fine poet and wrote a number of direct war poems in the Western Desert. He still seems to me sadly underrated. People don't seem to realize that he was as good a poet as most of the First World War poets and better, in fact, than many. But, on the whole, it is true, because there was this difference of feeling: it was a conscripted war, it was a disenchanted war. There wasn't the romantic feeling of self-sacrifice and heroism that was prevalent then, because values had changed generally. I mean, after all, we were children of the post-Freudian generation and we were more introspective and more sceptical, I think.

MORRISH: Did you write any poetry yourself when you were in the army?

SCANNELL: No, I didn't. I lived like an animal, a sort of khaki automaton, during the war and just waited till I could get out of it.

MORRISH: When did you start writing poetry?

SCANNELL: Well, I began as a child, writing appalling poems and still stuck all the way through to this obstinate idea that I was a poet, that I could write; and as soon as I got out of the army I began to learn my trade, as it were.

MORRISH: What writers or poets influenced you most, do you think?

SCANNELL: Auden, I would say. And I think it is true that most poets of my generation are, or have been, influenced by Auden. Certainly, I have an immense admiration for his work. I have never been influenced in the sense that I tried to write like Auden, because I know that I couldn't. He is, I should think, a completely different sort of person from myself: certainly he has a different kind of mind, a far, far better one. He is an intellectual and I am not. I respond more intuitively, I think, to experience.

MORRISH: Do you find writing poetry a sweat and a strain, something that is very hard for you?

SCANNELL: Yes, and more and more so as I get older. Not at first. When I first wrote, I would turn out five or six poems a week and they were all great poems, or so I fondly believed. But now, I do find it terribly difficult and I even try to think of excuses for not beginning. You know, I might get out a piece of paper and find to my delight and relief that my pen has been mislaid or run out of ink, and then I can go to the pub quite happily.

MORRISH: How long does it take you to write a poem, generally? Is it a long, laboured process?

SCANNELL: It varies a lot. It tends to become more and more laboured now because I am more critical, I think, of what I write myself. But once in a while, a poem does come very easily and very smoothly. That little poem, 'The Lynching', came like that, very easily indeed. And I am quite fond of that poem. I think it is quite a good little poem.

MORRISH: Was this the result of an actual experience, of a lynching in the States or something?

SCANNELL: No, no. Just the idea. I was just rather preoccupied and appalled by the treatment of Negroes generally. And it did strike me very forcibly, talking to bigoted people, that behind the colour prejudice is this strong sexual jealousy, based on a kind of lavatory-wall mythology of virile Negroes.

MORRISH: How does the idea of a poem come to you? Is it generally some outside situation, something you read in a paper, perhaps, or is it, maybe, a line?

SCANNELL: It's all rather mysterious how these poems do happen. But most commonly, I think, as an image; a certain image occurs to me, a certain line, perhaps, and gradually over weeks, or whatever it may be, the poem builds itself up. Other things, like the 'Walking Wounded', that's simply something that has haunted my imagination. There seems to me something terribly poignant about the 'Walking Wounded'. This was an actual incident in Normandy, seeing these men in the early morning coming back from an attack, and it has been lying there for nearly twenty years before I really found my way to writing it. I spent an enormous amount of time on that poem and did about ten different versions before I got it out, and even now I'm not really pleased with it.

MORRISH: There have been criticisms levelled against some contemporary poetry that it's concerned more with individual, emotional problems or human relationships and not with grand universal questions: beauty and truth and so on. Do you think it is, in fact, limiting or a development for the better?

SCANNELL: Well, I simply don't think it's true. I don't think that poets generally have been preoccupied with the great abstractions and eternal verities. I think they have always, the best of them, anyway, had their preoccupations rooted in lived experience. I think that must be so. I am very much opposed to a kind of poetry which is

221

being written now, a kind of abstract, making-word-patterns or poem-shaped pieces of writing, which appear to me to have no relation whatsoever to experience as I know it.

MORRISH: Have there been any specially important experiences in your life which have greatly affected you as a person and therefore as a poet? Or periods of your life, perhaps, that have been very fruitful to you?

SCANNELL: No, I don't think so. Obviously the war, yes, the war was a big sort of climacteric experience; getting married, having children, certainly. This opened up new areas of experience to me which I never knew existed. Parts of myself came to life which I didn't know were there even at all. The capacity for selfless loving, for one thing, which I thought I was quite incapable of.

MORRISH: Do you feel yourself to be one of any modern group of poets? Do you find that you have anything in common with any people writing today?

SCANNELL: No, I don't feel that. I don't feel that I belong with any group at all.

MORRISH: Do you read a lot of your contemporaries' work?

SCANNELL: Yes, I read quite a lot.

MORRISH: Do you approve of their work or do you have any particular dislikes amongst contemporary poets?

SCANNELL: I have likes and dislikes naturally. I admire, in England, Philip Larkin. I think everybody does probably now. I think everybody realizes that he is a very fine craftsman and a very good poet indeed. Of the younger poets, I like Anthony Thwaite very much and the Australian Peter Porter. The poets I don't like (perhaps I shouldn't name them, but they can probably be recognized by the description) are these abstract word-spinners who deal with metaphysical problems of one kind or another, and the contents of their poems look rather like the catalogue of an art exhibition. You know, they write about other art forms and so forth.

MORRISH: Yes, and this is a kind of poetry which somehow implies a special, rather limited group of people who are going to appreciate them.

SCANNELL: It does, yes, and I think they do a great disservice, too, to poetry because really very few people read contemporary poetry now, and I don't think I am exaggerating when I say that, beyond poets, would-be poets and professionals, teachers and so on, hardly anybody, in fact, reads poetry.

MORRISH: Are you conscious, when you are writing poetry, that you are writing for a relatively small section of the population?

SCANNELL: No, not at all. I am only conscious of trying to get the thing out for myself, to my own satisfaction. I am not aware of an audience at all. Afterwards, however, I would very much like to think that somebody is enjoying what I have written.

MORRISH: Do you like reading your poetry out loud or having it read out loud?

SCANNELL: I quite like to read poetry in public and on the radio and so on, but I do feel that the listeners should have the text in front of them, or know the poem anyway. I don't think that one can fully appreciate a poem on simply one hearing of it.

MORRISH: Do you feel very much at home in modern twentieth-century society, or is there much you dislike heartily about it?

SCANNELL: Naturally I am fairly concerned and worried about various problems that have emerged in this part of the twentieth century: the Bomb and this racial business. But really I enjoy the twentieth century and I enjoy cosmopolitan life. I enjoy the life of the city and I find this exciting and evocative. I couldn't imagine myself living in the Lake District and writing nature poetry.

MORRISH: Are you religious?

SCANNELL: Oh dear! Sometimes I am and sometimes I'm not. Sometimes I feel that I would like very much to be a Christian. There is something rather splendid and dramatic about the doctrine of the Fall, and it sometimes seems to make sense to me that really the heart of man is desperately wicked and the doctrine of Redemption and Grace makes sense and makes order of what otherwise seems quite mad and chaotic. But rationally, no, I'm not a Christian.

MORRISH: But when you say you are religious *sometimes*, you mean in the sense that you think that there is something outside the ordinary rational, material explanation for life?

SCANNELL: Yes, I have moods when I believe that this is so. And yet, from my reading of people like Frazer and Freud, *Totem and Taboo* and so on, it seems to me so clear that religion is something that has been created by man himself in order to explain the universe. It began with magic and it gradually became more and more sophisticated and I see no reason, if the human race continues, say, for another thousand years, why our present religions won't seem as strange and fanciful as the Greeks' or even earlier, the magical rites.

MORRISH: But as long as there are men there will be some need for magic or wonder?

SCANNELL: Yes. I think it was John Crowe Ransom who said that it is really the poets who make the religions, or at least, who vivify them. They make them living things and once the poetry, as it were, is excluded it dies. I feel these new translations of the Bible are tending to do this. All you're left with is a set of stale dogmas and nobody, I think, wants those really at all.

MORRISH: What do you think is the function of poetry?

SCANNELL: It has many: I think, at the practical level, the preservation of language. Language is abused in so many ways, as you know, by the press and by politicians and by advertising people, and the poet is using language scrupulously and honestly and with great care and respect for meaning and all possible meanings and associations. He is, in fact, trying to speak the truth. As Baudelaire said, he must be intelligent above all things – intelligent, using it in that French sense – and I agree absolutely there.

MORRISH: Why does he choose poetry rather than some prose form?

SCANNELL: Because poetry is, as it were, the quintessential literary activity. I think this is true. I have written novels myself and I know that when I am writing prose, I find myself writing much more slackly than under the strict and rigid discipline of verse. The fact that you are writing in a particular verse form focuses your attention on the use of every word and the relations between words.

MORRISH: How do you find problems of form help you or hinder you when you are writing?

SCANNELL: I think that a strict metre and rhyme scheme and so forth can be very valuable. It can give a tightness and tautness to your work. On the other hand, there is a danger that it can sound rather glib and smooth and mechanical, so that you have got to hit on a compromise somehow. Robert Lowell, the American poet, does this very well. He doesn't write the sort of loose, indulgent kind of free verse that lots of people are doing now, but while using a strict metric, he manages all the time to have the rhythms of common speech, of normal speech, working with and against this metrical norm.

9th September, 1963.

Stevie Smith

STEVIE SMITH was born in Hull, but moved to London at the age of three and has lived in the same house ever since.

Her published works include three novels, *Novel on Yellow Paper* (1936), *Over the Frontier* (1938), and *The Holiday* (1949); six volumes of poetry and drawings, *A Good Time was Had by All* (1937), *Tender Only to One* (1938), *Mother, What is Man?* (1942), *Harold's Leap* (1950), *Not Waving but Drowning* (1957), *Selected Poems* (1962). She has also published a sketch-book with comments, *Some are more Human than Others* (1958), and wrote the introduction and captions to a book of photographs, *Cats in Colour* (1959).

ORR: When did you begin writing poetry?

SMITH: Well, I wrote one or two poems when I was a child and then I had a tremendous period of not writing poems again until I was about twenty, I suppose.

ORR: Do you enjoy writing poems?

SMITH: Yes, very much indeed. I love it.

ORR: Is this the sort of thing that you would do even if they were not going to be published at all?

SMITH: Oh yes, you would: it gives you a wonderful pleasure. There's a certain amount of pain about it too, but hours and days can go by, one sort of throws it away and goes and digs it up and tosses it into the air and finishes it off or doesn't finish it off. Anyhow, I love doing it.

ORR: How do the ideas for your poems come to you? Do they come in the form of words, of pictures, of shapes, of sounds?

SMITH: Well, it's terribly difficult to say where one gets them from, and one feels one ought not to say in case one doesn't get them any more. It's like that famous line from Browning: 'Where the apple reddens never pry.' Sometimes it's an idea I want to get across very strongly

like 'Was He Married?', which is a theological poem, and I argue
those points to myself and then I notice this rhythm coming into it,
this strong beat, and then I try to make the argument in the poem.
There are different sorts of poems, you know, the argument poems,
the melancholy ones, the ones about death, and a tremendous lot
about witchcraft and fairy poems, which I suppose are memories
from childhood and Grimm's stories and the German fairy
stories.

ORR: Do you find theology plays a large part in forming or deciding
your themes?

SMITH: It plays quite a strong part, especially if I have been reading
theology, and there are very strong other threads coming in too. I
get inspiration from books, but they are always books which are not
in the least poetical; I mean, they are books about theology or history
which have nothing to do with poetry. But sometimes an idea will
flash across one's mind from these books which may be a counter-
argument, but it would form itself into a poem somehow and that,
I think, is what happens with a theological poem.

ORR: You've got a very strong sense of rhythm: I think this emerges
very clearly in your poems. Is this something conscious or is this just
something in your nature?

SMITH: It is something in my nature, I think. It is very, very strong, I
know, and that's why I like reading my own poems aloud—and
best of all, singing them—because you can't score a poem as you can
score music, so you can't really put the accents on paper so that other
people will inevitably read them correctly, you see.

ORR: So you do think when you are writing your poems of having them
read aloud?

SMITH: Well, no, of reading them myself. I don't really want other
people to read them.

ORR: But you think of the sound of them?

SMITH: Oh yes, very much: they are sound vehicles.

ORR: I notice that you like to put some of your poems to music, to
well-known tunes. Why is this?

SMITH: Well, there again, the rhythm. I think if you can fix it to a tune
you will be quite certain that other people will get the right rhythm.
It's a way of making sure. You see what a suspicious nature I have!
But I like, when I have written my poem, to make sure that if it ever
is read by somebody else aloud it will be read properly. This may be
very arrogant, you know: I mean, the way that another person may

stress the poem, it might be better than my stress, but naturally one wants one's own way in these things.

ORR: Are you a good judge of your own poems?

SMITH: I don't know, because I never judge them. I don't think my poems have changed very much since I started writing.

ORR: Does this mean that your own attitudes haven't changed very much?

SMITH: No, they haven't changed at all, I think. One has one's thoughts about things and one takes great pleasure in these thoughts and in working them out. But I should be very surprised, for instance, if one day I said, 'This is absolutely black' and the next day I said, 'This is absolutely white.'

ORR: Don't you think that more and more of our poets and writers today are concerned with problems of morality, even problems of survival?

SMITH: Yes, but I think all poems must be concerned with that and always have been at every age, surely. I am very concerned with that, though I don't mind much about survival. I rather like the idea of death, and I think a lot of my poems do treat of these subjects. It is like this man who I had a poem about. He took to journalism you see, to earn more money, as poets do quite often, and in the end he met his Muse in the form of an old gentleman and cut his throat, murdered him, and then kept hearing these ghost sounds which he had repudiated and refused to listen to. It's a very modern situation, but it crops up all the time through human life, surely.

ORR: You don't feel that we are more conscious today of the world around us than perhaps our parents were?

SMITH: I think the everyday things impinge tremendously and always have and the writer must learn to say no to them if they get in the way and are a bore and a nuisance, like the necessity of earning money, the necessity of keeping one's family, of having children. These problems go on and they press most terribly, and the world of my childhood, of course, was split with war, too. So aren't we being rather unphilosophical, parochial really, about this idea that life is so different today? We rather seem to pride ourselves like children saying, 'Never have things been so bad.' But they have been much worse, surely, in the past. This is a sort of childish boasting, I think—that we are in such a parlous state nowadays. I should think we are not really.

ORR: Don't you think, though, there is a growing consciousness in everybody's minds with mass communication, television, radio and so on, that the world is too much with us?

SMITH: Yes, but it needn't be, you see. This is the terrible excuse people make. They are free agents, they must learn to say no. They are not forced to look at television, though I think it would be foolish to say, 'No, I won't look at it at all.' I think choosing is using human freedom. You know Morgan Forster always said, 'Connect, only connect.' Well, I should say, 'Select, only select.' I would never refuse to look at the television because I disapproved of television. If it was something I wanted to see I would jolly well look at it. But I'd turn it off when I began to get tired. I once saw *The Trojan Women* on television. I wouldn't have missed it for anything. Wonderful. And so odd to have made Helen like a streetwalker, and to have missed the key to the whole play. I mean, in the line: 'If these thing had not happened to us, we should not be remembered.' Not quite an anti-war slogan that, eh? You see, if you say no to things, when you say yes you enjoy them much more because you come fresh to it.

ORR: Do you find that you are influenced by the work of other writers?

SMITH: Well, some of the past writers influence me. I think Gibbon's prose is absolutely wonderful and one clutches these wonderful sentences of his about the early Christians when he said, 'For it was not in this world that they were desirous of being either useful or agreeable.' I mean those superb adjectives 'useful or agreeable'. Indeed, it was not an idea that would have occurred to the early Christians. One gets such pleasure out of that, you see.

ORR: Do you find this has any influence on your own writing, though?

SMITH: Well, it sharpens it, perhaps.

ORR: Do you find echoes of other writers in your own poems?

SMITH: Not conscious echoes, but I dare say there are a good many. I don't read the contemporary poets, really not so much out of arrogance as that I feel one ought not to. One will get the lines crossed and begin writing their poems and they will begin writing one's own. But it's just as well everybody doesn't feel like that, of course. I like some of Byron's poetry very much. Especially some lines come into one's mind. You know those wonderful ones about the Athanasian creed in 'Don Juan': 'It illuminates the Book of Common Prayer, /As doth the rainbow the just clearing air.' I like romantic, sad poems, you know. I love Wordsworth's 'Idiot Boy'; I think it's a beautiful poem. I can't forget it, where she looks for him and he's riding his donkey in the moonlight through the Lake District. It's

absolutely wonderful. Then I love some of those lines in 'The Ancient
Mariner'. What a sustained poem that is! Not a single line is wrong,
not one foot is wrong. It's amazing!

ORR: So you wouldn't consider yourself a typical example of a 1961
contemporary poet?

SMITH: No, not just 1961, perhaps. But I'm alive today, therefore I'm
as much part of our time as everybody else. The times will just have
to enlarge themselves to make room for me, won't they, and for
everybody else. Being alive is being alive, and being alive now and
not in the last century.

ORR: I believe that you are publishing a collected volume of your
poems accompanied by some of your illustrations. Are these drawn
specifically to accompany certain poems?

SMITH: No, they aren't. I just sort of sit and draw sometimes. I am not a
trained drawer, you know. It's rather more like the higher doodling,
or perhaps just doodling without the higher. But I enjoy doing it,
and sometimes the dogs which come have such a look in their eyes
that you can't believe that you've done them. And the faces that
come!

ORR: They almost take you by surprise?

SMITH: Oh yes, yes. Some of these faces are indeed dreadful, and yet
some of them are beautiful.

ORR: Do any of your poems take you by surprise?

SMITH: Some of the lines I sometimes start off with that come to me
when I'm half asleep, they do take me by surprise. And you think, if
you are in your workaday mood (you have almost the financier's side
to you, you see, the stock exchange side, all that sort of thing which
is extremely shrewd) and then these lines come to you when you wake
up and you think 'What utter nonsense, hasn't the Muse anything
better to do than that, than to throw such nonsense about?', and then
you think, 'Well, you know, it's a gift', and then you play about
with it and then this tremendous pleasure comes, and then you think
of the drawings in the box and some of these faces and animals. The
animals are so extraordinary! This child with a terrible look on its
face! This one does not have a poem. I just wrote as an underline for
it: 'Eighteen months old and already odious'. Then I did one of a
despairing creature crawling out of the water and clinging to the
knees of a larger figure. And the saying underneath: 'Not everybody
wishes for eternal life'.

ORR: Do you attach much importance to the more conventional

devices and disciplines of poetry? I'm thinking of things like the sonnet form, regular metre.

SMITH: Yes, I do, because I can't work without this sense of rhythm and metre and sometimes it will not go right. It has to be worked at and worked at. It may take years. In one case, I remember, I put the thing away. It must have been fifteen years ago I started that wretched poem. I did in the end get the line I wanted. As for the rhyme, I think that the English language is rather poverty-stricken in absolutely correct rhymes: therefore you must use these assonances and broken rhymes. And then they are beautiful, I think, whereas an absolutely close rhyme in English can become a jingle.

ORR: Do you find that you seek the company of other poets and other writers?

SMITH: I like company very much. Of course, I live rather alone, really. I live with an aunt who is ninety. I'm very fond of her, but we live alone, and most of my friends are in London and I am a little way out of London. No, I see my friends and I like them, but they don't, most of them, seem to be writers. Some of them are. I don't know many poets. I know some novelists. But most of my friends are just friends and I don't really know what they are. They are married and have children, their husbands are barristers or something like that, lawyers, or civil servants. No, I wouldn't say I had a tremendous literary acquaintance. But when I do go to publishers' parties I do enjoy them very much. I like to meet writers. I don't know where they meet in London. I mean, they don't go and sit on the pavement cafés. But, of course, the pavements are so awfully cold. I don't know where they meet. I think you must be friends with them to begin with. You can't just go and say, 'You are a poet, so am I, so I am coming to dinner next Thursday.' But I think in France a lot more of the brains of the community, the intelligence, goes into the arts than it does in England. I think in England the intelligence of the country goes into the professions and government. And of course you might say for the country it is a good thing that it does, perhaps.

ORR: But do *you* feel this is a good thing?

SMITH: I don't think it does any harm. I think a poet should get on with his work and not be bothered what his status is in the community. In fact, they can be too spoilt, I think, and I'm not sure that they are not a bit too spoilt now.

ORR: So you don't think that the poet should occupy a unique or favoured place in society?

smith: No, I don't think he should at all. I think he should be just
made to get on with his writing: put in a room with pencils
and pen or a typewriter and then if his poems are no good,
then he must just be thrown out, I think.

6th December, 1961.

Bernard Spencer

BERNARD SPENCER was born in 1909, and educated at Marlborough and
Corpus Christi College, Oxford. He started to publish poetry while he was
at Oxford, and was editor of *Oxford Poetry*. He contributed to *New Verse*
in the thirties, and later became one of the editors of the Middle East verse
magazine, *Personal Landscape*. He served with the British Council in Greece,
Egypt, Italy, Spain and Turkey. He died in Vienna in 1963.

His published works include *Aegean Islands* (1946), *The Twist in the
Plotting* (1960), *With Luck Lasting* (1963) and *Collected Poems* (1965).

ORR: Mr. Spencer, can you remember when you first began writing
poetry?

SPENCER: I think I should say late in my public school period when I
was very much influenced by romantic poetry, by nineteenth-century
poetry, by William Morris, by Keats, and made discoveries of people
like James Elroy Flecker, and I think I wrote one or two poems then
on conventional subjects. I think I wrote one about Venice when I
was on a visit, which sounded extraordinarily like other people's and
nineteenth-century poets' views about Venice.

ORR: So these influences were very strongly apparent in your poems at
an early stage, were they?

SPENCER: Oh yes, I went through an absolutely normal stage of being
in love with poetry; reading all I could find, but especially the pulling
out from the shelves of romantic poetry. I would say it was mostly of
that period, although I do remember when I got a school prize at
about seventeen, I was much laughed at for having chosen George
Herbert as the book and everyone thought that was extremely stuffy
of me. That, I think, is important, because I have a great, great
admiration for the Metaphysicals now.

233

ORR: Apart from the Metaphysicals, what other poets have been an influence on you as a maturer writer?

SPENCER: I think Thomas Hardy, very, very especially. I like the down-to-earthness of his language and his observation. I also liked, at an early stage, Edward Thomas.

ORR: Do you find that it is difficult for you to assimilate these influences and then emerge with a style which is triumphantly and definitely your own?

SPENCER: It was difficult, I am quite sure. Looking back on the things that I used to publish in the early days, I was quite clearly writing under a rather strangling influence of what was considered right in those days and I am sure that Eliot and Auden were very strong influences. But I think that as one grows older, one just cuts the cackle and I have to turn more and more to my knowledge of myself, what I am really like, and steer away from any accepted style, as far as I know. There is one other point, of course, that I have lived a long while abroad, for about twenty-two years, and I have come a little bit under the influences of what I have read here and there, whether in Greece, with poets such as Elytis or Seferis. Although I don't write like them, it must have given me ideas of different ways of writing from those you would find in England or the States, I suppose.

ORR: It is definitely noticeable, on reading your poems and on hearing your poems, that you don't belong to the English pastoral school.

SPENCER: No, I think I am much more interested, really, in people in a landscape, with some dramatic situation. But very much, of course, in the landscape with them, because I believe the landscape is involved in their feelings. That is what, really, I am looking for all the time, I think, a dramatic situation in some landscape.

ORR: Do you find yourself bound by, or helped by conventional poetic forms, the pure mechanics of poetry, as one might write a sonnet of fourteen lines with a certain rhyme scheme or observe a certain regular metre or stanza form?

SPENCER: I do write sometimes in regular stanza forms, as were custo-mary years ago. But on the whole, I think, I write far more in irregular forms: let us say, not with a regularly recurring pattern, but the pattern growing up more or less like a plant according to the nature of what I am saying. I do think, though, that in each poem I write, I try to set myself a new technical problem. I think I have written very little in the same form from one poem to another, because it is famous that you should keep your mind on some technical thing. It helps the imagination to do its stuff, if you have your mind on a technical problem.

ORR: What about the sound of your poems? Do you think of your poems in musical terms, in terms of their being read aloud?

SPENCER: Yes, in the end I do, although I don't think it is necessary for all poets. But I myself am very attracted by the sound of words. Of course, everyone is really when they write. They hear an imaginary sort of voice, rather monotonous in their ear, chewing over what they are saying. What I hear in my ear is not really the way I would read it out in the end, when I had written it. But I think you hear in your ear a voice which is playing with the contrasting vowels and consonants and textures. That, I think, you hear and definitely I expect to hear it.

ORR: Do you expect your poems to make an impact on a first hearing, as distinct from the impact they may make when studied on the printed page?

SPENCER: Well, I don't think there is very much poetry being written nowadays which can have an impact on first hearing and I, who have to do a certain amount of lecturing and poetry-reading abroad, prefer to help an audience, if it is the first time they are going to be exposed to this poem, by pointing out a few things about the kind of poem it is. Because if you are reading by yourself a poem that is unfamiliar to you, you are in fact, through experience, already looking at the shape of it, and in the first few lines you are observing whether there is a rhyme going on or not. But it is much more elaborate than you can expect an audience of less trained people to be able to get at.

ORR: We hear a great deal today in the form of lament that contemporary poetry appeals to a very tiny audience in this country. Does this mean that the appreciation of poetry is becoming a more exclusive and difficult thing? We have heard it said, and I am sure you have, that poets are now writing for other poets.

SPENCER: I don't think there has really been much change from what there always was. I mean, in Shakespeare's time he and his contemporaries were not writing their lyrics for the general public, were they? In fact, they used to keep them in manuscript and pass them round to other writers and highly educated friends and later on they were published. But they didn't have very grand sales, did they? The plays are a different matter. So I don't think that there is very much change. I think new poetry will always be rather limited in its first audiences until it has been digested through the machinery of criticism and made available to a wider public, usually years after-wards.

ORR: Do you find yourself constantly in the company of other poets, other writers, and perhaps artists and musicians?

SPENCER: Well, I don't very much. Maybe partly by circumstances, because I don't live in an English-speaking community most of the time. But, frankly, I think I rather prefer not to be. I think I like ordinary people, because I am *listening*, because they are my subject-matter, and I think if I got among a group of poets or writers very often I should be put off. I like listening to the ordinary person talk, not the literary person.

ORR: You think it is better, do you, in your case for the poet to live in a kind of literary isolation?

SPENCER: Yes, because the nature of my life is that I have to keep a lot of company and I don't get enough loneliness, and possibly this is an effort to get a kind of mental loneliness. You must let the pressures build up inside you and not be diluted by literary talk.

ORR: Do you find an interest in or a knowledge of other arts, the visual arts of music, is helpful to you as a poet?

SPENCER: I have, I think, a very strong visual sense and I am practically unmusical (someone said I am tone-deaf), but as for the visual arts, I am very stimulated by them and I am very stimulated by sights and sounds and feelings in the making of a poem.

ORR: Are there any recurrent themes, dominating themes, which you can detect in your own poetry or any constant filter through which all your observation and imagery passes in order to produce your poems?

SPENCER: No, I don't think so: possibly there is one thing. I have been living for a long time near the Mediterranean, that is to say in the scene of various earlier civilizations, and I suppose inevitably there's a sort of excitement and a reference to other civilizations which I find continually stimulating me to write. I don't mean that is my only way of writing, but I do find that I have written a certain amount about such themes. The fact of being in some sort of continuity with earlier civilizations does have an exciting effect on me. That, I think, I can detect. It is about the only recurrent theme, if there is one, that I can think of.

ORR: Can you say, then, what is the sort of thing that prompts a poem in your mind?

SPENCER: I should say that I suddenly detect myself in a situation, out of which comes a so-far-unformulated excitement, and I suppose all poets must feel or learn to know this. It is like a sort of signal flashing on, or some particular kind of bell going. They know that there is a poem there, if they look attentively. One of the objects of writing is to explore and disentangle and put in some kind of form this nebula of feeling, which troubles and worries until it is listened to and dealt with and turned into a poem. It might happen at any moment and, no doubt, one sometimes does not hear the kind of signal to recognize one is in the presence of a poem. I rather like what a Greek poet said (it was Seferis) that you meet poems like people and certain kinds of poems in different places. A certain kind you may run into in a railway station, you can expect them there, and other kinds in, shall we say, the bathroom.

ORR: And it depends on the sort of poet you are as to whether you produce railway poems or bathroom poems?

SPENCER: Well, yes. What I really wanted to say was that poems are almost hanging about. Perhaps you may call them, if you like, but they only come up at that moment. But a lot of unrecognized poems, I think, are lived through every moment of your life. It depends on how alert or how undisturbed you are, or how excited and attentive you are at that very moment when the opportunity comes.

ORR: In the same way, perhaps, as it has been said of another art, that inside every unhewn block of marble there is a statue?

SPENCER: I suppose so. Something like that, yes. But definitely it is a feeling as if some sort of signal has gone on and the fact that inside you, from that moment, is a so-far-unexplored area of feeling and emotion, which is almost disagreeable to hold on to. And the poet, for all reasons, must then work on this or let it hang about, preferably for some time before he starts working on it, and this will turn into a poem, with luck.

ORR: And it is the exploration of this that makes the whole business of writing poetry worth while?

SPENCER: It isn't the only thing, but I think that is what leads one on at the first moment, if one wants to create something. But the first thing is really working on this: the exploring, trying to find out what it is. I suppose some sense of order is involved in trying to bring out, to give a shape to what is essentially, at the first moment, unshaped.

27th August, 1962.

Stephen Spender

STEPHEN SPENDER was born in 1909 and was educated at University College School and University College, Oxford. Co-editor *Horizon* Magazine 1939–41. Counsellor, Section of Letters, *UNESCO*, 1947. Co-editor *Encounter* 1953; Elliston Chair of Poetry, University of Cincinnati 1953, Beckman Professor, University of California 1959, Visiting Lecturer, North-western University, Illinois 1963. Hon. D.Litt. Montpellier. C.B.E. 1962. Poetry Consultant to the Library of Congress, Washington 1965. He is married and has two children. He is currently working on a long poem, *Pronouns in Time*.

His published works include *Poems* (1933), *The Burning Cactus* (1936), *Poems for Spain* (1939), *Ruins and Visions* (1941), *Life and the Poet* (1942), *Poems of Dedication* (1946), *The Edge of Being* (1949), *World Within World* (Autobiography, 1951), *The Creative Element* (1953), *Collected Poems* (1954), *The Making of a Poem* (1955), *Engaged in Writing* (1958), *The Struggle of the Modern* (1963).

PRESS: Have the other arts, apart from poetry, either influenced you in your daily life or, directly or indirectly, in your poems?

SPENDER: Well, I think painting probably has, although I've hardly ever written about painting directly. As a matter of fact, the thing I wanted to be almost more than to be a poet was to be a painter when I was young, and painting is a tremendous interest for me. I think I'm really too visual as a writer because I always tend to think of things in terms of paintings.

PRESS: And in your poems would you say that you proceed by images rather than by sound and by musical themes?

SPENDER: Yes. I mean, I really only feel safe when I am working on an image, otherwise I feel rather lost always.

PRESS: You don't write a poem to be read aloud?

SPENDER: When I read my poems aloud it worries me because I am visualizing them the whole time. They have a sort of romantic kind of musicality, I think. But all the same, what I am following the whole time is the imagery, and this always worries me when I am reading it because I wonder whether I can get the meaning and the imagery across at the same time.

PRESS: Does a poem take its shape in your mind first as an image or as a sound half-heard, apprehended? What is the origin of a poem?

SPENDER: It occurs to me really as an idea which I can crystallize in an image. For instance, in the long poem I'm writing, although it will take me an enormous amount of rewriting and working on (and I have been five years writing six sections of it) all the same, I know absolutely what I want to do, because the images and the ideas are very strong indeed.

PRESS: And have most of your poems been based on some very deeply felt personal experience or on some wider public theme?

SPENDER: Well, I think most of them have been about personal experience. I feel very hesitant about writing about public themes, because although I think about them quite a lot and I even read the newspapers with interest, all the same I'm very suspicious whether one doesn't flatter oneself when one thinks one cares about even the most dreadful things like concentration camps and so on, and I think that one can only really test oneself by what one really does feel in a personal kind of way. Therefore I am very suspicious of things like the Theatre of Cruelty and so on because I think just the cruelty gets across, but the deeper experience gets across in a purely meretricious kind of way.

PRESS: Did you feel this in the nineteen-thirties?

SPENDER: Yes, I did, certainly. I thought then perhaps it was a duty to try to write about suffering, to try to experience it and so on, but I always felt there was a great gap between my own life and the kind of lives which moved me and which seemed to me, well, much more important in terms of suffering than my own life. There was always this great difficulty: there was the person who somehow was the victim of this terrible kind of history in which we live, but who is inarticulate, and there was the person who was articulate but not sharing this victimization: and I asked myself how to establish the connection between the two. This is a problem, I must say, which certainly preoccupies me all the time.

PRESS: What do you feel about verse drama? I think you've written no verse drama since the thirties. Do you think there is a place for it in the contemporary theatre?

SPENDER: Well, I think there is, but I think that the poetry of the theatre is something separate perhaps from the poetry of verse and it's more important to write the poetry of the theatre than it is to get verse on to the stage. I think there is a dilemma here, because poets are too often pre-occupied with getting verse on to the stage. And this sums up for them poetic drama. They think somehow that verse on the stage is a Good Cause. Even Eliot has been misled by this, not thinking really of the poetry of the stage, which sometimes consists of stage properties and scenery and so on, the symbolism of the picture which is the frame on the stage. Even Eliot seems to give little thought to this and to ask himself how on earth am I going to get this audience to sit down and listen to my poetry. His answer to his own question is, he has to dilute his poetry a great deal and lead the audience gently towards the 'real poetry' of certain passages. But I think the poetry of the stage is something different from just putting verse speech into actors' mouths. I think always in this connection of Ibsen, who began by writing poetic drama and ended by writing extremely realistic prose drama which, nevertheless, uses a great deal of poetic symbolism, in fact, *is* poetic symbolic drama.

PRESS: And would you say the same is true of Chekhov and Beckett in our own day?

SPENDER: Yes, certainly I would. In fact, I think the great achievements of poetry in the theatre have not been by vocational poets. I think poets have nearly always been diverted into the dreary crusade of trying to get the audience to like poetry.

PRESS: Do you feel there is still a place for the long poem?

SPENDER: Yes, I do. I have always thought of poetry as making some kind of statement about life, about experience, and as one gets older this leads one away from the lyrical short poem towards thinking one ought to try to make a kind of summing-up statement about the whole of one's experience.

PRESS: As an editor, do you find there is a sharp distinction between contemporary American poetry and contemporary English poetry?

SPENDER: I think that the great tradition of English poetry is to a very large extent amateurism. I mean that poetry has always been looked on by the English as a kind of fit exercise for a man when he was being a courtier or a lover. One might almost say amateurism was the main line, or the parallel main line of English poetry. The poetry of gentlemen comes from the Elizabethans, and continues right through the seventeenth century. There is a certain sort of professionalism in the eighteenth century, of course, but amateurism—apart from the great 'pros', Tennyson and Browning—recurs again in the nineteenth century. On the whole one can find oneself preferring the amateurs in the nineteenth century to the great professionals like Browning and Tennyson. One can think it was a mistake of theirs to try to be so professional. Hardy looking at them considered himself an amateur. One can really think of Shelley as an amateur, a gentleman, like Byron. But I think that the Americans have never had this attitude. The Americans have always been deadly serious, have always had a very professional attitude. They began by thinking that their professionalism consisted in following English models and being American writers within the English language, in which there was no really great distinction between the nineteenth-century American and the English, until there was Whitman's revolt. Now, of course, they have developed the idea that American poetry is different from English poetry, and they are highly professional at their own kind of writing. By 'professional' I mean academic to a great extent and the English are tagging along afterwards. The English are now trying to be as American as they can, I think, especially the young poets.

PRESS: Do you think that this is a bad thing, the imitation of the American, that it is something alien to our traditions?

SPENDER: I think we have learnt something from it. We have learnt something from the professionalism of American poetry, just as the English painters learnt something from the professionalism of French painting. But on the whole I don't think it is very good for us. I mean, I think that probably English poetry and the whole English attitude to poetry is different from the American and that although one can learn a great deal from studying Wallace Stevens and writers like that, on the whole I think that one ought not to try to imitate them.

PRESS: You think that Larkin by remaining obstinately English is—

SPENDER: Is much the best? Yes, I do.

PRESS: Have you found it harder to write poetry as you have grown older? Do you write less frequently, with more difficulty?

SPENDER: Yes, I should say so. At the same time, I have more confidence in a way, in that I feel that I know what I can do, whereas when I was young there were a great many things that I wanted to do which, when it came to trying to do them, I just wasn't confident and couldn't do them. Also, of course, as one gets older I think one gets terribly involved in life, one gets terribly taken up by business and involved in all sorts of external activities. So I rather agree with Empson that probably most poets write very well when they're young and then perhaps they have a chance of writing well again when they're old—I mean, this one really has to look forward to. There are some poets who manage by sheer devotion to go on writing all through their lives, like Auden for instance, but on the whole I think the middle-aged poet is a bit of a bore. I haven't published— deliberately—a volume for about twelve or fifteen years, because I thought the whole idea of producing the little but regular slim volume every three or four years is really rather boring. I rather like the idea that people forget I write poetry. And then you get a great deal of satisfaction if actually you are writing every day, which I do, as a matter of fact. Then you hope you are preparing a big surprise just when they think you've stopped.

PRESS: Do you think that there is any specially good way for a poet to earn his living? Do you feel that teaching and what one may call cultural diffusion are liable to weaken a poet's gift?

SPENDER: Well, that is what we always say and I think that if one was going to advise a poet—a young poet—what to do, one would say, 'Well, be a truck driver rather than a schoolmaster', but at the same time in one's heart one knows it's rather rubbish, I think. One knows that poetry is, after all, an intellectual activity though maybe a poet should resist becoming an intellectual. One knows that one wants to read a great deal and one knows that one wants to meet other writers, other poets and so on, and this is the life that one has chosen. The only thing is, of course, that literary life itself is rather disillusioning. It has its prizes and acclaim, but these things have absolutely nothing to do with one's poetry. The prestige which one gets indirectly as the result of being a poet and writing poetry is nonsense; or, if it is not nonsense, positively harmful, and one should try, anyhow in one's mind, to keep absolutely clear of public labels. Writing poetry is something which has to come out of qualities untouchable and authentic within oneself, unaffected by literary contacts or any other kind of contacts which haven't become one's deepest personal experience. The danger of the literary life is that it makes one fed up with literature, because one sees that so many people are using it either for ends which are really the politics of literary groups or for furthering their own careers: or, what is even worse, people nowadays use the arts to produce an absolutely empty kind of work which is about nothing at all but which is rather skilfully done. I think the real reason that one feels that perhaps a poet would do better as a truck driver than in literary life is because one feels that literature, the literary life, is the most unreal kind of life. By this I mean the unreality of the kind of life that you and I lead: you know, editing, being cultural agents, reviewing one another's books and so on; we feel it is a kind of emptying out of the real content of experience and substituting for it something which is void.

PRESS: Have most of your friends, nonetheless, been either writers or people engaged in the practice of one of the arts?

SPENDER: Yes, most of my friends are either writers or painters, and I still think that, in spite of everything, artists are intelligent people and also people of the greatest understanding and of the deepest experience. You see we have always (I say 'we', my generation—I dare say it's true of later generations), ever since we were young, we have been awfully worried about the problem of what is real and what is unreal, how do you lead a real life? We used to discuss what is real when we were Oxford undergraduates. But when you live amongst people who live real lives, what are called real lives, as most of us did during the war for instance, you discover that the degree of reality is not established by external activities but by what happens inside you, and that people can lead extremely real lives externally without anything happening inside them at all. So that on the whole it is the artists one knows who do really have the closest contact with reality—the good artists—and in whom some kind of development seems to be going on throughout the whole of their lives.

PRESS: You don't have any audience consciously in mind when you write?

SPENDER: No. Of course, with one side of my mind I would like to be successful, and I would like to get a big prize and to be able to go away and to devote myself to living the kind of life I want and writing the kind of poetry I want instead of having to earn my living, but this is absolutely unimportant. For instance, if I thought that by publishing a poem that I was writing, but which I wasn't quite satisfied with, I could immediately get a large prize, this wouldn't affect me; I wouldn't publish it. I wouldn't publish it until I thought I had done what I wanted to.

26th August, 1964.

Anthony Thwaite

ANTHONY THWAITE was born in 1930 in Chester. He spent 1940–44 in the United States, and on his return to England continued his education at Kingswood School and Christ Church, Oxford. He was visiting lecturer in English Literature at Tokyo University 1955–57, B.B.C. producer, sound radio, 1957–62, and literary editor of *The Listener* 1962–65. At present on leave of absence from the B.B.C., he is assistant professor of English at the University of Libya, Benghazi. He is married and has four children.

He has published two collections of poems, *Home Truths* (1957) and *The Owl in the Tree* (1963), and a critical work, *Contemporary English Poetry: an introduction* (1959). He was joint-editor of the *Penguin Book of Japanese Verse* (1964).

ORR: How long ago did you start writing poetry?

THWAITE: When I was fourteen. I can almost fix the date. I hated poetry until I was fourteen. I had read very little of it, and the little I had read I'd read in school. I happened to spend the war in America as a child: I was educated there and had great chunks of Longfellow shoved down my throat, and I reacted against all that. I came to poetry at fourteen, I think, simply because the English master one day read out in class an Anglo-Saxon riddle in translation. I was taken with this. It seemed to be an exciting way of using words. This was a poem, I was told, and I think this riddle element, this business of solving something, has always appealed to me in poetry.

ORR: And did your *appreciation* of poetry come at the same time as you started writing poetry? Did you enjoy *reading* poetry then?

THWAITE: Yes, I started reading it almost immediately. I read very widely and I think deeply, as far as a fourteen-year-old can do. I was reading at the same time Rupert Brooke and T. S. Eliot and Patience Strong and all kinds of people, some good and some bad and I really had very little discrimination. I just ate poets whole.

ORR: Can you detect any influence on your style from these or other writers?

THWAITE: The people I was reading then, in my teens, I think have had no influence on me at all. In the poems I am writing now, I think I have been influenced by people, but only superficially. I admire, for example, the poetry of W. H. Auden very much and I think one can tell that from my work. On the other hand, I don't think I derive *very* closely from Auden. Philip Larkin is another poet I admire very much. Sometimes I find irritating traces of his work in my own. But I think, you know, as one gets older (I am not talking about whether one gets better or not) at least one does develop one's own voice whether it is good or not, and one leaves behind the more direct influences of one's teens.

ORR: Do you write anything else, other than poems?

THWAITE: I write a good deal of criticism, reviews, and so on. I have attempted to write novels. I have always got to chapter three and have looked back on the first two chapters and have suddenly realized: 'Oh! this isn't me at all. This is me trying to be Kingsley Amis', or 'This is me trying to be C. P. Snow', and this irritates me.

ORR: You think originality and sincerity to one's own beliefs and feelings must emerge in a poem or a novel?

THWAITE: Oh, I think so, yes. And this is what has stopped me writing novels, because these people have been treading on my heels, whereas with a poem I feel I have got away from that. I am, on my good days, in my good poems, doing something which only I can do. With novels I feel that other people could have written them really, and could have written them better.

ORR: Do you find that there has to be a conscious effort to avoid writing like other people?

THWAITE: Actually, in my job, I have to read a lot of poems by other living people and occasionally I feel this blunts the edge of what I want to do in my own work. But I do find, in some curious way, that on the whole what I am writing myself and what I am reading as an editor can be put into different compartments and that the one doesn't influence the other.

ORR: Have you ever wished to turn your hand to poetic drama?

THWAITE: I *have* wished that, but not for a long time. I remember when I was nineteen I finished a most dreadful piece of Christopher Fry-like pastiche, but since then I have not attempted poetic drama. I do not

246

think I could. I think it may have something to do with the fact that I am not very good at extended schematic writing; that most of my poems really do take just one thought, one anecdote or one concept and explore that pretty briefly and, I hope, deeply; whereas with a play or with a novel one has to have a sort of time sequence, quite different from the sort of lyrical or elegiac poetry I write. I do find this a difficulty.

ORR: Looking a little more closely at the pure mechanics of your work, can I ask you how much value you attach to the more conventional structures of poetry: rhyme schemes, regular rhythms, the sonnet form, for example?

THWAITE: Yes, I do find received forms fruitful as far as I am concerned. I feel that what I have to say does, on the whole, fall into some sort of received form, not necessarily the sonnet (in fact I have written very few sonnets) but into some structure such as iambic pentameter, probably with a rhyme scheme. I feel that this sort of framework does give my work an edge which it would not have otherwise. I do see the dangers of falling into a rut in this way: that one finds oneself rather like Wordsworth later on, being able to encapsulate one's thoughts so neatly, I mean as he did in blank verse. I find a six-line stanza in iambic pentameter terribly easy to do, for example, but, of course, not easy to do well, and I think I have got enough self-criticism left to know that this is something I just have to be on the lookout for the whole time. I do not find it at all easy to write free verse. I think Eliot is perfectly right: there is nothing more difficult than writing free verse well. My experiments there are only experiments. I have never tried to publish them and I think, in fact, I only write free verse sometimes to loosen myself up.

ORR: Do you see in your own poems, when you look at them at a later stage, any recurring themes, any dominant imagery? For example, there is a good deal of what we might call domestic suburban scenery and a sort of *Gemütlichkeit* in a poem like 'The Hedge'. Are you conscious of this?

THWAITE: Yes, I am conscious of this and even if I hadn't been conscious of it myself it would have been borne in upon me by the sort of things people say. I can see dangers here, too, of sticking perhaps a little too rigidly and cosily and safely to this sort of domestic suburban theme. But I think that in some of my poems I've used it simply as a point of reference: the jumping-off point is this local scene, this grey little anecdote, and I hope that some of them, anyway, just go beyond that a little. There are dangers of being type-cast as a sort of 'nappy and bottle poet', but I do keep my eye on that!

ORR: Let's turn to something else. Is poetry significant? (It's an awful word to use, I know.) Does poetry make an impact in the same way that contemporary drama makes an impact; that the films, that the more public art-forms make an impact?

THWAITE: No, it doesn't. I don't think it ever has had the impact of any one of a number of arts at any one time, and it certainly has a pretty small impact on the generality of people nowadays. It is sometimes a chastening thought that the total number of people in Britain who are eager to read new poetry and to hear about it is probably no bigger than the capacity of a West-End cinema. And that is rather frightening. On the other hand, the small size of this audience isn't necessarily a very bad thing if you have got people who are reading with a good deal of passion, which, I think, one has got in this very, very small poetry audience today.

ORR: Isn't that the danger, though? It has been said that contemporary poetry is written by poets for other poets.

THWAITE: Yes, of course that's true if you pick up one of those little magazines written by poets for other poets, which hardly anybody else bothers about. But then I don't know! I do a fair amount of lecturing here and there to extra-mural classes and that sort of thing and I do find quite a general interest among these people in poetry: that is, people who are not poets and who are not trying to write the stuff themselves (or, perhaps, have tried to at one time and given it up) but who do keep on reading poetry and take an active interest in it.

ORR: Some of your poems must have a specialist appeal. We were talking just now about poets writing for other poets, but I was thinking of a poem like 'The Boys'. Do you think this poem would make an impact on people who don't know this sort of scenery and this sort of situation?

THWAITE: Yes, I think really, you know, the influence of the army, the sort of thing I am talking about there, should come across to most English people. If one is going to use concrete imagery, one can't hope for universal poetry all the time. There is a splendid poem by Louis MacNeice in his volume *Solstices*, which is all about English Literature abroad and the difficulties of talking about something like Keats's 'Nightingale' in the middle of India where they have no nightingales. This sort of difficulty of communication is something which is just part, I think, of using specific images. One can perhaps get a more universal audience by using abstractions, but I find this difficult. I need to pin my poems down with specific references and if most of these specific references are English, well, I suppose that's because most of my experiences are English.

ORR: Do you envisage your poems being read in a hundred years?

THWAITE: I think any poet, any artist, must feel that something is going to survive. But I don't bank on this.

ORR: That's not why you do it?

THWAITE: That's not why I do it, no. I do write poems to preserve things: to put it simply, things that have happened to me and made me think about them, and this preservation of things, I suppose, is a part of the poet working towards eternity, or a kind of literary eternity.

ORR: That's preservation, but there must also be communication, mustn't there?

THWAITE: Communication? You mean, is my imagery so localized, so pinned down in time and space? I don't know! I don't think honestly this is a very fruitful sort of line for the poet to follow. You cannot write for the future in this way. Who knows what the future is going to be?

ORR: You've never been drawn, have you, to take an easier way out and to do something with which you can be more sure of having satisfaction, like growing roses?

THWAITE: Well, I do other things as well. I do grow roses in fact, though not very well. I also have a family. I think it is probably fairly obvious from my poems that I am devoted to this family even though in poems like 'The Hedge' and 'Night Thoughts' I am narking a bit and kicking against the pricks. I am devoted to lots of other things. I think it is entirely necessary for a poet to have a wide range of interests. I know 'wide range of interests' sounds a dreadful thing, the sort of thing one puts down on application forms for jobs, but it is so. I think fruitful poetry comes from a man who does have wide interests, a variety of interests, and I do. Quite naturally, I don't force myself into liking things I don't like, but I do like quite a lot of things.

ORR: But poetry is important to you?

THWAITE: Poetry is enormously important to me, yes. I can't imagine living without it, living without writing it.

9th July, 1962.

Charles Tomlinson

CHARLES TOMLINSON was born in 1927 in Stoke-on-Trent, and read English at Queens' College, Cambridge. He worked for several years in a London elementary school, and subsequently as a private secretary in Italy. He then did research at London University and is now Lecturer in English at the University of Bristol. He visited the U.S.A. between 1959 and 1960 on a writer's fellowship and again between 1962 and 1963 as Visiting Professor to the University of New Mexico.

His published works include *Relations and Contraries* (1951), *The Necklace* (1955), *Seeing is Believing* (1960), *A Peopled Landscape* (1963), *Versions from Tyutchev* (1960, in collaboration with Henry Gifford), *Castilian Ilexes: Versions from Machado* (1963), and *American Scenes* (1966).

ORR: Were there any distinct influences on you, in your composition of poetry, that you can detect yourself?

TOMLINSON: Well, I think I would say that I have been definitely influenced first of all by a prose writer, and that is John Ruskin, in actually looking at nature and considering what it has to offer one; and secondly, that from the point of view of metre and so on, I have been influenced by Marianne Moore and Wallace Stevens, the American poets, more so, I think, than any other English poets that I particularly care for.

ORR: Can you say why, or is that too difficult a question?

TOMLINSON: Well, I think that one has an apparatus, so to speak, in the work of people like Stevens, like Williams, like Marianne Moore, for dealing with the external world. When I started writing poetry, I suppose round about 1948, the atmosphere was still dominated by Dylan Thomas, and I think this prevented many poets from finding their own voice and from looking very clearly at the world outside themselves. It was mostly the job of articulating their own subjective feelings in a rather cloudy manner, with a good deal of the Thomas rhetoric laid on. Now, at this time I happened to have read Stevens and Marianne Moore and later I read Williams, and it seemed to me that here was a clear way of going to work, so that you could cut through this Freudian swamp and say something clearly, instead of wrapping the whole thing up in a rhetoric which is foreign to oneself or which, I think, was in a way foreign to my generation, though my generation hadn't found the proper voice. Many of them tried to find it by going to Empson. But in that kind of poetry, fine as Empson is at his best, I think you are at a dead end if you try to develop it. Whereas there is something that can be developed out of the American tradition.

ORR: And is this an apparatus of both thought and diction?

TOMLINSON: It's partly diction. I think one's got to beware of the excesses of Stevens's diction, but if you take Marianne Moore, she has this Ruskinian open-ness to the creative universe in looking at the surfaces that it offers one, just as Stevens at his best has. It was from the clear verse of Stevens, as distinct from the tremendously over-aestheticized verse, that I found some way of articulating my own feelings. But at the back of it was always the sheet anchor of having read Ruskin, who is now out of favour; and I think unfortunately so, because he has got a good deal to teach English poets.

ORR: Of the contemporary English poets, are you consciously influenced, do you think, by any of the older generation?

TOMLINSON: Well, I think one is inevitably influenced by Eliot. There's no way of getting away from the fact that Eliot has something to supply, and here you've got a useful antidote to what is wrong with Stevens. I mean, in Stevens you've got a strong mannerism, whereas in Eliot, I think, in the 'Four Quartets', you've poetic manners as distinct from mannerism. This is something one can learn from, whereas you have to beware of the mannerisms of an American like Stevens. Again, I think from Pound at his best one can learn a good deal about the nature of the way the word must fit the deed and the way in which you must not simply invest all your powers in the beautiful cadence, which the neo-Thomas writers did.

ORR: Now, you mention some American poets whom you admire as a poet yourself. Are there other American poets whom you admire as a reader?

TOMLINSON: I think Robert Lowell's poetry at its best is very fine indeed.

Again, I like also the poetry of Elizabeth Bishop and Robert Frost. I like Frost immensely, though I think that that large *œuvre* does boil down rather to a few obvious masterpieces.

ORR: So can I deduce from what you have been saying that you would think that the American poets are much less subject to influence, that they are adopting a much freer line in their composition than contemporary English poets, who, as you say, may be under the influence of Dylan Thomas, T. S. Eliot, or whomsoever?

TOMLINSON: Well, I think the thing about American poets is that they realize that they have simply got to read the poetry of other languages, they have simply got to read French poetry, whereas so many English poets are so pleased with the parish pump it doesn't seem to concern them that they ought to know what happened in French Symbolism from, say, 1870 to round about 1920: from Rimbaud up to Valéry. All that phase interests me immensely, and I think it has obviously fed the American poets as well, whereas writers of my own generation were not, I think, as poets, particularly interested in that kind of thing. If you go to the works of someone like Larkin you don't touch that level at all.

ORR: So do you think the influence of Dylan Thomas upon younger poets writing in English today has been a bad one?

TOMLINSON: By and large, yes, a very bad one. But it is more or less over now, isn't it? It began to fade in the late forties and early fifties. But the question is whether any adequate diction has replaced that overblown rhetoric which was degraded Thomas. Thomas at his best can obviously be very fine; but the kind of verse that was written by poets like the New Apocalyptics, who were all the rage when I was beginning to write, that kind of thing was impossible to build on. You couldn't build a solid and trustworthy poetic architecture out of the kind of diction, out of the kind of imagery which was available at that time. It simply needed something new, and for my own case I found that the Americans helped here.

ORR: Do you think in English poetry today there is a new style, something which we can mark down as English poetry of the nineteensixties, in the same way as one could identify quite a deal of the verse which was being written at the time of Wyatt and Surrey?

TOMLINSON: Oh, I think there's a horribly common style, I mean that 'man-of-world' off-handedness, that rather rootless wit, which is the other extreme from the kind of thing you get in Dylan Thomas and the complete commitment to 'emotion'. I think you've also got a common diction in a good deal of poetry which doesn't commit itself to very deep emotion, and therefore feels the need to congratulate itself. I think that is unfortunate. There are two characters in *Ulysses*, Phillip Drunk and Phillip Sober, and I think the neo-Dylan Thomas stuff was Phillip Drunk and now I think we've got Phillip Sober. I don't like either of them personally. I think it needs a greater richness than you can do either completely drunk or completely sober.*

ORR: And you think you can find this in American poetry of the present day?

TOMLINSON: Well, I think that you can certainly find something. For myself, I did find something which released me from the dilemma of either Dylan Thomas or William Empson. It did seem to me that there was a real opening of horizons there, and it gave one a means of using one's knowledge of French poetry, because it seems to have been so absorbed into American techniques. If one had read one's French Symbolists and then one came to read one's Americans, it was, stylistically, suggestive and helpful.

ORR: Now, you've been in America for some time, Mr. Tomlinson, and perhaps you may have had the opportunity of comparing what happens on that side of the Atlantic with what happens here. Would you say there is any difference in the attitude towards poetry?

TOMLINSON: Well, I get the impression (of course it can be very false when you just travel around from place to place) but I get the impression that there's far more enthusiasm about it in America, that you can give a poetry reading and feel that people have felt it. Whereas in England they are all a little blasé about poetry: they know it all, they've grown up with it, or imagine they have, and I think it brings us back to the fact that the Americans have read their French Symbolists and have absorbed them. The Briton, on the other hand, presumes he doesn't need to, that he can be like Thomas Hardy and just use what is to hand. Now, I think one gets this feeling in English audiences at times, that they lack the enthusiasm of discovery.

ORR: Is this anything to do with the fact that there isn't really a long-standing tradition of poetry in America?

TOMLINSON: It may indeed be that. That does help, at any rate on the positive side of things, it does help to undermine this horrible certainty that one finds on the part of English people.

* I had not at the time of this interview read Ted Hughes, whose work obviously changes the balance here.

ORR: You mentioned Thomas Hardy just now. One can go through English literature, I think, decade by decade and one can probably come across a Thomas Hardy in almost every generation in British poetry, can't one?

TOMLINSON: Yes.

ORR: Now, is it right to say this sort of thing doesn't happen so much in American poetry, that it hasn't had time or hasn't had the soil in which it could happen?

TOMLINSON: I think that's very true. I mean with Hardy, you've got Hardy drawing on a whole peasant tradition, which simply hadn't solidified in America. There is nothing one can compare with Hardy. Frost really is a different thing, isn't he?

ORR: Now, you write only poetry, don't you? What I mean is, you've never wanted to write plays or fiction—novels?

TOMLINSON: Oh yes, I have got drawers full of these things. But I wouldn't show them to anybody. I have written a novel which is quite useless, and a number of short plays and short stories and so on, but I think this was merely apprentice work which was helpful finally, in some mysterious way, for my poetry.

ORR: Can you say what led you to poetry as the final medium of expression?

TOMLINSON: Well, I don't know whether I can answer your question, but I can describe vaguely what happened. It began, not with my writing poetry but with my being influenced by and interested in the film medium, and I began by writing film scripts, none of which were ever made into films. They always came back from the film companies marked 'This lacks the element of popular appeal', but at all events that's why I started writing. From there I went on to writing short stories and also a novel, strongly influenced by filmic techniques, and I think it was all this visual thing which I felt the need to consolidate and crystallize; and bit by bit I came to write verse and I found that this could crystallize it and hold it more containedly than prose, at least *my* prose.

ORR: Don't you find that a lot of contemporary English poetry seems to be written for other poets rather than for the general reader?

TOMLINSON: Well, this is one of the problems: there being no general reader, for whom should one write it? I think the terrible interbred feeling of so much poetry does put one off immensely from wanting to read it.

ORR: So you don't think there is a large public?

TOMLINSON: No, there's no large public at all. One can't hope for that; I wish one could.

ORR: So it requires a considerable effort of will to go on writing poetry, does it, for such a small circle of readers?

TOMLINSON: I think, you know, it would require an effort of will to write anything, even if you had a large public. Just the sheer discipline of getting the thing right whether you've got a big public or a small public is effort enough.

ORR: But it's worth it in the end?

TOMLINSON: I think it's worth it in the end.

4th January, 1961.

Rosemary Tonks

ROSEMARY TONKS lives in London. She mounted a new experiment in poetry readings, called Sono-Montage, combining poetry with specially composed electronic sounds, for the Hampstead Festival in 1965.

She has published a volume of poems, *Notes on Cafés and Bedrooms* (1963), and two prose works, *Opium Fogs* and *Emir* (both 1963). She is now completing a second volume of poems.

TONKS: I think it diabolical, this getting of a poet out of his or her back room and the making of them into public figures who have to give opinions every twenty seconds. I know this is what the French do, but I don't approve of it.

ORR: You don't think it helps, do you, for a poet to talk direct to his public, otherwise than through his poetry?

TONKS: Well, I avoid this on every possible occasion, first of all because it means a loss of something like two weeks' work, during which time I worry about it, and then I get over it. When one is writing one is an introvert, and when one goes on to a stage one must make oneself into an extrovert.

ORR: Unless, I suppose, one is a Dylan Thomas kind of person who enjoys that sort of thing enormously?

TONKS: Yes, but it killed him eventually, the enormous strain of each performance, for a man who was both, of course, but who found it progressively more strenuous and who wrote less and less poetry, so that every time he went on the stage he knew that he was giving up another poem, practically, which he could have written. You either read and you give talks and you become a public person, or else you write consistently and every day and think on a certain level.

256

You can't go back to that deep level of thinking if you are too much a social person.

ORR: Does this deep level of thinking preclude the idea of an audience?

TONKS: I could communicate if only the English weren't quite so English, but you know they don't finish their sentences; and anyway they are not passionately concerned with their subject, and so the conversation tends to turn into a series of already-hammered-out academic platitudes, which means to say you are not going to break fresh ground, you are only going to exchange academies.

ORR: Does this mean you keep away from the society of other poets as much as you can?

TONKS: No, I try to seek it out. At one time, of course, when I was alone, I frightfully wanted to meet other poets. Now I go and meet them occasionally as a duty but they are rather a lost set, you know, here in London. They form movements.

ORR: Do you feel, then, that contemporary poetry is a bit of a dead end?

TONKS: It could be a great deal more exciting. I don't understand why poets are quite ready to pick up trivialities, but are terrified of writing of passions. I remember it was Stendhal who was praising Byron at the time, because he said here is a great contemporary who writes of human passions, and this is something which has completely gone out of fashion, if you like. You can write if you are disgruntled, in the present day. This is quite enough to carry a poem, so current thought has it. You can have a tiff with your wife and that is enough. But all the really tremendous feelings you live by have been ignored, or people just get round them.

ORR: So the real poetry to you is a kind of elemental poetry?

TONKS: Dealing with the things which really move people. People are born, they procreate, they suffer, they are nasty to one another, they are greedy, they are terribly happy, they have changes in their fortune, and they meet other people who have effects on them, and then they die; and these thousands of dramatic things happen to them, and they happen to everybody. Everybody has to make terrible decisions or pass examinations, or fall in love, or else avoid falling in love. All these things happen and contemporary poets don't write about them. Why not?

ORR: You don't feel now that we are more conscious, say, than people were two or three hundred years ago of the world around us, the world outside us, of things which are happening in the world like starvation and (a trite thing again to say) the shadow of the hydrogen bomb?

TONKS: I think they are academically conscious of these things and that is no bad thing, because to be conscious of them at all is very important. But that is a dry consciousness. Mass starvation is an enormous theme and you need a large soul to be able to tackle it. You can't tackle it with a trivial, off-hand sensibility.

ORR: You mean you have to be able to comprehend this effect of starvation, and to feel it?

TONKS: You must feel it: otherwise how are you going to make a poem about it? It's better in prose.

ORR: And is this something that you would feel would be, for you, material for a poem?

TONKS: Well, you see, I would have to experience it. I have been to countries like India, where people are deformed and ill, and I became ill myself. It was, frankly, almost too terrible to write about.

ORR: You mean, it was too close to yourself there?

TONKS: Yes, you see, essentially, although my poems are a bit dark in spirit at the moment, I want to show people that the world is absolutely tremendous, and this is more important than making notes on even the most awful contemporary ills. One wants to raise people up, not cast them down. Or if you are going to write of these desperate things, then you must put them in their context and show the other side of the picture. This is very much a duty, isn't it?

ORR: How much of the tone of what you write depends on how you yourself are feeling at a particular moment? I mean, if you get up in the morning bad-tempered, do you write a bad-tempered poem?

TONKS: No. Because first of all, I live with the idea of the poem, think about it before I write it, and then I find the right vocabulary for it, and then I find exactly what I want to say, then I test it a hundred times with life to make sure it's true, so that it isn't thrown off quickly.

ORR: So that the writing of a single poem is a long and rigorous experience for you, is it?

TONKS: It sounds long and rigorous, but it isn't like that at all; it is frightfully exciting. All these poems have taken quite a long time, a couple of months, because there are layers of thought under them. Now I am trying to express the thought in a much lighter fashion with a colloquial comment. I am trying to develop an idea with a comment like Aristophanes. Cavafy comments also and, in fact, in the case of Cavafy the whole poem is held together by the quality of the comment, almost, which is the comment of a delightfully wryly-humoured man who has seen every kind and turn of human circumstance.

ORR: So do you feel at some point in the poem that the poet has to emerge as an editorial figure, let us say? Does he have to take sides, does he have to emerge, as one poet put it, as a bully or as a judge?

TONKS: I'm not sure about this. I don't know whether this is raising a moral question or not. Everybody who writes takes a moral decision straight away, with the very act of putting down one sentence or another, there's a moral bias to everything you write. I couldn't take up one cause especially, and I don't think I even want to stand outside my causes when I am writing about them.

ORR: Do you find yourself drawn to any particular set of themes?

TONKS: It depends. In this book, *Notes on Cafés and Bedrooms*, the themes, although different, are under the same driving force.

ORR: They're urban mainly, aren't they, with, perhaps, rural incursions, if I can put it that way?

TONKS: I'm a tremendously lyrical poet and this has had to be cut away. My poems are strongly backboned and thought out, and I would write one poem after another about nightingales and leafy grots, but I can't get a satisfactory poem out of it.

ORR: Does this mean, then, that you are very critical of your own work?

TONKS: I judge it the whole time. Only, if a poem has come off tremendously quickly, I am a bit doubtful about the language, but the actual theme of the poem has sharp scrutiny from the very first moment it enters my head, and it usually comes in after I have had conversations with people about their lives. That is what sets it off.

ORR: Do you find inspiration from *literature* in any way: not particularly poetry, drama, but, maybe, historical works?

TONKS: Oh, yes, historical stories, not historical works, which are usually so terribly badly written, because historians can't seem to learn how to write. I find French nineteenth-century literature tremendously exciting and inspiring. Once you have learnt that you can advance human sensibility in a certain way, you look at life in a new way; then you look back to literature, then you look out at life again. That's how it works, isn't it?

ORR: Have there been any writers, though, that have been a notable influence on you?

TONKS: All the great writers from Shakespeare to Chekhov, practically all French literature.

ORR: You have never found yourself writing like them and having to stop yourself consciously?

TONKS: Everybody does. The best thing about an influence is to realize it and to swallow it, and never to throw it away. It is like throwing away all the advantages of metre or rhyme, everything must be grist to your mill. You want to be on guard, but not afraid.

ORR: Somebody I was talking to in this vein recently said, 'When you say so-and-so is influenced by, let us say, Dylan Thomas, what you really mean is that he isn't sufficiently influenced by all the other writers in English literature.' Is this a point of view you would agree with?

TONKS: Yes, one always tends to find somebody who is closer to oneself than the others, or whom one admires so desperately one wants to write like him, but this can be cured. You will only find your own idiom if you are grown up. If you are a person, in addition to being a well-read person, then you can cure your reading with your life.

ORR: In fact, the main stream of inspiration is a thing or environment which is around you and pressing on you directly?

TONKS: No, which I make. Inspiration is a home-made thing. Poetry is an artificial art. The assumption that it is like dancing and singing, very close to nature, is an absolute fallacy. It is artificial from start to finish. You make it, but if it isn't based on life, however much it is praised at the time, it will die. If it works it is almost more powerful than life, in the end.

ORR: Is the sound, the physical, audible sound of your poems important to you?

TONKS: Yes, it is. But I don't think a poem is only a poem to be read. I mean to say, it has a life on the paper which is quite as good as the life it has when it is read. It does not necessarily have to be read.

ORR: But you don't feel, do you, as some of our contemporary poets do, that their poems exist really and fully on the printed page, but they don't care how they sound when they're read aloud?

TONKS: Well, you see, there is an excitement for the *eye* in a poem on the page which is completely different from the ear's reaction. Some poems, the eye can see nothing in them, literally, until they are read aloud. Basically, it would be fine if a poem could do *both*, but there are certain poems which never will do both, and are great poetry anyway.

ORR: So that you don't feel that poetry is purely and simply singing?

TONKS: No, it is not. It should do both. And, in fact, there are poems of mine which are quite difficult, but which I have put an awful lot of trouble into making musical, and the music has come over. 'Poet as Gambler', in which I laboured on the music, is difficult to read, but, in fact, it is successful, I think.

ORR: You see, when I pick up a volume of verses by someone whose verses are unknown to me, my temptation is to read them aloud to myself.

TONKS: Really? But isn't this because your ear is so well-trained that you want to test it on the part of you which is best trained to take it?

ORR: That may be so, but on the other hand, this would destroy for me the enjoyment, if I applied it all the time rigorously to every poem written for the printed page. But what I meant to ask you is, you don't have a person like me in mind when you write your poems, then, do you?

TONKS: No, I don't actually. I wish I had somebody in mind, but I feel extremely alone, I may say.

ORR: But the idea of communication, of somebody receiving, is important to you, is it?

TONKS: Yes, because one writes poems to be read, doesn't one, and there is no nonsense about that. If I make what I want to say well enough, somebody will respond to it, perhaps. I have to create my own sensibility forcefully enough for them first of all to recognize that it is valid, and also to like the sort of world I am giving them, because I am giving them a new world.

22nd July, 1963.

Rex Warner

REX WARNER was born in 1905 in Birmingham, and educated at St. George's, Harpenden, and Wadham College, Oxford. He has taught in England and Egypt. He was Director of the British Institute, Athens, 1945–47, lecturer at Berlin University, 1947–48, and Tallman Professor at Bowdoin College, Brunswick, U.S.A., 1962–63. He is married and has four children.

His publications include *Poems* (1937), *Men of Stones* (1949), *Men and Gods* (1950), *Pericles, the Athenian* (1963). His translations include Euripides, *Medea* (1944), Aeschylus, *Prometheus Bound* (1947), Thucydides, *The Peloponnesian War* (1954), Plutarch, *The Fall of the Roman Republic* (1958).

SCOTT-KILVERT: How have subjects for your poetry presented themselves to you? Have your poems been written long after the event, or as an immediate inspiration?

WARNER: I think one could say a bit of each. A lot of them one gets from a particular event, but what's really set it off is something that's happened a great deal earlier. And every now and then one tries to do something purely descriptive, like some of those poems on birds; but, in fact, one knows one's getting in all sorts of other things which have got nothing to do with the birds, and past experiences are somehow getting in, if one finds the right sort of symbol for them.

SCOTT-KILVERT: Now, your own poetry seems much more personal and in a way less inspired by topical events or by contemporary history than your novels have been. Is this still your view of poetry?

WARNER: I think that it is one of the most difficult things of all to write any poetry with a political content, but I don't see why it shouldn't be done, and I think it has been done terribly well by Yeats, in particular; also one or two by Seferis. But there are very few writers who seem to be able to manage to get their sincere political convictions into something which, at the same time, makes poetry. It is a terribly hard thing to do, and those are the only people I can think of, apart from Milton, who have really done it.

SCOTT-KILVERT: And as far as you were concerned, this was a theme which could be more easily handled in fiction than in verse?

WARNER: Yes, though I must say I wish I could do it in verse, but I obviously can't. I've tried and when I try and write a political poem it's usually pretty awful.

SCOTT-KILVERT: Well now, has your poetry been strongly influenced by any particular writer, either early in life or later?

WARNER: I should think it was a good deal influenced by Gerard Manley Hopkins, who had a big effect when I was about eighteen, nineteen or twenty, and I think I can say that I was one of the very first people at Oxford who read him and passed it on to Auden and Day Lewis and others who also, I think, have been influenced by him, but particularly Auden.

SCOTT-KILVERT: Well, one certainly notices that you make a very great use of alliteration in your verse. Would you like to enlarge on that, on what it means to you in particular, and what kind of effect you are aiming at?

WARNER: I suppose in the end it comes down to the ordinary sort of onomatopœia and, of course, simply that one likes the sound. I think, possibly, that it gives emphasis to an idea if you have a repetition of consonants and vowels. It is difficult to say, but that's a question of feeling, I think, rather than of theory.

SCOTT-KILVERT: You have used this in your own poetry much more than you have in translations. There are people who use it quite a lot in Greek translation, but on the whole you haven't done so.

WARNER: No, I think that's because I try to be rather puritanical about translations and as nearly as possible try and get almost word for word, chiefly not to distort the meaning of the original. This has its weakness, because one may be missing a good deal of other things.

SCOTT-KILVERT: Do you consider regular verse forms, for example the sonnet form, have a particular value for the poet?

WARNER: It really depends entirely on the poet. I think it's got a certain value for me and for many others simply because it gives a sort of discipline: the framework which is useful to anybody who has got a mind that's apt to wander and go off at different angles. That helps a lot.

SCOTT-KILVERT: Has your environment played an important part in the kind of poetry you have written?

WARNER: Sometimes one's environment hits one a good deal and sometimes it doesn't. I should think for me the country has played a large part and, if you can call education an environment, then certainly having spent a good deal of time studying Greek and Latin.

SCOTT-KILVERT: I would like to turn to your translation of Greek tragedy. In tackling Greek tragedy, do you think one ought to try and find an English equivalent for, let us say, Greek iambics and then translate into that, or do you think one ought to keep as close as possible to the original metrical form of the Greek, so that you make it sound quite unlike anything else in English literature?

WARNER: Ideally, I think one should try and get it as near an equivalent as possible. I think it is a mistake to translate iambics into, say, English heroic couplets like Gilbert Murray does: better to have something which conveys something of the rhythm of the original, which I have certainly tried to do, with or without success. I think it's easier to do the dialogue of Greek tragedy. I use a long line, a semi-Alexandrine thing, based on a six-foot line rather than a blank verse line, which is certainly more familiar in English. I think if one could, it would be better to do the same thing in the choruses, but they are too difficult. One can't get that into an equivalent at all in English; and after all, one misses the dancing. But I think that by far the most like Greek is Milton in *Samson Agonistes*. He really has got something there, I think, which nobody else has, unlike anything else in English. I know T. S. Eliot says that he ruined English literature because he was so good, but it's always seemed to me not a very good argument.

SCOTT-KILVERT: Do you find blank verse is too compressed for the sense of a six-foot line, so that one is constantly having to overflow the edges, so to speak?

WARNER: Yes, exactly. And I do think it is rather important, certainly in Euripides, that each line does tell by itself; and if you have to overrun the sense of one line and put it into the next line, then you are losing something, whatever you are gaining in other ways.

SCOTT-KILVERT: Do you think a poet ought to try to lose his own poetic personality when he is translating a master like Aeschylus or Euripides? Or ought he to try and recreate his author, as it were, in his own idiom? I mean, as for instance Yeats has done in his *Oedipus* translation?

WARNER: Well, I think it entirely depends on the poet. I mean, Yeats is a great poet himself and he may do something which is not at all like Sophocles, but is very like Yeats and is, therefore, perfectly good in itself. If one is attempting to really *translate*, I still think one ought to keep as close as possible to the original. One can't exactly make oneself like the original, simply because one knows one's not so good as Aeschylus or Sophocles, but one can at least try and give the words, which is about all one can do. All translation of poetry is bound to be defective, I think. But give what the poet's *meaning* is first, because there's a great danger, if you start making it like your own favourite poem or poet, you may make something which pleases you, but gives a totally false idea of the original; whereas the meaning does give you something, anyway.

SCOTT-KILVERT: Would you say your approach was like Browning's, who, I think, said, 'I will make it as Greek as words can stand', or words to that effect?

WARNER: Yes, in theory. I think Browning did make it pretty nearly impossible in his translation of the *Agamemnon*, but I rather admire it, all the same. I think that is the right way, though Browning introduces Browning a good deal and makes it harder than Aeschylus to understand.

SCOTT-KILVERT: Did you have any particular reason for choosing Euripides rather than Aeschylus or Sophocles? Did you feel it was more sympathetic for a modern audience?

WARNER: I think that Euripides *is* more sympathetic for a modern audience. Also I think he's easier to do, apart from the choruses. I mean, the ideas are very modern indeed and easily recognized by any modern audience, whereas the ideas of Aeschylus take a bit of understanding, and one wants a bit of knowledge of the background and everything, and also, of course, a much grander style altogether; whereas Euripides conforms to what Aristotle says, I think, that the iambic is the nearest thing to prose and the particular sort of poetry that Euripides uses is a sort of fifth-century poetry of ideas which is similar to everything we are used to in England.

SCOTT-KILVERT: Were you thinking in particular of a stage production or a radio production, or had you any particular medium in mind?

WARNER: I think I was chiefly thinking of having them read and making them readable, but there is no reason why they shouldn't at the same time become playable. I was very conscious that, particularly with Euripides, it is perfectly playable in modern terms, and in fact more modern than many modern things are.

SCOTT-KILVERT: Well, now, about your translations of Seferis. Can you say what are the particular qualities which attracted you to his poetry?

WARNER: Again, awfully difficult. I always liked the poetry from the first one I saw, which I think was 'The Argonauts', and I had a go at that immediately I saw it, knowing even less Greek than I know now. There is a quality about him which I think is unique, and the kind of themes that come into him the whole time, exile, loss, tragedy, certainly, and yet there's an enormous vitality in it all, and he sees the interpretation of the past and the present in a way that very few others do. I suppose it's really because I myself have a very strong feeling about Greece in general, and the thought that it's just the same as it was, but different, and Seferis is one of those who certainly feels that himself. I suppose it's something like that. But, of course, it's hard to say, because one simply likes the poetry and I'm also a great friend of his and am extremely fond of him and so I like it all the more.

SCOTT-KILVERT: Would you say that one had a much more vivid appreciation of his poetry as a result of having been in Greece?

WARNER: Well, I think so, but I don't think that one need go to Greece in order to see that his poetry is extremely good; that's quite unnecessary, but it helps, certainly.

20th February, 1962.

Vernon Watkins

VERNON WATKINS was born in 1906. Both his parents were Welsh; he now
lives on the Gower coast, near Swansea, and works as a clerk in Lloyds
Bank. He is married and has five children. He was visiting Professor of
Poetry at the University of Washington, Seattle, during 1964.

His published works include *Ballad of the Mari Lwyd and Other Poems*
(1941), *The Lamp and The Veil* (1945), *Selected Poems* (1948), *The Lady with
the Unicorn* (1948), *The Death Bell with Poems and Ballads* (1954), *Cypress and
Acacia* (1959), *Affinities* (1962); his translation of Heine's poems, *The North
Sea*, was published in Britain in 1955. He was editor of Dylan Thomas's
Letters to Vernon Watkins (1957).

ORR: Mr. Watkins, did you start writing poetry when you were very
    young?

WATKINS: Yes, I think I must have been seven or eight when I started.

ORR: And you've been writing steadily ever since?

WATKINS: Well, I've only had one interruption that I can remember,
    and that was my first year at a public school. When I was fourteen
    or fifteen I dropped it for about eighteen months.

ORR: Tell me, do you find writing poetry easy?

WATKINS: I should say it's increasingly difficult, for me, because I have
    a natural facility and my poetry has to battle with that.

ORR: After you've written a poem do you find that you make a lot of
    alterations in it before it achieves its final stage?

WATKINS: I make a succession of drafts. If the first draft has unity, then
    I know that the poem is likely to get finished eventually. I make a
    large number of drafts over a period of time (it might be three or four
    months or it might be ten years) in which time I might have made a
    hundred poems, but the last is nearly always close to the first draft.

ORR: So that the substance of it doesn't really change, it's only the detail that changes?

WATKINS: Well, I do make different poems and a lot of them are rejected, but the thing falls into place quite suddenly. I should say that composition is a very quick thing, not a deliberate thing: quick at the beginning, quick at the end, very deliberate in the effort to get it right over the years or months, whichever it is.

ORR: Do most of your poems have the original impetus of a deeply-felt personal experience?

WATKINS: That's rather a difficult question. It's true of some, I think, but what I feel strongly is that a poet can't choose his material, that it is literally handed to him, and I think in this I probably differ from a lot of my contemporaries. I find that however much I think I might be able to perform something very different, I am always pulled back to what I feel I have to do.

ORR: Are there any particular poems of yours which have been the result of a deeply-felt personal experience?

WATKINS: Yes, many.

ORR: Are there any that you would like to mention particularly, and perhaps tell us a little about the experience?

WATKINS: I think the most obvious example is the long poem, 'Yeats in Dublin', which was written after meeting Yeats. I think that what led to the poem was that I had read Yeats continuously for ten years and was very much moved by every new poem as it came out, and meeting him made a great impression on me. But the poem is largely a report of the meeting. I wrote it very, very quickly at the beginning. I should say about that poem that when I left him I made a very large number of notes about the meeting in the train going back, about everything he said. Well, in the next nine months I wrote the poem, but during that time I never looked at my notes, and when I finished the poem nine months later I found that nearly everything in the notes was in the poem, but it had got in in a different order. And the poem was revised a year or two later again.

ORR: What about this more recent poem of yours, 'In the Protestant Cemetery, Rome'? Does that arise from a personal experience?

WATKINS: Oh certainly. I went to Rome in 1927 when I was twenty and saw the graves of Keats and Shelley. I was at that time very much under the influence of Shelley and, I should say, really very unhappy. Twenty-six years later I saw the same graves again. That was in 1953 and the poem was composed in the following year.

ORR: Do any of your poems arise out of a particular mood, a mood of unhappiness or of jubilation rather than a particular experience?

WATKINS: I don't think so, really. I don't think moods govern my work very much.

ORR: You find your mood, as far as writing poetry goes, remains pretty constant?

WATKINS: I think there is a single pivot for all my work, really.

ORR: Do you read much contemporary poetry?

WATKINS: Yes I do, quite a lot. I am not absolutely up to date, you know, because I like really reading one poet at a time. On the whole, I don't like reading anthologies. Whenever I read an anthology during an evening, I feel depressed at the end, even if the anthology is very good, because it's an uneasy mixture of very different poets. I think the main value of an anthology is in leading one to the works of individual poets.

ORR: Are there any contemporary poets who have impressed you greatly?

WATKINS: I never give a written judgement about contemporaries. I think there are some extremely good young poets, and some extremely good poets of my own age, here and in America.

ORR: Do you find that you have been influenced at all in your own writing by the work of any other poet?

WATKINS: Stylistically, I think very much by Yeats. People have pointed that out, and a long time ago T. S. Eliot wrote to me and said 'I look forward to seeing your work when it has emancipated itself from the influence of Yeats'; and I wrote back and I said 'I develop very slowly and that's going to take a very long time.'

ORR: Does it take you a long time to write a poem?

WATKINS: That, again, varies so much. I have done a poem which I have never altered, at once, in half an hour. But, on the whole, a fair average would be many months; anyway six months, and very often six years to finish. It's nearly all there: it's only just the final thing that takes a long time.

ORR: And over this period of time you never lose touch with the original idea of the poem?

WATKINS: I think it's held there in the unconscious mind, but I work on different poems over the years, and I think it's rather a great difference between me and Dylan Thomas (I was so close and friendly with Dylan) that he, on the whole, set one poem before him over a long period and rarely did many while it was in progress.

ORR: Does the imagery which you use in your poems come usually from one particular source, or spring from any environment which is known to you particularly?

WATKINS: A certain amount of the scenery of my poetry comes from the scenery immediately below my house (as I live on a cliff), rocks and sea, particularly in my ballads. Yes, that is recognizable.

ORR: What part of the country is that?

WATKINS: The Gower Peninsula, about ten miles from Swansea.

ORR: Now something more general. Do you think, Mr. Watkins, that poetry has the same significance to people today as it did, let us say, in the time of Elizabethan lyricists? Is poetry an important factor in everyday life today?

WATKINS: I think the importance of poetry is continuous and life-long, but I don't think it's as immediate. I mean, a tub-thumper in Hyde Park will get an immediate audience and an immediate reaction, but I think the audience for a poet is always an audience in depth, and he mustn't really mind if even fifty years or a hundred go by before his work is felt by people exactly attuned to it, because that's happened to very great poets in the past.

ORR: Do you believe that the poetry of any particular age communicates to people reading it, let us say, two or three hundred years later, the spirit and feeling of that age?

WATKINS: Well, it's very difficult, because, you see, I'm a metaphysical poet and for me Blake's words are true, that 'all ages are equal and genius is always above its age'.

ORR: I don't know if you noticed in the newspaper the other day, there was a report that in Rumania poets had been advised to write less about love, and nature, and write more about contemporary things such as hydro-electric plants and farm development schemes. Would you say this was a good thing or a desirable thing for contemporary poets, to write about the material things around them?

WATKINS: Well, I can only speak for myself. It is extremely undesirable for me because I would be really a non-starter. I mean, I know my practical adaptability well enough to say with almost certainty, I think, that the hydro-electric plant would be itself quite out of date by the time I had mastered it.

ORR: Do you believe, then, perhaps, with Dr. Johnson, who said that there are some things which are fit for expression in poetry and others which are not? Do you believe hydro-electric plants are not a fit subject for poetry, perhaps?

WATKINS: That again is rather a difficult question because it depends, I think, on the idiom and style of the poet. I mean, Ezra Pound has evolved a style which will really take anything into that particular rhythm at which he is so brilliant. But I think, I believe really, that lyric poetry should be exalted or else I don't think it's worth writing.

ORR: Do you think that the actual writing of poetry has a beneficial or any other sort of effect on the poet himself?

WATKINS: It's a very great discipline. One can't really tell. It can make you very irascible with other people, and bad-tempered, and behave in an incorrect way while a poem is not right. I don't think there is anything that gives greater exhilaration than getting a poem right. I think poetry is immensely rewarding, but I think the interval between the first draft and getting it right can be very trying.

10th October, 1960.

David Wevill

DAVID WEVILL was born in 1935 in Japan and educated in Canada and at Caius College, Cambridge. He taught in Burma for two years 1958–60, and spent six months in Spain on a Gregory award. He is now a freelance writer. He is married.

He has published a collection of poems, *Birth of a Shark* (1964), and is represented in *Penguin Modern Poets 4* (1963).

ORR: David, let's begin by hearing something about your personal history. Where were you brought up?

WEVILL: I was brought up in Canada during the war and up until 1954, when I left to come to England.

ORR: You have, in fact, done quite a deal of travelling, haven't you?

WEVILL: I have. A lot of it was forced on me. I was brought up travelling. I was born in Japan and we moved to Canada. I travelled a lot in Canada when I was a child and I find I have a certain restlessness, you know, an inability to stay very long in one place. But I keep coming back to England as a home, for some reason.

ORR: Now, do you consider yourself a Canadian poet writing in England or an English poet?

WEVILL: I consider myself a Canadian. But I haven't thought about this much. Everywhere I've been I seem to have been the only Canadian in sight, so this has given me a rather isolated position in my own eyes. I think in relation to current Canadian poetry I tend to be more English.

ORR: Would you find it difficult, then, to go back to Canada and continue writing poetry there?

WEVILL: Broadly speaking, no. But I think the difficulty there is one of living—making sufficient money to keep up, because it's a country with a high standard of living and it's a country of great dispersal. It's wide, it's got only about five people to a square mile as compared with about five hundred in England.

ORR: You find the metropolitan concentration here suits you?

WEVILL: Yes and no. It throws me out: it makes me want to be out in the country, in the open. But when I go out in the country on my own I feel my alienation. In fact, I think one has to balance it somehow: be able to shift from city to country and get the benefit of both.

ORR: Having done a lot of travelling, do you find that you're drawn to write poems about places that you've seen and places that you've visited?

WEVILL: Yes, but I find I can't write a poem about, say, Granada or Rangoon or London as such. But the backgrounds have a way of worming in, so it really becomes a question of your mind moving through different geographical areas and planes and collecting details rather like a magpie, and these details crop up in rather surprising combinations, usually as an accompaniment to some memory or some more immediate state of mind.

ORR: Do you think, then, that if you were living in one place for a long time you would find it difficult to write a variety of poems?

WEVILL: No, I wouldn't. But I think, quite literally, I would write myself out of a place and then feel the need to move on. This would not mean I'd exhausted the place, but probably the place had exhausted me in some way.

ORR: Do you project your poems when you're writing them consciously towards a person or a type of person or a group of people? In other words, do you have a specific audience in mind?

WEVILL: This is a great problem. I prefer to have *one* person in mind all the time, because I find that personal, direct communication tends to unleash a lot more than if you are thinking in terms of a mass of people. As far as an audience or a crowd or, say, a body of listeners goes, that's a different matter. I believe when you are thinking in terms of an audience it can be dangerous. You can find yourself writing too publicly and simplifying yourself into a kind of loudspeaker, if you're not careful.

ORR: Do you write your poems with the idea that they are going to be read aloud, or is it the look of the poem on the printed page and its content that can be derived straight from the printed page to the mind that interests you?

WEVILL: I think a poem has to both read well and look well. I don't believe a poem is good enough if you can't read it aloud. But I think it has to have that dual nature to it. I get no pleasure from poems (for instance Mayakovsky's later poems) which are really public poems spoken in a public voice. When you read them on the page, they seem somehow shallow. They have a hollow ring to them.

ORR: But do you pay conscious attention, when you're writing or when you're revising a poem, to the sound it's going to make?

WEVILL: I do, yes: I find this is natural. I find that I often have to beat the sound element out of it, a sonority develops which I have to be cautious of: the usual things, alliteration and assonance and effects which tend to be natural to your mind when you're writing poetry.

ORR: What about the more formal discipline of poetry: sonnet forms, rhyme schemes, regular metres and so on? Do you feel drawn to employ these, do you respect them?

WEVILL: I respect them, but I don't feel drawn to employ them. I think because by experience I've learnt that they don't really suit my needs and that I'd much rather pay greater attention to individual words and phrases and cadences, and that the moment I strait-jacket myself with a strict form or metre I'm not free to say what I want to say. This doesn't mean that one writes in a completely undisciplined way, but you've then got to impose your own set of rules and that's a very personal thing.

ORR: So that the discipline isn't immediately apparent to a reader?

WEVILL: The discipline is often *not* apparent to a reader and you get criticized on the basis of poor prosody and this sort of thing. Here is where reading aloud can help. You can convince an audience that this is a natural speech rhythm, whereas on the page it may sometimes look as if it's a little jagged or uncontrolled.

ORR: Do you want to write things other than poems: novels, short stories, essays, plays?

WEVILL: Yes, I'm interested in plays. At the moment I'm trying to write short stories as well. But I think the idea of drama is fascinating, particularly for poets, because it's difficult nowadays to think of *good* poetry as a medium for drama, as a tool for drama.

ORR: Do you think this is because of the age we live in, a sort of anti-poetic age?

WEVILL: No, I don't think it is an anti-poetic age at all. I think it is an age which has changed the nature of poetry, but I think poetry is adapting itself to the age in a strange way. I think it's rather that the frontiers between poetry and prose are very hard to define, in many

ways, and what you are writing in verse can sometimes express itself
in prose just as powerfully, if you're thinking in terms of drama.

ORR: This is interesting. Do I take it, then, that you think poetry and
prose in this mid-twentieth century are perhaps coming closer
together and beginning to overlap?

WEVILL: I think they are, because I think a lot of prose being written
now is very powerful and intense prose, which is the quality of a lot
of poetry that's now being written, poetry which nowadays lacks the
kind of artificiality it had. Fine though it was, I think Dylan Thomas's
later poetry had this artificiality to it: it was sonorous and it was in
some ways meaningless. But I think nowadays people are a little
more concerned with the meanings, the actual prose meanings the
poems have.

ORR: One of our contemporary poets was talking on the B.B.C. the
other day about what he labels the 'New Criticism' and he said the
danger of the new criticism was that it tended (I'm simplifying his
argument) to applaud complexity in a poem for its own sake. Do
you think this is a danger in contemporary verse: that *complexity*
will attract the attention and applause of critics, rather than the real
virtues of a poem, whatever they may be?

WEVILL: I think this may be a danger. I mean, I think critics very often
like complexity because, in the same way one likes reading thrillers
sometimes, one likes to unravel a mystery.

ORR: Like a crossword?

WEVILL: Like a crossword. I think the *kind* of complexity again is very
important. One instinctively feels there are certain things which have
to be kept simple and other things which cannot be simplified. To
over-simplify or understate something which is very complex such,
I think, as was happening here about ten years ago in poetry, the so-
called movement, is just as bad.

ORR: You're thinking there of the *New Lines*.

WEVILL: Yes. I find the whole attitude behind *New Lines* unsympathetic.
I think it tends to discount a great many areas, very fruitful areas, of
writing.

ORR: Of course this was, wasn't it, a reaction against the Dylan Thomas
sort of poetry?

WEVILL: Yes, I think that's true.

ORR: And they said, I think, that they were trying to reassert the virtues
of eighteenth-century poetry, of clarity and of purity?

WEVILL: Yes, but eighteenth-century poetry was very graceful as well and I don't think anything in *New Lines* can, strictly speaking, be called graceful. I think what is often lacking is what I can only call intuition, the transforming quality of mind and the senses. For me a poem is good if it tells me something fresh, tells me something which I hadn't really thought of, or which I might have had an intimation of, but wouldn't have expressed as the poet did. And I find that when a poem is too concerned with telling me the obvious, whether it's complex or simple, then I just lose my interest in it. I think the eighteenth century did have this graceful, intuitive quality which, after Freud and psychiatry and mass communication, now becomes mere jargon. You know, people just use these insights as counters to play with. They're not really personal insights, they're something which a man in his reading learns and then uses in his poetry, and they tell me nothing about the person who is writing and they tell me nothing about myself.

ORR: They become mere ciphers?

WEVILL: They become ciphers. There is also a tendency to say everyone is governed by the same motives, feelings, and I don't think it's true. I think very few people have direct insights sufficient to let them write a really original poem.

ORR: What about the influence of other writers whom you've read, influences on your style, your thought? Do you find yourself relatively immune to this, or is this something you're conscious of and fight against?

WEVILL: I find that this is something hard to define. I think that the first modern poet who influenced me was Ezra Pound, and not the 'Cantos', but the shorter poems, the earlier poems he wrote. I like the cleanness of his lines and the simplicity of his pictures, the images he built up, and this appealed to me when I was in Cambridge. I also was, and still am, very fond of Garcia Lorca, who is another poet who is almost a classic of how to describe by using metaphor, simply and imaginatively. But I find that on the whole with one's contemporaries, though one can admire their work, and there might be a natural similarity sometimes between your work and theirs, strictly speaking there is no influence because you are both developing simultaneously and very likely you're heading in different directions, and I always think influence is in the eye of the perceiver. I think you should always look for what is unusual in a writer, what is personal and may be unique.

26th May, 1964.